The Acid Diaries

"A unique account of a courageous psychonaut's journey into the preternatural depths of human consciousness."

MARTIN A. LEE, COAUTHOR OF *ACID DREAMS*

"*The Acid Diaries* is the best insider's portrait of the psychedelic journey I've ever found; the writing is stunningly beautiful in its effervescent candor. *The Acid Diaries* is an exceptionally honest and unguarded book."

DR. CHRISTOPHER M. BACHE, AUTHOR OF *LIFECYLES, DARK NIGHT/EARLY DAWN,* AND *THE LIVING CLASSROOM*

"Instant enlightenment? Hardly. One has to work for it, as outlined in this book . . . highly recommended . . ."

JONATHAN OTT, ETHNOBOTANIST, WRITER, TRANSLATOR, PUBLISHER, NATURAL PRODUCTS CHEMIST, AND BOTANICAL RESEARCHER IN THE AREA OF ENTHEOGENS

"Like any strong acid trip, there is both existential angst and cosmic bliss, and many states in between. *The Acid Diaries* is a contemporary classic of personal psychedelic exploration."

MICHAEL HOROWITZ, TIM LEARY'S AUTOBIOGRAPHER

"All psychonauts will admire and profit from this amazing gift."

". . . a rich, dense, philosophical, and psychological trip memoir."

"If you have any interest at all in acid, then get your hands on this book!"

The
Acid Diaries

A Psychonaut's Guide to the
History and Use of LSD

Christopher Gray

Park Street Press
Rochester, Vermont • Toronto, Canada

Park Street Press
One Park Street
Rochester, Vermont 05767
www.ParkStPress.com

Text paper is SFI certified

Park Street Press is a division of Inner Traditions International

Originally published in the United Kingdom in 2009 by Vision under the title
The Acid: On sustained experiment with lysergic acid diethylamide, or LSD

Library of Congress Cataloging-in-Publication Data

Gray, Christopher, 1942–2009
  The acid diaries : a psychonaut's guide to the history and use of LSD /
Christopher Gray.
       p. ; cm.
  Originally published as: The Acid : on sustained experiment with lysergic acid
diethylamide, or LSD. United Kingdom : Vision, 2009.
  Includes bibliographical references.
  ISBN 978-1-59477-383-9 (pbk.)
  1. Gray, Christopher, 1942–2009 2. LSD (Drug) I. Gray, Christopher, 1942–
2009. Acid. II. Title.
  [DNLM: 1. Gray, Christopher, 1942–2009 2. Lysergic Acid Diethylamide—
Personal Narratives. 3. Spirituality—Personal Narratives. QV 77.7 G778a 2010]
  BF209.L9G73 2010
  154.4092—dc22

                                                                        2010024351

Printed and bound in the United States by Lake Book Manufacturing
The text paper is 100% SFI certified. The Sustainable Forestry Initiative® program
promotes sustainable forest management.

10   9   8   7   6   5   4   3   2   1

Text design and layout by Virginia Scott Bowman
This book was typeset in Garamond Premier Pro with Caslon 540 as the display
typeface

For the Children

Who, if I cried, would hear me among the angelic

orders? And even if one of them suddenly

pressed me against his heart, I should fade in the

strength of his stronger existence. For Beauty's nothing

but beginning of Terror we're still just able to bear,

and why we adore it so is because it serenely

disdains to destroy us. Every angel is terrible.

RAINER MARIA RILKE, *DUINO ELEGIES*

Contents

Preface

WHAT FOLLOWS IS A report on a self-experiment with the psyche-delic drug lysergic acid diethylamide (LSD).

There are two main parts to it: first, what happened to me over the period I took the drug, which was close on three years; and sec-ond, accounts, in their own words, of other people's experiences before it was banned in the mid-1960s, plus a synopsis of what little theory there is as to what the drug does to you.

The LSD used was black market and high quality. I always took it alone, at regular two- to three-week intervals, gradually stepping up the dose. For the first year I made a systematic attempt to turn the drug's energy inward, using methods pioneered during the decade before its criminalization—that is to say, with the subject reclining, using a blindfold, and listening to music on earphones. After that first year I took it outdoors, though still on my own, deep in woodlands close to where I live.

Roughly speaking, the experiment could be divided into three stages. The first was about personal, biographical issues. The second was about boundary and ego loss, sometimes harrowing, and not infrequently associated with the supernatural. The third consisted of glimpses of something transcendent and deeply sacred. The three inter-penetrated and overlapped, but those were the basic themes.

Case history . . . ghost story . . . and finally theophany.

I have used first-person narrative throughout, both to convey the immediacy of the experience, and to underline that any speculation I may make is entirely my own responsibility. I have felt myself to be in the position of geographers or explorers of an earlier age, as they pushed into terra incognita. I am still not sure myself of exactly what happened, or of what I saw. In the words of Terence McKenna:

> The early approach with psychedelics was the correct one. This is the notion that intelligent, thoughtful people should take psychedelics and try and understand what's going on. Mature, intelligent people need to share their experiences. It's too early for a science. What we need now are the diaries of explorers. We need many diaries of many explorers so we can begin to get a feeling for the territory.[1]

1

Batch 25

EARLY IN 1943, AT the height of the Second World War, a research chemist called Albert Hofmann employed by Sandoz Pharmaceuticals at Basel in Switzerland accidentally absorbed a tiny quantity of a chemical he was working with. The compound, originally synthesized for its possible use in obstetrics, had previously only been tested on lab animals, where its effects had seemed negligible. Now, however, Albert Hofmann felt as though he were drunk. The world seemed dreamlike, colors began to glow with a deep inner light, and his sense of time became erratic. After about two hours these phenomena gradually faded away, leaving no aftereffects; but the chemist, his curiosity piqued, decided to run further tests.

Lab-coded LSD-25, the compound was the twenty-fifth of a series of lysergic acid derivatives—analogs of ergot, a naturally occurring fungus that grows with particular vigor on rye and has been used widely in folk medicine since at least the Middle Ages. Three days later, Hofmann took what he considered a minuscule dose, 250 micrograms—that is, 250 millionths of a gram. His lab notes read:

April 19, 1943: Preparation of an 0.05% aqueous solution of d-lysergic acid diethylamide tartrate.
4:20 P.M.: 0.05 cc (0.25 mg LSD) ingested orally. The solution is tasteless.

4:50 P.M.: no trace of any effect.

5:00 P.M.: slight dizziness, unrest, difficulty in concentration, visual disturbances, marked desire to laugh . . .

At which point the notes stop abruptly. Hofmann found he could no longer write, nor even think, clearly. Starting to panic, he asked his lab assistant to accompany him on his bicycle journey back home, but no sooner had the two set off than the drug's effects became positively alarming. "I had great difficulty in speaking coherently," Hofmann later recorded. "My field of vision swayed before me, and objects appeared distorted like the images in curved mirrors. I had the impression of being unable to move from the spot, although my assistant told me afterwards that we had cycled at a good pace."

By the time he finally arrived home, the structure of time and space was coming apart. The outer world was undulating and hallucinatory; his body image was distorted, and he was finding it difficult to breathe. Colors turned into sounds and sounds into colors. During brief moments of lucidity, he could only imagine he had poisoned himself with the drug and was dying; or, alternatively, that he had driven himself irrevocably insane. Later he described the height of his delirium.

> The worst part of it was that I was clearly aware of my condition though I was incapable of stopping it. Occasionally I felt as being outside my body. I thought I had died. My "ego" was suspended somewhere in space and I saw my body lying dead on the sofa. I observed and registered clearly that my "alter ego" was moving round the room, moaning.

I quote this in full. While Hofmann's tripped-out bicycle ride was to become iconic for the 1960s and '70s, this other part of his report, at the very height of his intoxication, has been comparatively neglected. Hofmann himself seemed uncomfortable with it. Was he noting this sense of dissociation as a particularly outlandish hallucination—or was he half-suggesting that he had somehow "left his body"?

However, this was to be the climax of his experience; shortly afterward, some six hours after he first took the drug, its effects started to ebb. Slowly things began to return to normal, and finally he fell asleep.

One last feature that struck Albert Hofmann was how positive and healthy he felt on awakening the next morning.

A sensation of well-being and renewed life flowed through me. Breakfast tasted delicious and was an extraordinary pleasure. When I later walked out into the garden, in which the sun shone now after a spring rain, everything glistened and sparkled in a fresh light. The world was as if newly created. All my senses vibrated in a condition of highest sensitivity that persisted for the entire day.[1]

2

Wonder Drug

SANDOZ PHARMACEUTICALS WAS BAFFLED as to what its chemist had discovered. Further experiments with lower doses seemed to bear out Hofmann's own provisional conclusion, that the drug precipitated a temporary mental breakdown. LSD-25 was a test-tube case of schizophrenia; and it was as such that Sandoz began, tentatively, to explore the possibilities of marketing it. The first samples of the drug were sent out to psychiatrists and hospital workers and—picking up the tag "psychotomimetic," or imitating psychosis, along the way—began to circulate as an educational tool: as a possible means of understanding, of experiencing from the inside, what mental patients were going through.

Yet from the first there were dissenting voices. Repeatedly, experimental subjects insisted that, far from being delusional, they were seeing the workings of their minds with exceptional clarity. "I can watch myself all the time as in a mirror and realise my faults and mental inadequacies," wrote one in an early report.

With hindsight, you can see what a nightmare Sandoz must have had trying to profile the drug's effects.

In the first place, the drug didn't affect any two individuals in the same way. Not only that, but it didn't always affect the same individual in the same way. Any single session could break down into different episodes, often bearing no apparent relation to one another; furthermore, the same individual might have wildly different experiences over a series of sessions. Pragmatically, the first thing Sandoz established was that only very low doses—within the 50 to 100 microgram range—were suitable if you wanted to keep one foot in the world of madness and one in the world of sanity. No other drug in the world was effective at such tiny dose levels.

But no sooner did researchers begin to get a handle on dosage than it became apparent that the milieu in which the drug was taken was also a major factor in what happened. The psychotomimetic, or "model schizophrenia," approach broke down when it was observed that if lysergic acid was administered in a hospital setting, with white lab-coats and harsh lights and hypodermics, subjects were indeed likely to become psychotic . . . however, the paranoia was being caused by the doctors as much as by the drug.

The chemical appeared to be chameleon-like, and the ensemble of factors shaping its effects in any one case gradually came to be conceptualized as *set and setting,* the *set* being the psychological makeup of the subject and the *setting* the environment and its associations. It was from exploring different combinations of these—plus adjusting the hair-trigger dosage—that the first major use of lysergic acid emerged, as what was referred to as an "adjunct" to conventional psychoanalysis.

Given a relaxed, relatively informal analytic setting and a lowish dose, what happened was that patients got in touch with long-repressed feelings, which they could both express and analyze for themselves with remarkable fluency. Bonding with the analyst occurred easily, traumas seeming to leap into consciousness of their own accord.

Depression and anxiety were particularly responsive to treatment, and by the mid-1950s, lysergic acid was beginning to look like a major breakthrough in the entire field of analytically oriented psychotherapy. The drug worked equally well for Freudians, Jungians, and any other major school of psychoanalysis, and a variety of new approaches to treatment began to appear.

A patient might, for instance, be seen the day before a session with the drug, be supervised for the session itself, then be seen again for a follow-up session the following day. This made work with patients much more intense, but it was estimated that the overall length of individual analysis could be reduced to one-tenth of what it had been. At last there was the real possibility psychoanalysis could be applied on a mass level.

Particularly promising work was being done with alcoholics, largely in Canada; and it was here lysergic acid suddenly proved that its creative potential had still barely been touched.

While the doses used as an adjunct to analysis were on the low side, alcoholics were found to respond much more positively to high ones. Alcoholics Anonymous (AA), during the time the "model schizophrenia" concept was still in vogue, had suggested that high doses—300 micrograms or more—could simulate delirium tremens and the harrowing experience of "hitting bottom," which for AA was the key to successful rehabilitation. However, when this was tested out, it was found that, on the contrary, a large number of alcoholics had eminently positive experiences that they insisted were deeply religious and that the insights they brought back had enormously healing effects in their own right.

In fact, when high doses began to be explored systematically, they were found to stimulate seemingly mystical feelings in a high proportion of people. Whether such individuals had previously been "religious" did not seem to matter. At one or another stage of their session, they would undergo a meltdown of everything they had previously taken for reality and glimpse what they claimed was the sacred core to existence. Furthermore, there were scattered but persistent reports of telepathy, extrasensory perception, and other cases of esoteric and paranormal experience.

Dosage was finally established around the mid-1950s. One hundred micrograms was low, 200 was medium, 300 and above, high. And the two major schools of LSD psychotherapy that evolved were defined primarily by the dose range they employed.

The first school used relatively low doses for session after session, or "serially," as it was called, an approach that became known as psycholytic therapy. The second was based on the concept of the "single overwhelming dose," sessions never being given more than twice or at most three times, the purpose of which was to shock patients out of their obsessional behavior and give them a glimpse of transcendent reality. Sacred music, religious statues, or other imagery could form part of the setting in this second approach—as could natural beauty— which became known technically as psychedelic therapy.

The first was the dominant school in Europe, the second in the United States.

By the early 1960s, well over a thousand research papers and several dozen books had been written on the subject; and lysergic acid diethylamide, or LSD, as it was already becoming known, seemed set fair to become the wonder drug of psychotherapy for the second half of the twentieth century.

3

The Doors of Perception

WHAT NO ONE DREAMED was that the drug was about to become part of the roller-coaster political ride of the 1960s. The first step toward this happening was that the drug began to break free of doctors and psychoanalysts. During the early '60s, LSD was still perfectly legal. Providing you had halfway reasonable professional qualifications, independent research projects could be set up with relative ease.

Oscar Janiger, a Los Angeles psychotherapist, was the first person to study the effects of LSD on a wide range of people not suffering from any particular psychological problem. Janiger's approach was very largely nondirective: the setting was a ground-floor apartment, part of which was a well-equipped art studio for anyone who wanted to paint. (Janiger was especially interested in the drug's effects on creativity.) It had a comfortable modern living room with a record player for anyone who had brought music they wanted to listen to, and French windows giving on to a secluded garden for those who wanted to sit quietly on their own. You could take a walk through the neighborhood so long as you were accompanied by a member of the staff.

The emphasis Janiger put on painting, and on studying the effects of LSD on creativity more generally, indicates how far the drug had already slipped from psychiatric control. LSD was being taken up by avant-garde artists and intellectuals, at first by painters amazed by what the drug could do to form and color; then by writers, musicians, and philosophers equally astounded at what high doses could do to cognition.

Mescaline, which had hung fire since its synthesis just after the First World War, was found to resemble LSD very closely in its effects, and for several years the two drugs were used almost interchangeably. As a consequence, the peyote cactus cult of the Native Americans of the American Southwest was suddenly treated with new respect, and the anthropological dimension to hallucinatory drug use began to open up. Gordon Wasson, a New York banker, and his wife, Valentina, tracked down a functioning magic-mushroom cult of what seemed great antiquity deep in the mountains of Mexico. Could hallucinatory drugs have played a much more dynamic role in tribal religions and primitive societies in general than had been previously imagined? The word *psychedelic* entered the language.

In fact, it was mescaline rather than LSD that proved the inspiration for what was to become the most famous of all testimonials to psychedelics, Aldous Huxley's *The Doors of Perception*.

Little more than a lengthy essay, the book opens one May morning in 1953 with Aldous Huxley being given 400 milligrams of mescaline sulfate by Humphry Osmond, an English doctor responsible for much of the research into LSD and alcoholism in Canada.

Huxley was at his home in the Los Angeles hills, and having taken his dose, he lay down and closed his eyes. All he had read about mescaline's effects led him to expect that within half an hour or so he would begin to see shifting geometric patterns in brilliant color, which would then gradually transform into fantastic landscapes and jeweled architecture. However, as time passed, no such thing took place; there were a few colored shapes, but they were devoid of interest. Not until he opened his eyes and sat up did the drug kick in.

Huxley found himself sitting in a transfigured room. Furniture and walls of books were glowing as though lit from within. The jewel-like colors for which mescaline was celebrated were there . . . not inside, but out, the spines of the books glowing, he wrote, like rubies and emeralds and lapis lazuli; and when he looked down at his own body, the very material of his trousers had become a source of wonder.

Beside him was a small vase with three flowers in it, a casual combination of a rose, a carnation, and an iris, but what he saw took his breath away.

> I was seeing what Adam had seen on the morning of his creation— the miracle, moment by moment, of naked existence. . . . Flowers shining with their own inner light and all but quivering under the pressure of the significance with which they were charged.

World authority on comparative religion and leading exponent of Indian Advaita Vedanta, Huxley may well have been—but nothing had prepared him for this, this beauty of everyday objects that led him deeper and deeper into is-ness. Perhaps that was the most striking thing *The Doors of Perception* did; it replaced the concept of hallucination with that of *vision*.

> What rose and iris and carnation so intensely signified was nothing more, and nothing less, than what they were—a transience that was yet eternal life, a perpetual perishing that was at the same time pure Being, a bundle of minute, unique particulars in which, by some unspeakable and yet self-evident paradox, was to be seen the divine source of all existence.

Equally important was that Huxley was the first person to point to *boundary-loss* as being the keynote psychedelic experience. He noted the way the grid that the mind or ego imposes on perception loosens and dissolves, the way phenomena breathe and pulse as they lead you deeper and deeper into themselves. In many ways Huxley's experience that spring day was more typically Platonic than Indian *advaitin*. Beauty dissolved into is-ness, and is-ness into intelligible Being.

He looked away from the flowers and books, and some furniture caught his eye: the composition formed by a small typing table, a wicker chair, and his desk. At first what struck him was the intricacy of their spatial relationships observed from a purely artistic viewpoint, as a still life, something that could have been composed, he writes, by a Braque or a Juan Gris.

> But as I looked, this purely aesthetic Cubist's-eye view gave place to what I can only describe as the sacramental vision of reality. I was back where I had been when I was looking at the flowers— back in a world where everything shone with the Inner Light, and was infinite in its significance. The legs, for example of that chair—how miraculous their tubularity, how supernatural their polished smoothness! I spent several minutes—or was it several centuries?—not merely gazing at those bamboo legs, but actually being them—or rather being myself in them; or, to be still more accurate (for "I" was not involved in the case, nor in a certain sense were "they") being my Not-self in the Not-self which was the chair.

Here both Eastern and Western religion began to transform into something qualitatively new, stretching Huxley's spiritual articulacy to the breaking point. This was, in fact, to prove the climax of his trip, and shortly after this passage he starts to fall back from the existentially searing quality of such nonduality and relate his experience to philosophy more generally. Earlier in his essay he had referred to possibilities broached by the English philosopher C. D. Broad.

> The function of the brain and nervous system and sense organs is in the main eliminative and not productive. Each person is at each moment capable of remembering all that has ever happened

to him and of perceiving everything that is happening everywhere in the universe. The function of the brain and nervous system is to protect us from being overwhelmed.

Now Huxley replaced this with a much more vigorous paraphrase:

Each one of us is potentially Mind at Large. But in so far as we are animals, our business is at all costs to survive. To make biological survival possible, Mind at Large has to be funneled through the reducing valve of the brain and nervous system. What comes out at the other end is a measly trickle of the kind of consciousness which will help us to stay alive on the surface of this particular planet.[1]

What mescaline does, Huxley suggests, is temporarily bypass this "reducing valve" function of the brain, allowing through a flood of data that had previously been screened out as it served no "practical" purpose . . . a speculation that has remained the guiding image of theories as to how psychedelics work.

4

Psychopolitics and the Sixties

DURING THE LATTER HALF of the 1950s, self-experiment with cannabis, mescaline, and LSD began to spread across Europe and the United States. By the early '60s mescaline had been overtaken by LSD, and LSD was swept up in the snowballing "youth revolt" of the time.

Psychotherapists bitterly attacked what they saw as irresponsible, purely recreational use of enormously potent drugs. Yet it was difficult not to agree with the lobby for the legalization of drugs, headed by crusading ex-Harvard psychology professor Tim Leary, that psychedelics weren't the private property of psychotherapists to dictate as to how and when they should be used.

Moreover, even the most cursory examination of young people's use of LSD would have shown that, far from being merely recreational, what was happening was that features of an entirely new set and setting were beginning to appear. Outside the analytic setting the drug lent itself to something far more Dionysian and celebratory. "Acid" could melt the boundaries between individuals and bond large groups of people.

While researching this book, I reread Martin Lee and Bruce Shlain's *Acid Dreams: The CIA, LSD and the Sixties Rebellion*. Not only is the

book the best history of LSD, it's the best history of '60s counterculture as a whole: an eyewitness account of just how close the West, in
particular the apparently monolithic United States, came to internal
breakdown in the late '60s. I was beginning to think I had imagined it
all, so outrageous did the things we had done seem in the light of the
past twenty-five years' abject political and cultural conformism—but
no, everything was there in *Acid Dreams* . . .

During the early '60s a large, and certainly the most spirited, part
of the post–Second World War generation started to drop out of society. They dropped out of school, college, and steady jobs and lived off
expedients in inner-city slums and threadbare country communes.
While all were actively against the Vietnam War, their politics weren't
so much focused on specific issues as on a gut-felt sense that society as
a whole was bankrupt and that it could be meaningfully opposed only
by living a different way of life here and now.

By the middle of the decade so many young people were dropping
out that it looked as though "youth" was becoming a social class in its
own right, one about to inherit the revolutionary dynamism Marx had
ascribed to the industrial proletariat.

For between the two world wars, capitalism had cut a deal with the
traditional working class. The worst of the exploitation would be relegated to the Third World, and workers in the West would be given a
larger slice of the capitalist pie—providing they stayed in line. Over the
following years, standoff had become status quo; more than that, the
ever-increasing consumption of goods by the updated, mid-twentieth-
century working class had become an essential part of capitalist economy, one without which it couldn't continue to function . . . but the
exclusion of the vast majority of people from any real control of their
own lives remained untouched.

What the hippies were saying was that poverty and exploitation
hadn't been done away with, they had merely been modernized.

The overcrowding, hunger, and disease of the nineteenth-century
working class had been replaced by the loneliness, tension, and free-

floating anxiety of its twentieth-century equivalent. Poverty had become psychological, and this at a time when there was logically no need for poverty at all. Technologically, humanity had reached the point where basic material survival could be assured with much less labor than ever before. In principle, at any rate, we stood on the verge of a new age of leisure.

"Workers of the world disperse," as one hippie graffito put it succinctly. That was the negative side of the '60s political program, the refusal to work, the embracing of a degree of voluntary poverty. The positive side lay in trying to prospect the values of the new Renaissance now possible. If consumer goods are a mockery of true human desires, then what exactly do we want? Most of the '60s experiments in creating a new lifestyle can be seen as an attempt to answer this question.

Acid Dreams zeroes in on the Haight-Ashbury district of San Francisco as reflecting most of the themes of such a "revolution of everyday life" . . . Sexually, free love and the dissolution of the nuclear family in a new tribalism . . . Socially, the bid to create much smaller communities, where everyone knows most everybody else, with a politics based on consensus and direct action continually fed by, and overspilling back onto, the street . . . Culturally, a huge stress on individual creativity, not creating the "art" of middle-class spectator/show culture, but something genuinely interactive—something closer to children's play—games directly creating experience itself . . . Spiritually, the "Acid Tests," the fusion of music, dance, and psychedelics originally devised by ex-novelist Ken Kesey and the Merry Pranksters, in which the whole community could participate in celebratory loosening of boundaries and ego transcendence . . .

So what role did LSD play in this?

In *Acid Dreams,* Shlain and Lee suggest that essentially LSD functioned as a rite of passage.

What's the simplest way you can sum up the drug's effects? Surely by saying it reveals that evolution is in no way complete or even stable. Life has been frozen in its present form, and we have been informed that this is objective reality . . . while it's no such thing. Life is wild and free and a total unknown, and taking acid was initiation into this awareness. "That," write Shlain and Lee, "was what Kesey and the Merry Pranksters meant when they invited people to try and 'pass the Acid Test.' The willingness to endure what could be a rather harrowing ordeal was for many young men and women a way of cutting the last umbilical cord to everything the older generation had designated as safe and sanitized."[1]

I think Shlain and Lee have put their finger on what really was a breakthrough in the hippie use of LSD. What hippies sensed was the initiatory and ceremonial side of the drug . . . the social, not to say communistic, dimension that psychotherapists, with their fixation on individual subjectivity, had completely blanked out.

Ultimately, both hippies and the New Left saw individual isolation and the separate self-sense as being the crucial revolutionary issue of the time. What had to be created was a new culture offering the transcendence of these: a body of sacraments, available to everyone, at the heart of social life. Arguably this insight, on the part of people barely out of their teens, was as profound as anything psychotherapists had to offer.

5

Bad Trips

THE FIRST TRIP I had was mescaline. I took it in Paris when I was twenty, and it didn't do anything. The problem wasn't the mescaline. The friend I took it with got off all right, off to a classic bummer.

We were sitting in my hotel room waiting for the drug to come on when he suddenly caved in on himself. "I am seeing terrible things about myself," he said, looking at me with this strange, stricken expression. He had gone as white as a sheet. I had no idea what he was talking about, and when someone took him off in search of antidepressants, I was left to go wandering on my own through the Latin Quarter. Apart from one brief moment when all the flowers in the Luxembourg Gardens lit up as though they were neon and someone had tripped the switch, nothing happened at all. Somehow I had managed to stop the trip dead in its tracks.

Mescaline didn't come my way again for nearly a year, by which time I was living in Tangier along with a pileup of other young misfits and adventurers, getting our first taste of the Third World.

My dud trip in Paris didn't lead me to expect anything very much, so I decided I would take the capsule of white powder at night and go down to a small bar on the Tangier waterfront that had a collection of jazz records.

I was sitting quietly in a corner listening to whatever was playing, the initial nausea fading and the trip just starting to come on, when suddenly someone knocked the record player behind the bar. The needle skidded across the vinyl, producing a shriek hideously amplified by the drug.

The very fabric of reality sounded as though it had been torn, and before I knew it I was on my feet and blundering through the door. However, no sooner was I outside than I saw I had been quite right: the veil of the world had indeed been rent.

The palms, which fringed the boulevard, had all shrunk to a fraction of their former size. What had been trees now resembled a row of houseplants.

Everything else remained unchanged, which had the effect of making whatever fate the trees had met even more scary. I looked around the empty boulevard and felt horribly vulnerable: it was as though some threat of a qualitatively different order was hanging over me . . . as indeed it was. Deciding I'd be better off in my room in the medina, I made my way back along the deserted waterfront, then up the steep flight of steps through the old city wall. I passed the fleapit cinema and The Dancing Boy (a dope café where a boy in drag danced to a small live band), finding my way instinctively through the grimy labyrinth behind the Socco Chico.

I climbed the stairs to my room, thinking, Thank God for that, as I shut the door behind me. Fumbling in the dark with the matchbox, I lit a couple of candles . . . to illumine a room I had never seen before, one hallucinatory beyond belief. In the flickering light the arabesque tiles on the walls had not only become lustrous in their colors, but as I watched, first one then another section started to move, until there was an enormous and insanely complex system of cogs turning busily all around me. The walls had vanished; there were just wheels upon wheels revolving as far as I could see. I was in the center of a throbbing, incandescent machine.

Suddenly there was a blinding flash of pain in my head, and I staggered back.

The pain faded, but in its place I found something had gone wrong with my breathing. I couldn't tell what it was, but I felt I was about to suffocate. Then, to my horror, the pain in my head started to come back—not too badly at first, but slowly building up in waves to the point that it felt like my head was splitting, then ebbing away . . . only to build up again, in a rhythm that was to continue throughout the night.

I was terrified.

Whatever was happening contravened everything I knew of what the world was and the way it was supposed to work—yet my fear went beyond anything you could analyze. It was terror in its raw state. Like slipping on an icy pavement, when your feet shoot out from under you and for a single suspended moment you know you're falling, but you're so disoriented you don't even know the direction you're falling. Like that—but being frozen in that moment forever and ever.

For there was no sense of time, absolutely none.

The only thing that helped was to try to walk. If I kept on stumbling up and down, I found I could retain a semblance of subject/object relations. In some corner of my poor mad mind was the memory that vitamin C was supposed to cut bad trips; and, with the promptness of things in a dream, I found I had half a lemon in my hand, which I was trying desperately to suck. That was as good as it got in the thinking department. Most of the time I couldn't remember having taken a drug at all; or if I did remember for a moment, I couldn't work out what taking a drug meant.

This was eternity. This was it.

A vase of flowers, like flowers in a Chagall painting, hung impossibly in midair. The blossoms were tastefully arranged, as though in a bowl, but there wasn't any bowl; they weren't held up there by anything at all. Rainbow-colored strips of light from the Moroccan slit windows crept across the walls and floor in a strange jerky manner, like miniature Technicolor searchlights. I shambled backward and forward, sucking my vile half-lemon, trying to avoid stepping in the machinery or the searchlight beams, through this unspeakably evil Wonderland . . .

Never afterward could I work out how such hallucinations were possible. On present evidence I was in another dimension, separate from but closely adjacent to this, one whose nature was predicated on timelessness, incandescence, and torture. Clearly, looking at it afterward, wherever I had been corresponded in shocking detail to the Christian concept of hell, shot through with the most terrible conviction that this nightmare was what lay, and had always lain, behind the affable world of appearances. Biding its time . . .

But how could that be? Apart from chapel at boarding school, I had never been particularly exposed to Christian conditioning.

At some point the peak must have leveled off into a plateau, one which stretched throughout that eternal night, only to disappear—almost in a matter of seconds—as the first light of dawn slipped across the roofs of the medina. Horribly, the speed and ease with which it vanished seemed a token that it hadn't gone very far.

6

The First Maps

LOOKING BACK ON THAT time, what seems so incomprehensible is that we never took LSD more seriously. How was it we failed to grasp its importance? For the concept of deconditioning was at the heart of the New Left of the time. If any single feature set '60s and '70s radicalism apart from any previous insurrectionary politics, it was insistence that individual subjectivity had to be transformed. The political was the personal. Politics were psychopolitics. Our own hearts and minds were precisely where the old order was ingrained—and if we couldn't change ourselves, then what hope was there we could ever change the world?

The near hysterical hostility of psychotherapists toward hippies didn't help. It made us disregard everything else they said, which was stupid. The best summary of research until then, Robert Masters and Jean Houston's *Varieties of Psychedelic Experience,* came out in 1966, and there was much we could have learned from it.

Masters and Houston start by asking the basic question facing anyone who becomes involved with LSD—how can individual trips differ so wildly from one person to the next?—and drawing on several years of research, they speak of "four levels of the drug experience hypothesized as corresponding to major levels of the psyche," levels that they proceed to characterize as follows:

the sensory level

First, LSD brings changes to perception, most obviously to sight, but more generally to the body image—which can appear to grow or shrink, age or become youthful—changes tending to congregate in the early stages of a session, while the drug's effects are still mounting.

the recollective-analytic level

This general loosening of one's perception of oneself and the world, plus the massive influx of energy, allows unconscious material to begin to work itself free. This was the level that so excited psychotherapists. There was no longer any need to go digging for repressed emotions or memories; they burst into consciousness with little or no prompting. Using the term loosely, this could be described as the Freudian level of the drug's action.

the symbolic level

If the session goes deeper, a further level is reached. Personal identity starts to thin out and disappear. Phenomena don't just become more beautiful physically, they become more densely charged with meaning. They become mythopoetic. The personal unconscious appears to be becoming replaced by something you could well call the collective one . . . the theater of ritual and myth. Masters and Houston call this the "symbolic level"—and it could, again using the term loosely, be characterized as the drug's Jungian dimension.

the integral level

The sensory . . . the autobiographical . . . the archetypal. A typical session would be multilayered with these three levels shifting in and out of one another. However, there was one final, qualitatively different variety of psychedelic experience, reported by Freud and Jung, that in a few cases appeared to be religious epiphany. This had always been the most contentious implication of psychedelics, the possibility that God could be put in a pill; and Masters and Houston, while admitting themselves baffled as to how any such thing could be happening, were forced to acknowledge that a small number of their subjects did appear to be having authentic mystical experiences.

By their very nature, such maps are bound to be oversimplified, but analyzing a session in terms of these four levels can provide surprising insights. Look more closely, for instance, at something as celebrated as Aldous Huxley's mescaline trip in *The Doors of Perception*. Why has no one else, or at least no one on record, ever managed to reproduce his experience?

If we look at Huxley's trip in terms of Masters and Houston's schema, we can see that it started off with a highly positive experience of natural beauty, which then shot straight to the symbolic or archetypal—"I was seeing what Adam had seen on the morning of his creation," and so forth. Apparently there was no intervening biographical or recollective-analytic level . . . but anyone familiar with Huxley's life knows that he is withholding a vital piece of information here. As a schoolboy Huxley had contracted an eye disease that had made him unable to see for a matter of weeks, and left him with appallingly bad eyesight for life—so bad that at times he'd been forced to use a guide dog. *Huxley was all but blind.* Could he, as he sat gazing at his little nosegay of flowers, have passed quickly through something you could well describe as recollective-analytic? Realized in a flash that he was seeing far better, better qualitatively, than most people ever see? His blindness had been healed. Essentially, he had experienced a classic miracle.

I'd suggest he was swept up by such a wave of gratitude and trust that it bore him effortlessly through the symbolic level up to the nonduality of Masters and Houston's "integral level." But had this breakthrough not been based on such positive emotions, it could equally well have lurched into schizophrenic terror.

Perhaps Masters and Houston's book simply came out too late. By 1966, you could feel the impending violence in the air. That's something *Acid Dreams* conveys so well, the huge groundswell of collective energy, then the riptide that surged through '67 and burst into '68, revolutionary year of miracles . . .

Politically, the first thing to happen in 1968 was the Vietcong's Tet Offensive, which proved that a peasant army could whip the most powerful nation on Earth. A few weeks later in early April, the rioting, looting, and arson after the assassination of Martin Luther King seemed to have brought the war back home to America. There were 125 cities on fire in the United States, twenty thousand people arrested, and fifty thousand troops on the streets. Nothing like it had happened since the Civil War. Shortly after, Europe erupted with the Paris May Days, when a student occupation of the Sorbonne sparked a nationwide wildcat strike that brought France in its turn to the brink of civil war, with President de Gaulle, if rumors were to be credited, getting ready to bomb Paris.

And these were only the spectacular highlights of something far more serious: the ongoing dropping out of the most intelligent and adventurous young people of the time, which for several years seemed to promise a massive, all-inclusive general strike, one not only against the economy, but against the entire capitalist version of reality. Sustained psychedelic research was well-nigh impossible amid such apocalypticism—but this was only the first part of the Sixties Rebellion, and events were to develop still further . . .

Historically, "the '60s" never dovetailed with a decade. The period of maximum turbulence was much more like 1965–75, with "the Movement" peaking politically in '68 and '69, then collapsing at what was apparently the height of its strength. The headline-grabbing tactics of the hippie terrorists of the early '70s—Baader-Meinhof in Germany, the Weathermen in the States, the Angry Brigade in England, the Red Brigades in Italy—were not only a disastrous political miscalculation, but they served to confuse a far deeper and more significant reorientation of opposition.

Rather than the terrorists, it was the early feminists who dealt capitalism the body blow. Their work offered the first critique of

Western society as a whole and provided the first tools with which revolutionaries could begin to revolutionize themselves—to question their very concept of identity: their mind or ego. During the early to mid '70s, erstwhile militants in droves took to individual and group psychotherapy and later in the decade to various spiritual practices. This was the time the counterculture really tried to come to grips with deconditioning in an organized manner. And this was the time you would have expected a proper exploration of LSD . . . but no such thing took place.

Why? For myself, I had gone on tripping after my nightmare in Tangier—as a self-styled rebel, one had little choice in the matter—but always with a whipped-dog wariness. Basically, I never trusted LSD; and despite all the song and dance about psychedelics at the time, I suspect that a large number of my peers didn't either. Amazing eye-opener LSD might be, but it seemed too volatile, too violent to be workable. Had we known of the research Stanislav Grof had been doing in Prague—with its high doses, dozens of sessions, and openness to religious or paranormal experience if it occurred—we might have changed our attitude, but Grof's *Realms of the Human Unconscious* was not published until 1976, and by then it was already too late.

By that time the possibility of any real revolutionary confrontation was draining away. While a few experimental cults, such as Osho's or Adi Da's, were to continue into the '80s, the zeitgeist that had inspired our generation was all but played out. Perhaps we had destroyed too much and failed to replace it with anything positive, leaving the next generation with no alternative but to back away from the yawning void we bequeathed them. The impotence of the Left became patent, and through the '80s and '90s, yuppie neoconservatism swept all before it. Nothing was done to contest the ever-increasing totalitarianism introduced by the Reagan and Thatcher regimes, or even to publicize the corporate World State agenda that lay behind it.

Perhaps revolts that fail always create this murderous backlash. Ringleaders are either dead or thoroughly discredited; and the rest, however sick at heart, have little option but to try to pick up the pieces and lead some semblance of normal life, to curl up with a lover and a couple of kids and draw the curtains on the horror outside. Acid and the revolution dropped out of sight together; and there the matter stood until . . . well, I'd say, comparatively recently.

7

Sleep—
and Waking Up

ONE LAST THING BEFORE leaving this background material and entering into the experiment that is the subject of this report.

As I've been saying, there was widespread interest in individual and group therapy, in esoteric traditions, and in Eastern religions during the early and mid-'70s. Personally, as a young Marxist, religion had always been anathema to me, and it was only because I was ill in bed and couldn't find anything else to read that I opened Ouspensky's *In Search of the Miraculous,* a book I had been sedulously avoiding for years.

But the psychology I stumbled on was the last thing I had been expecting.

"Everyone you see is asleep," Gurdjieff tells Ouspensky early in the book. "Asleep and lost in dreams." This hit me like a bucket of cold water. Perhaps it was particularly shocking for me personally because of something that had happened in a car crash—that had happened twice, in fact, and both times in car crashes. During the last seconds before impact, time had gone into extreme slow motion—or perhaps it would be more exact to say it was both moving and frozen at one and the same time. There was absolutely no fear. On the contrary, I was euphoric: I seemed to have become an integral part of Being itself and felt enormously safe. I wasn't myself at all, yet never before had I been myself so intensely.

To say I had briefly "woken up" would express perfectly what had happened. And as I read more of Ouspensky's book, I realized I had known this strange state before. Falling in love had taken me there; so had Third World travel; so had political activism when it involved crime. I remembered how, in moments of danger, my voice had sounded as though it was someone else speaking.

This was a eureka moment for me. I thought I had found in Gurdjieff's ideas of "sleep" and "dreams" and "self-remembering" and "waking up" the basic vocabulary of the revolutionary psychology we had been searching for. Part of the thrill of direct action had always been the transformation of consciousness that being totally in the present moment brought about. Demonstrations, particularly when they turned into riots, could create just the same mental silence, even the same sensation everything was happening in slow motion. The placards, the rearing horses, the flying mud . . . and inside the quiet and emptiness, the oddly straightforward happiness.

Unfortunately, like many others before me, I found I couldn't stay in a state of "self-remembering" for more than a few seconds at a time.

Late at night, I'd go for walks through the streets saying to myself, I will stay self-aware until I reach the next tree in the pavement. But it was like trying to balance on a tightrope. I could never catch the moment it happened, but within seconds I was lost in thought again . . . only waking from some daft conversation with myself a couple of trees farther down the street. Quite literally I had been sleepwalking. For the first time I saw that my mind was totally out of control and could not meaningfully be called "my" mind at all.

After the best part of a year, my failure to make any progress at all had brought me close to nervous breakdown. In fact, I think I would have cracked up (Gurdjieff students do) if it hadn't been for my discovery of vipassana, the Buddhist meditation technique in which you concentrate on your breath to give yourself some purchase on the present moment.

That made it easier, and for several years I was to give vipassana my best shot. I kept touching that abrupt awakening in the midst of things, when the inner monologue stops, the mind is empty, and one accesses a strange intuitive wisdom—silent, timeless, spaceless. But such moments always slipped through my fingers. I spent years in India, nearly becoming a Buddhist monk in the process, but in the end had been forced to admit defeat and give up any attempt at practice.

This had taken me a long way from anything currently understood as politics . . . only to dump me back in much the same impasse. Spiritual alternatives didn't work any better than political ones, and as I watched the final collapse of the counterculture in the early '80s, all I could feel was despair. By then I was pushing forty; I had been on the road since I was sixteen, and I was dog-tired. I had fallen deeply in love with a woman I met in India, and we came back to England where we settled down and brought up our child together. In many ways those were the happiest years of my adult life—but, for all that, underneath everything there was a sense of profound failure, of lost ideals, that was eating away at me like a cancer . . . This, so many years later, was to be the context of my rediscovery of LSD, and the story I want to tell.

8

Realms of the Human Unconscious

FOR ASTROLOGY THERE ARE two particularly critical junctures in the life of any individual, the first at the end of their twenties, and the second at the end of their fifties.

Called the Saturn Return, these are the two occasions the planet Saturn completes its orbit around the sun and returns to the position it occupied at your birth. Seen negatively, these times border on nervous and mental breakdown; seen positively, they are crises that put you back in touch with your own deeper nature. I can't answer for the theory, but I can vouch for the fact that these two occasions were the times of the most dramatic self-confrontation in my own life; and it was with the second of the two that LSD was to reenter my life.

What happened at first, however, seemed far removed from anything to do with drugs. My relationship with my lover, which had lasted all these years, came apart—and badly—and the son so much of our life had revolved around was now well into his teens. I started living on my own and for the first time in years was alone.

The subject of aging and death is so taboo that we know next to nothing of what each of us goes through as we are forced to admit we have grown old. So I couldn't say whether what started to happen to me is something that happens to many people or not—although it was simple enough. My sense of time started to break down.

I found I no longer had anything new to look forward to. Perhaps in itself this wasn't such a dreadful thing, but it soon became a sense that I didn't have any future at all. And with the disappearance of the future everything else started to come apart. The imaginary point at which everything was finally going to be resolved—which had dangled in front of me all my life, like the proverbial carrot— was suddenly gone, and I saw that it had been the basic way I had structured the world.

Without it, I found myself dumped in a present moment so form- less as to be almost void. Nothing had any proper shape. Everything was in such flux there was no point at which I could say, this is the present moment, this is now—for the instant I said so, it was already gone. The world seemed to be permanently vanishing. Nothing was fully real. My ability to impose any sort of conceptual grid on life was disappearing . . . and what started to surface were strikingly vivid memories of early childhood.

. . . Suddenly I would be five or six again, and back in the rambling garden of my Gran's house outside Liverpool.

I would be sitting fishing beside the biggest of the ponds early on a summer's morning. The sea-fog would just be lifting, and I was watch- ing the float on the surface of the water, waiting for it to twitch. I could see the smallest details of the fishing rod I had made, the bam- boo cane I had filched from Maudsley's potting shed, the black thread with a matchstick at the bottom as a float, and a few inches below that the worm wriggling in a crude knot. I was after the minnows and sticklebacks, crouched in my favorite spot, where there was a flat stone to sit on and a yellow rose overhung the water.

Was this what happened when you no longer had anything to look forward to? That almost automatically you started to look back? But if this was meant to be nostalgia, you could have fooled me. There was nothing fond about these memories; they hit me like a blow. My body quivered, and the sense of loss—as though I'd lost everything, absolutely everything—was so intense as to be almost unbearable.

Those memories hurt . . .

Suddenly, I'd be nine or ten again, and back at my first boarding school. The image of a boy from my class or dormitory would slide between me and whatever I was doing. Tin and Day and Derbyshire, Pongo and Hey-Heddle—there they all were, school friends who had never so much as crossed my mind during my entire adult life. My recall of the school was phenomenal. In a ghostly way I could hear the lids of the small wooden chests, what we called tuckboxes, slamming in the dank, abandoned eighteenth-century kitchen where we kept them. I could smell, almost taste, the rust of the disused flue where I used to stash my disguises, my money, and my matches during tuckbox inspections.

I used to collect old coins, and the tuckbox room was where I did a swap for my best coin, a George III twopenny piece. The coin was huge. At the time it was minted it must have been literally two pence worth of pure copper, and it was the most magical thing I had ever set eyes upon. I could remember walking away with it in my hand, thinking that if I could count slowly up to ten, the other boy wasn't going to realize the huge mistake he had made and come chasing after me.

The poignancy of these memories conveyed an urgent, almost didactic quality. It was as though they were trying to tell me something— apparently that I'd been far happier as a child than I had ever been as an adult. At any rate, these memories stopped abruptly when I turned sixteen and dropped out of the second of my boarding schools . . . leaving me staring into space, haunted by the ghost of my George III twopenny piece, as though in the whole of my subsequent life I was never again to possess anything half so valuable.

So much for the fancy stuff. What started to happen as fifty-eight became fifty-nine, and fifty-nine, sixty, was unmistakably universal. The failing powers, the deepening solitude. The insomnia, the embittered life-review. Like a fair number of my generation, I had just been diagnosed as having hepatitis C, and effectively had little to look forward to apart from increasing ill health. I started to see old people everywhere, and things I had been observing for years (the shakiness, the threadbare self-respect, the blank fear never far from their eyes) now made perfect sense. All at once you get hit with the bill for a lifetime's pretending you are never going to die. And it's enormous. In the morning I would awake, not knowing for a moment who or where I was, and then there'd be this icy dread, this sense of being trapped inside a body with only a short time left to live. Worst of all was the impotence, the feeling there was no way I could come to grips with what was happening.

What made me sit down and reread Stanislav Grof's *Realms of the Human Unconscious* at precisely this point? I just don't know. Several times in the following narrative there are going to be examples of events I can understand only as direct intervention of the unconscious in my daily life, and perhaps this was the first of them.

I had read the book several years before, on the insistence of a friend who swore it was one of the few masterpieces of contemporary psychology and philosophy; and having read it, I could only agree with him. On that first reading the introductory chapters seemed to be in agreement with what little I could remember of Masters and Houston's *Varieties of Psychedelic Experience*. Grof's argument, like theirs, was based on a fourfold classification of LSD's effects . . . though Grof spoke of "realms" rather than stages or levels.

the aesthetic realm

Here Grof's observations were very close to those Masters and Houston made of their "sensory level." This was the celebratory, "recreational" dimension to the drug. You experienced a blast of psychic energy, and the world could suddenly go hilariously funny, or grotesque, or fairytale pretty. You were open to the moment and to other people. But psychologically, all this was peanuts compared with what the drug could really do.

the psychodynamic realm

Grof's second realm, with its focus on personal biographical material, also corresponded closely to Masters and Houston's second, or "recollective-analytic," level. But Grof was much more hardcore. As against Masters and Houston's one or two sessions, Grof's psycholytic approach could entail up to a hundred, administered on an implacable once-weekly rhythm; and he was perfectly prepared to use high doses, 500 micrograms or more if necessary. But then he was dealing with some seriously traumatized people.

the perinatal realm

Perinatal means "relating to birth," and this was where Grof began to diverge from *The Varieties of Psychedelic Experience.* On the strength of the 3,500 sessions he had personally supervised—his clinical experience was far greater than that of anyone else in the field—Grof maintained that reliving your own birth lay at the heart of psychedelic experience. With ongoing psycholytic therapy, not only would patient after patient regress through childhood and infantile trauma, but sooner or later they would reexperience what appeared to be authentic memories of both the later stages of life in the womb and of birth itself.

the transpersonal realm

One of Grof's most provocative findings was that birth and death appear to be deeply interrelated in the unconscious mind. Reliving their own birth, subject after subject believed they were in fact dying—dying for real—and, emerging from their ordeal, claimed to feel spiritually reborn. They reported a sense of identity that had at times expanded far beyond ego boundaries and transcended the limitations of time and space. Paranormal or esoteric and religious capacities could be briefly activated. Grof cited various out-of-body phenomena: among others, telepathy, precognition, clairvoyance, clairaudience, meeting with deities, and space and time travel. And with an open-minded but noncommittal review of such experiences, *Realms of the Human Unconscious* closed.

The first time I read *Realms,* I had backed off from this climactic "transpersonal" material. What had me sitting bolt upright in my chair was some of Grof's material on the birth trauma.

For this did not, as I had always imagined, consist of the shock of being expelled from the security of the womb, nor even of trauma incurred during delivery. No, what Grof drew attention to was experience in the womb immediately prior to birth, particularly to the period between the onset of contractions, during which the baby is subject to savage and unrelenting pressures, to what is probably the worst pain most of us will experience during our lives, hours and hours of it before the cervix finally dilates and the baby becomes engaged in the birth canal.

On that first reading, what set my spine crawling were some of his patients' descriptions of those last hours in the womb. *For what they described were, blow for blow, the very things I had experienced that awful night in Tangier.* Same terror, same sense of suffocation, same splitting pain in the head. Same sense of timelessness. Same sense, in a word, of hell. Before this I had never heard any kind of explanation, however abstruse, of what had happened to me during that trip. But, in Grof's terms, mine hadn't been some borderline psychotic response; others too told an identical tale of having descended into the Inferno and been faced with the prospect of eternal fear and pain.

9

Session 1

A Low-Dose Trip

MY SECOND READING OF *Realms of the Human Unconscious* had a much stronger, more decisive impact. Not that it made me want to embark on a course of LSD psychotherapy, had such a thing even been possible. No, but somewhere around the middle of the book I found that I had decided, in a perfectly matter-of-fact way, that I was going to try some LSD again. Oddly enough, above all it was Grof's modus operandi that fascinated me.

I found that I had taken on board, without demur, his insistence that energy should be turned inward and that, practically speaking, the best way of doing this was to lie down comfortably, put on a blindfold, and listen to music on headphones. The idea of being so vulnerable, so much at the mercy of my own mind, was scary, but I thought that if I was going to do it I should do it totally.

I decided I'd take a trip alone, at home, and with a blindfold.

Home was a small apartment in a Victorian tenement in North London, close to Hampstead Heath. The block was tucked away, almost secluded, and for London the apartments were exceptionally quiet. In the summer, even with the bedroom window open, you couldn't hear any traffic, just the birds singing. In fact, it was in the bedroom I wanted to do the trip. It was a plain little room, with nothing much in it, but I had painted it a warm yellow, and the window looked out on an elder and an ancient, ivy-covered brick wall.

I already had a Walkman and a sleeping mask I bought at the local drugstore.

The problem was the LSD. I had been out of touch with the drug scene for years, and I hadn't realized how elusive LSD had become. The only time you ran into it was at raves, used in tandem with Ecstasy, as an energy boost if you wanted to keep on dancing all night; and even then only in 50-microgram doses. Finally, however, I lucked out and got a small sheet of what turned out to be high-quality blotter acid, with several dozen small perforated sections of 100 micrograms each.

So it was, early one Saturday afternoon in the spring of 2001, that I peeled back the plastic film from my little stash, carefully cut out one of the tiny dotted squares, and washed it down with a glass of water.

About twenty-five minutes later I started to feel slightly nauseated, then giddy, and I went into the bedroom. Somewhat defiantly, I clipped Terry Riley's *In C* into the Walkman, lay down on the bed, and settled the blindfold and earphones.

Ten minutes or so into Terry Riley, a twitch started in one leg, turned into a tremor, and moved to the other leg; then both legs started to tremble simultaneously. Shortly after, I noticed my sense of body temperature had gone haywire: I was either too hot or too cold, but bizarrely, I couldn't tell which. There was a mounting sense of psychosomatic pressure I could neither define nor locate.

Then it hit.

Dionysian was the first adjective that came to mind—and it conveys the surge of warm, almost drunken energy that started to course through me. Behind the blindfold there was a burst of images and snatches of dialogue. In a warped, almost multiple-personality way, I seemed to have become a different person, someone who was a warrior and a poet in another time. At one moment I experienced myself as being this other person, at another I was observing him from the outside; equally at times my mind was racing with "my" internal monologue, at other times with snatches of conversation in what seemed alien voices.

Bits I could remember afterward, others not.

There was one very clear episode where a sort of voice-over was saying how the only authentic life was one lived in the light of death; and then with no apparent connection, there was a series of sharply focused images. A headland, trees, a bay. Why, that's Ireland, I thought in surprise. Jostling one another, images came faster and faster . . . a low-ceilinged, ill-lit room . . . a dark wooden counter . . . Elizabethan tavern, was it? . . . overlapping and succeeding one another. Something about a fine woman, about a castle or ancestral house, about war and more about the presence of death. This was much the way I had always imagined lucid dreaming to be . . .

How much time passed, I'm not sure. At any rate, *In C* had played out long before I took the earphones and blindfold off and looked around the little bedroom. The yellow was deeper and richer than before, but not wildly so. I felt fine. I went into the living room, put some Mozart on the CD player, then ran a bath.

Enthusiastically I added large quantities of bubble bath, so there were emerald mounds of bubbles. Where the taps splashed, there were bursts of stars in the air like the ones from the fairy godmother's wand in a Disney cartoon. So absurd were they the years fell away, and I clapped my hands with delight like a child and laughed aloud.

I was wallowing happily in the suds when, without a moment's warning, I went through a complete emotional *volte-face*. I remembered my friend Anna, who had just been diagnosed with cancer, and found there were tears rolling down my cheeks. Anna was one of my oldest friends in London; we went way back together, back to India in the '70s. When I went to see her at the hospital, she had said the cancer was inoperable, but that she had come to terms with it. Deep down, what she had wanted was a shock strong enough to force her to meditate with real passion—and she believed this was it.

I hadn't been able to cry for her before; truth to tell, I always found it hard to cry, and I was amazed by the ease with which I could do so now.

This seemed to bring me back to normal perception, and as the water in the tub began to cool I decided I was street-legal enough to get dressed and go for the walk I had promised myself. Easier said than done. I found myself going around and around in loops . . . trying to make a cup of tea . . . turn everything off . . . find my keys and money . . . only at this point I couldn't remember whether I had made the cup of tea or merely thought I had done so, and I had to go around looking for it . . . only to misplace the keys.

I was laughing at myself when, for a second time—and equally without a moment's warning—the LSD swerved around on itself. Abruptly I felt pinned in a searchlight. This was what I did, day after day, go around and around in these few rooms. I felt as though the ceiling had been taken off the apartment, and I was peering down watching a rat obsessively scurrying around its model labyrinth.

For the first time I fully appreciated what my friend in Paris all those years before had meant when he said, "I am seeing terrible things about myself." Then there was a flash of insight.

What LSD does is awaken your conscience.

But no sooner had I closed the apartment door behind me than I was swept up by a wave of happiness. Outside it was a spring afternoon, the sun was shining, and I set off on one of my favorite walks, across the Heath to the Vale of Health pond, around the Vale of Health village, then up the steep path through the gorse to the top of the hill, past Whitestone Pond, and then down the hill again through the back streets of Hampstead Village.

Nothing could have been further from the stark Gurdjieffian light in which I had seen my daily life in the apartment. Blossom . . . glowing old brickwork . . . mysterious gateways. Spring flowers everywhere. I half-expected passersby to stop, spread their arms, and break into "The Sound of Music."

This was the way tripping was supposed to be, when we were young and the world was poised on the brink of revolution and Renaissance. It all came back in a great warm rush. What on Earth had I been worried about? How could I ever have forgotten the way LSD turns the skyline into something out of a fairy tale? Always in front, and enchanted, and beckoning—and always looking like this next bit was really it, you were right on the point of stepping into another realm altogether.

10
The First
Group of Trips

I TOOK TO MADNESS like a duck to water. I couldn't remember when I'd last spent so enjoyable an afternoon. This dimension of magic, of the unknown, was precisely what had been missing from my life: and I didn't just mean the funny or pretty bits. Right from the first I appreciated the self-confrontation. What I had needed was to stretch the envelope.

Doing some more the next weekend did cross my mind . . . but then I reflected, no, that's rushing it a bit. But the weekend after that, I thought, well, I can't see any reason not to. The 100-microgram dose seemed plenty to be going on with, and so I got out my sheet of blotter and carefully cut out another one of the perforated squares.

I tripped in the bedroom again, and again had a wonderful afternoon, which I spent in almost exactly the same way—the most intense part of the trip with the blindfold and earphones, then the bath, then the walk on the Heath.

In fact, from the first my tripping tended to ritualize itself. I began to take a 100-microgram trip every second or, more frequently, every third weekend. To my surprise, the blindfold and earphones worked brilliantly. The blindfold allowed me to let go of the world and other people completely, while the music was like an Ariadne's thread I could follow through whatever happened. Should things threaten to become overwhelming, I just went back to concentrating on the music. Rather than feeling at the mercy of my mind, I felt more open and relaxed than I ever had when I tripped in my youth.

The real change the blindfold brought was to make me more aware of my emotions. As the trip came on, it made them bigger and clearer, like a magnifying glass. Yet at the same time I would have been hard put to verbalize what I was feeling so intensely. Something incredibly poignant was trying to thrust itself into my awareness, but I still couldn't see what it was. I kept arching my spine, trying to loosen the tension I felt in my lower back.

When it came, the rush was like a dam breaking. Psychologically I was bowled over by a wave of collective and symbolic material. LSD must be God's gift to the Jungians, I remember thinking, during one of the moments I surfaced from the flood of visions, voices, and emotions. These followed one another so fast I had difficulty keeping up with them, dazzled by the bravura of the . . . psychedelic language, or so I came to call it.

For the pace of its delivery was manic. Scenes zoomed in and out and were jump-cut. Voice-overs and snatches of dialogue came and went. Most of the material was realistic, but sometimes scenes slipped into cartoon. Sometimes words were printed; there were even, as I recall, occasional diagrams. Technically, if the visions brought anything to mind, it was movie trailers or TV commercials. There was the same almost Cubist abandonment of any single viewpoint. Was this where the media drew their hypnotic power from, I wondered, from stumbling upon, then systematically exploiting, the language of the unconscious mind?

By the second or third trip, however, specific themes were beginning to stand out and evolve—and the serial approach began to make self-evident sense. I had marked a passage from *Realms of the Human Unconscious* where Grof discusses this development of material from one session to the next.

Rather than being unrelated and random, the experiential content seemed to represent a successive unfolding of deeper and deeper levels of the unconscious. It was quite common that identical or very similar clusters of visions, emotions, and physical symptoms occurred in several consecutive LSD sessions. Patients often had the feeling that they were returning again and again to a specific experiential area and each time could get deeper into it. After several sessions, such clusters would then converge into a complex reliving of traumatic memories. When these memories were relived and integrated, the previously recurring phenomena never reappeared in subsequent sessions and were replaced by others.[1]

Mother and child, that was probably my first clear "cluster of visions, emotions, and physical symptoms." As with the warrior/poet of my first trip, this archetype was something I perceived from different viewpoints, sometimes from inside, sometimes from out. Sometimes I saw the child through the mother's eyes, sometimes the mother through those of the child. There were confused episodes where I seemed to have become a woman myself and be giving birth to a child; and despite my intoxication, I became surprisingly embarrassed by this and tried to pretend it wasn't happening.

During one of these early sessions I switched the music on the Walkman from *In C* to Henryk Gorecki's 1975 Third Symphony: his *Symphony of Sorrowful Songs,* with its three songs in which different women are lamenting death. Attraction to this particular symphony was definitely a prompt from the unconscious, for it both mirrored and magnified something I was feeling more and more . . . a kind of passionate grief. Then each time, as the trip began to level off, I would remove the mask and earphones and run a bath.

There I basked in the suds while the collective unconscious or whatever it was continued to throb, though more evenly now, through my veins. Ego loss crept upon me without my even noticing. Several times, half-submerged amid mounds of foam sparkling like a Christmas tree,

I realized I had completely forgotten who I was. Once I had to get a glass of water from the kitchen and wandered, dripping wet, through the living room. Glancing at the long pine table with the computer on it, the few books, the window box full of summer flowers, I wondered briefly who lived there . . . only to climb back in the bath and promptly forget about it.

What a paradoxical space acid accessed! Hardly ever had I felt I was myself so intensely, yet at the same time I hadn't a clue who I was! Never had I imagined personality to be something so superficial, something you could peel off so easily, peel off without impeding the normal functioning of the mind . . . peel off, in fact, without even noticing it had gone!

By the late afternoon the drug's effects had started to ebb, and I would go out for a walk on the Heath.

I headed for the Vale of Health, which, with its wildness, its unkempt banks of bramble and willow herb, was my favorite part of the Heath. I would wander around the woods or sit quietly on the bank of the pond, watching the mallards and moorhens.

As early as those first sessions, I noticed the way trips fall into two halves, the first half tending toward self-confrontation, while the second is more about integrating what you have experienced. And the extent to which you managed to assimilate everything was, or so it seemed to me, the extent to which the world became so lovely.

And by and large, that was it. By the time I got home from the Heath I would be getting tired, not so much physically as drained emotionally. I tended to spend the evening quietly at home; and rather than go through what I remembered as LSD's hours of twitching half-life, I took a mild sleeping pill and went to bed early.

However, there was one last and, so far as I was concerned, essential part to the session. First thing the next morning I'd write up everything I could remember of the day before; I did this religiously in a fancy hardback notebook I'd bought.

Rereading those early entries today, they seem dominated by

two particular themes: first by Jung and his concept of the collective unconscious; and second by speculation as to the extent the collective unconscious could be mapped over the right hemisphere of the brain as understood in terms of the "twin"- or "split"-brain theory.

From what I could remember of '70s pop psychology, the gist of split-brain theory was that the two hemispheres of the brain were specialized to very different ends and played widely differing roles in our daily lives. Physically, the left lobe of the brain controlled the right side of the body, while the right lobe controlled the left side. In terms of cognition, the left hemisphere was the seat of language and reason—of analysis, linear time, and numeracy—while the right was the locus of something trickier to define, a capacity to process large amounts of data at great speed, to perceive intuitively and express understanding in terms of symbol and myth. Put in terms of a much simplified diagram:

LEFT HEMISPHERE	RIGHT HEMISPHERE
word	symbol
thought	emotion
logic	intuition
analysis	synthesis
time	simultaneity
technology	art
history	myth

For centuries, Western industrial society has overplayed the importance of the left hemisphere, referring to it as the major hemisphere, while systematically downgrading the right and calling it the minor hemisphere. The idea I was pushing around in my journal was that LSD brought about a revolutionary reversal of this hemispheric dominance.

Could Aldous Huxley's "reducing valve of the brain and nervous system" be delineated more precisely, as something specifically designed to throttle the contribution of the right brain? A reducing valve that, when "bypassed" by mescaline, LSD, or other psychedelics, could no longer prevent the left brain being flooded by the very different way the right perceived, allowing a glimpse of the possibility the two hemispheres could one day be harmonized, bringing about a far richer, literally stereoscopic vision of life in the world?

As a theory, this didn't seem particularly implausible.

Historically, split-brain research did become the theater of a last-ditch attempt by '60s and '70s counterculture to draw a profile of precisely what was being repressed by industrial society.[2] For when Huxley writes that what comes out of the reducing valve is "a measly trickle of the kind of consciousness which will help us to stay alive on the surface of this particular planet," I think he's being distinctly ingenuous. What comes out is more precisely the type of consciousness demanded by industry, wage labor, and class society. Arguably, it's not helping us stay alive particularly well at all; and undeniably it is banning 50 percent or more of our nature to unconsciousness . . . to sleep, and to dreams.

11
Session 6
Doubling the Dose

THOSE INITIAL TRIPS SAW my anxiety about aging and death disappear. For the first time in years I had found something that fired my imagination. "Acid's one hell of a hobby," I joked with friends, who did not seem especially amused. In fact, when I tried to tell them what I was doing, they quickly grew uncomfortable.

Old friends in particular (and these were the very ones who prided themselves on having tripped when they were young) looked at me with such incredulity it would have been comical were it not that they must have been regarding their own youth with the same blank incomprehension.

I began to suspect that bad, or at least grueling, trips had been far more widespread than anyone in the '60s and '70s had cared to admit. In itself this wasn't a problem; it only became one because of insistence on the part of Tim Leary and the underground press that almost everyone had feel-good "mystical" trips; those who did not were made to feel there was something wrong with them. A sort of sullen resentment at such misrepresentation (rather than media scaremongering) strikes me as being at the root of much of the demonization of LSD that has lasted until the present day.

Whatever the reason, I found myself alone; and this was to prove a handicap.

Several entries in the trip journal complain that during the peak of a session I felt that everything was happening so fast I was missing much of it and that what I needed was a close friend who shared my enthusiasm and with whom I could have swapped sessions as a "sitter"—ideally, someone who could implement whatever agenda we had agreed upon (using a tape recorder, for instance) and generally keep the trip on track. This, I realized, was going to become even more important when it came to experimenting with higher doses, which by now I fully intended to do.

Blanket negativity on the part of friends ruled out any possibility of collaboration, and I found myself edged into a course that was to become increasingly solitary. So perhaps there was more than mere bravado—a flash of anger, perhaps—when I thought, to hell with this, I'm going to double the dose!

Probably it was a blessing none of my friends saw me on my first 200-microgram dose, as their fears would have been amply confirmed.

The rush was alarming, by anyone's standards. My legs were not just vibrating; they were drumming on the bed with such fury I lifted the blindfold to stare incredulously. Then my teeth started to chatter, and my whole body to shake: yet, perversely, none of it dissolved a sense of numbness that became steadily more oppressive. Repeatedly I tried to stretch, as though there were muscles I could loosen by main force.

Several times I tore earphones and blindfold off and mooned around the apartment, moaning melodramatically to myself. I knew I was hamming it up, but that was beside the point: the distinction between imagination and reality was wearing paper thin.

The apartment looked wrong. Normally I loved its raffishness, but now both apartment and its contents looked seedy to the point of being sinister. Gazing around I thought, Christ, what a dump! How has my life come to this? Which wasn't without a certain humor, since I was rapidly losing any idea of where I had come to, period. Peering through the living-room window, I failed to recognize the buildings on the other side of the lawn. The lawn itself appeared baked and drought-ridden, which led me to believe I was in California, possibly in the suburbs of Los Angeles.

At the moment I turned away from the window, my mind went into overdrive. Everything started to happen so fast it became a blur. I don't know how long this lasted, just a minute or so, I imagine, when equally abruptly everything started to decelerate again . . . like a movie that has been on fast-forward returning to normal with a jerk.

Phew! I thought, what was that? My mind had become disconcertingly clear; I no longer felt high at all. I went back to the bedroom, lay down on the bed, and dutifully replaced headphones and sleeping mask . . . but no sooner did I press Play on the Walkman than everything went crazy again, seriously this time.

If there was any music on the headphones, I never heard it. Instead my mind was filled with . . . something I don't know how to describe, except by saying it was a huge breakthrough in anything I had previously considered to be "psychedelic language." Technically there was the same high-speed trailer or TV-commercial delivery I've already noted, though now the voice-over was much more forceful. In fact, I seemed to have tuned in to something resembling an educational program: to my astonishment, I found I was being lectured. What was so fantastic was the way the information was being conveyed. For I was being taught from the inside, as it were: as though I had looked something up in an encyclopedia, but instead of reading the entry, I was actually experiencing it. The text was lived existential states.

So amazed was I that it took me several moments to realize that the lecture, or whatever it was, was about Zen Buddhism. Parallels between Zen and LSD were announced as though bullet-pointed:

- same zeroing in on the present instant
- same passion for beauty
- same spiritual violence

Overwhelmed as I was, I started to get indignant. What was this madness that had been turned on in my head as though I were a radio? Perhaps I shouldn't have been disrespectful, for the tone, which originally had been one of bonhomie—very like the diffuse jocularity of talks on the radio—began to slow down and even sound faintly threatening.

Finally, the lecture led up to the statement that for Zen, everything is interconnected: the heart of mysticism is knowledge that the part can contain the whole.

Now the earlier jokiness vanished without a trace—and the argument became swift, silent, and exclusively visual. At its climax, there was a brief series of images projected against a glaring white background, flickering and scratched a little, like an empty movie screen.

The first was a faint outline of perfect lips, pale gray against the white, about to speak one last word . . .

The next, of a fine and very beautiful hand about to make a single gesture . . .

Finally the outline of one leaf whose fall would express absolutely everything . . .

The little yellow bedroom had grown ominously quiet.

In a single paranoid flash I saw where it was all heading . . . and my skin started to crawl. Each image had been of the whole about to manifest in the part—but I knew with every fiber of my being that if the whole manifested here and now, the bedroom and I would be instantly annihilated. I couldn't breathe, and for the first time I reconnected, reconnected with my whole being, with the sick terror of that night in Tangier.

Again I was frozen in the split-second before the universe dissolved: before I was swallowed and sucked into a hideous writhing vortex. From somewhere I heard the phrase "cosmic engulfment."

This couldn't have lasted more than a few seconds before I leaped to my feet, throwing mask and headphones aside. I blundered into the bathroom, turned on the cold tap, and repeatedly splashed water on my face. Then I went into the living room and, like that night in Tangier, began to pace up and down; and, just as it had all those years before, a shaky apology for normal subject/object relations began to reestablish itself.

After a few minutes I remembered I had a bit of dope somewhere; I managed to find it and roll an equally shaky apology for a one-paper spliff. I took a hesitant drag, as I thought the smoke might make it worse . . . but no, whatever it was had gone; gradually the smoke calmed me down.

The next morning I sat staring blankly at the trip journal. What on Earth had happened? Was that Grof's "transpersonal realm"? If so, describing it as "multilayered and multidimensional" was putting it mildly. How did such an amalgam of diverse elements—astoundingly sophisticated communication, buffoonery, and stone-cold terror— belong together?

Above all, what got through to me was the fear.

So nothing had really changed. LSD still had the power to terrify me in a way nothing else had ever done, with a quality of the super- natural, of metaphysical damnation nothing else could command, and that an intervening lifetime had done nothing to diminish. At the heart of LSD was something that scared the living daylights out of me . . . but what was it?

Confused and upset, I turned to Aldous Huxley and reread *The Doors of Perception* and found, much to my surprise, that Huxley had gone through something very similar.

I had forgotten a key passage in his essay. His trip had not, as I remembered, peaked in the living room, the is-ness of which had been so miraculously revealed to him. Not in his perception of his books, nor his vase of flowers, nor his furniture . . . no, the climax had come just after that. Huxley had wandered out of the living room into the garden, dazzling in the L.A. sunshine, and been stopped dead in his tracks by the explosion of terrifyingly beautiful color into which a gar- den chair had turned.

Confronted by a chair which looked like the Last Judgment—or, to be more accurate, by a Last Judgment which, after a long time and with considerable difficulty, I recognized as a chair—I found myself all at once on the brink of panic. This, I suddenly felt, was going too far. Too far, even though the going was into intenser beauty, deeper significance. The fear, as I analyse it in retrospect, was of being overwhelmed, of disintegrating under a pressure of reality greater than a mind, accustomed to living most of the time in a cosy world of symbols, could possibly bear.

Magnificent description that this was, and while I could recognize much of my own experience reflected there, I felt there was something missing. Huxley suggested such visions were purgatorial. "The literature of religious experience," he continued, "abounds in references to the pains and terrors overwhelming those who have come, too suddenly, face to face with some manifestation of the *Mysterium tremendum*."

I wasn't sure about this. Obviously any premature revelation of God, or naked Being or whatever you want to call it, would induce the most primitive religious or ontological terror . . . yet this still didn't fully explain my own reaction. What had been truly horrible was the sense I knew more about this terror than I could remember. Somewhere, or so I suspected, I had known it before. Deep down, it was familiar.

12

BPM 2

WHILE *THE DOORS OF PERCEPTION* did corroborate my experience, it failed to explain it. Where, for instance, did the demented lecture on Zen fit in? I fetched my copy of *Realms of the Human Unconscious* and sat down to reread the chapter dealing with Grof's "perinatal": the realm in which the traumas undergone by the physical body, in particular the birth trauma, are coded. Almost immediately I stumbled on the expression "cosmic engulfment." So that was where that came from, I thought, and I continued reading all the more attentively

Something I hadn't realized was the extent to which tales of the religious experiences accessed by LSD had drawn attention away from reports of very different effects the drug could also have—especially episodes of physical pain and apparently unmotivated terror.

These couldn't be brushed aside as either slipshod set and setting, or only typical of neurotic subjects. Earlier I mentioned the independent research project run by Oscar Janiger, the L.A. psychiatrist who pioneered the study of the effects of LSD on normal, well-adjusted people. Janiger's set and setting had been impeccable. First, volunteers were screened for any sign of instability; then they were given their trip (generally a moderate dose in the 100–150 microgram range) in a laid-back, nonconfrontational setting, with professional assistance at hand should it prove necessary—yet the number of complaints of physical pain or other bizarre bodily sensations was surprisingly high.

"I feel paralyzed . . ." "I feel choked . . ." "I can hardly breathe . . ." "My body is being pummeled, squeezed, knotted, or twisted . . ." "I thought I was strangling . . ." "I am in agony . . ." These are all quotes from Janiger's subjects, and there are plenty more of them. Equally striking were what you could perhaps describe as cosmic panic attacks. "Everything seemed to fall apart . . ." "There was nothing to hang on to . . ." "I had a feeling of falling into some bottomless place which was simply terrifying . . ." "I was afraid of being absolutely and irrevocably obliterated . . ." "I have never known such a complete and utter state of helplessness . . ." "I was terrified, only it was a terror beyond terror . . ."[1]

By no means were such reactions universal, but Leary and the underground press, obsessed with promoting LSD, had downplayed if not ignored their very existence. Not only was this intellectually dishonest, but it blinded them to the cutting-edge research going on at the time. Stanislav Grof, still working in Prague, had witnessed far more alarming physical symptoms than any of Janiger's subjects had reported: patients who appeared to be suffocating, changing skin color, undergoing muscular seizures, cardiac irregularities, and projectile vomiting. But Grof had based much of his understanding on observation of such phenomena.

What he suggested was that such subjects were reliving aspects of difficult births. In itself this wasn't unduly contentious. Freud himself had drawn attention to the similarity between symptoms of acute anxiety attacks and the subjective experience of birth; and it was one of his most promising disciples, Otto Rank, who broke with the master because Rank insisted that what he named "the birth trauma" played a much more significant role in individual development than the Freudian Oedipus complex.

Throughout the history of psychoanalysis there had been isolated incidents of patients apparently reliving their births—all that LSD had done was open the floodgates to them. All Grof did, on the strength of his clinical observations, was amplify Rank's concept and suggest there were four major, and clearly differentiated, categories of prebirth experience. These he characterizes as follows:

cosmic unity

The deepest strata of memories accessible to us are those of simple happiness. Reflecting our original symbiosis with the mother and the universe, they confirm everything popular imagination has always ascribed to life in the womb. Once everything was perfect just the way it was. Relived on LSD, this is expressed as moments of feeling an integral part of the whole: of transcendence of space and time, and participation in the sacred. This is the nirvana of Buddhism, or Christianity's "peace which passeth all understanding."

"cosmic engulfment" and the "no-exit" situation

The second major strata of memories—which correspond to the first clinical stage of delivery—are entirely at odds with the first. Rather than being of serenity and bliss, they are of fear and pain. There are two distinct groups of such memories. The first is panic, then terror, at the first uterine contractions and the baby's perception that its life is threatened from an unknown source. This Grof refers to as fear of "cosmic engulfment." Second is physical torture, as the contractions increase, bringing enormous pressures to bear, while the cervix still refuses to dilate. This is the "no-exit" situation.

the death/rebirth struggle

The third great matrix—corresponding to the second clinical stage of delivery—consists of memories of the birth canal. While still subject to the pain of contractions, the cervix is now open, and the baby is fighting desperately for its life. Recurring on LSD, this is reflected as any sensation or vision of a struggle to survive calling for heroic effort. Battles, storms, natural disasters, titanic or apocalyptic conflict are all typical. (When I first read Grof's account of this third matrix, I remember thinking that if he was right, then this fueled the plot of practically every Hollywood movie ever made.)

delivery

The final strata of our most primitive memories, corresponding to the third clinical stage of delivery, are of birth itself, of separation from the mother and successfully attaining independent life. This is the matrix of spiritual rebirth, the archetype suffusing all the blissful trips with which the history of LSD abounds. Grof notes as particularly characteristic:

> enormous decompression, expansion of space, visions of gigantic halls; radiant light and colors (heavenly blue, golden, rainbow, peacock feathers); feelings of rebirth and redemption; appreciation of simple way of life; sensory enhancement; brotherly feelings; humanitarian and charitable tendencies.

At the time I didn't know what to make of any of this—and all I am doing at the moment is to give a quick synopsis of what I read. For the really important bit came next. Grof suggested that these primal experiences, our very first taste of sentient life in the world, were of an intensity that nothing in our subsequent life could rival, and as such they formed existential cores around which all subsequent experience tended to congregate and classify itself.

In fact, or so it struck me, he was proposing a new body of archetypes, although, perhaps because of the overriding Jungian associations, he did not want to use the term. Instead he called them Basic Perinatal Matrices, abbreviated (mercifully, I remember thinking at the time) to BPM. Thus mystical experiences, experiences of cosmic unity, were referred to as BPM 1; classic bad trips were BPM 2; experiences of heroic effort in life-threatening circumstances were BPM 3; while those of spiritual rebirth were BPM 4.

In his experience of hands-on LSD psychotherapy, Grof said, if an individual's memories of pleasure or pain were traced back through his or her life, they would betray increasingly clear features of their origin in the perinatal realm. Consciously reexperiencing the core memories themselves could help cure physical and mental problems as surely as remembering crucial postnatal trauma. However, full reliving of the core experience (and this was something he stressed) was not always essential. Matrices could become conscious in various symbolic or even philosophic forms and be successfully integrated on this level alone.

Finally, in his observation, BPM 2 tended to be the first material from the deep unconscious to be activated by LSD. As a rule of thumb, the order in which the matrices manifested was BPM 2, then BPM 3, then BPM 4—and only last of all BPM 1, the realm of nondual perception.

As I said, I didn't know what to make of any of this, which made it all the weirder that my next trip, my 200-microgram session, did evidence exactly such a progressive unfolding of BPMs 2, 3, and 4 . . .

I was lying down, blindfold and headphones in place, listening to the Gorecki Third as the trip came on. The recording was of the Krakow Philharmonic with Zofia Kilanowicz. At best, this gives a somber interpretation of the first movement, which was further amplified by the LSD; and by the time Zofia Kilanowicz started to sing the first of the three songs, the drug was conjuring up the totalitarian nightmare of the twentieth century.

Darkness lay over Europe, an omnipresent brooding evil, and I was transfixed by the despair of hundreds of thousands of people. I lay motionless on my bed, watching the series of movielike dissolves that had begun to appear behind the blindfold . . . Troop trains, the smoke from their funnels dirty against the dark sky . . . Barbed wire . . . Sentries . . . Turrets . . . The death camps . . .

By the end of the first movement, the acid was about to rush. The Krakow Philharmonic recording was live; in the pause between the first and second movements I could hear people coughing and resettling themselves, and it felt as though I was in the concert hall in person. Then there was silence, and sudden attentiveness. Everyone was rooting for Zofia.

The second song is the prayer scratched into the Gestapo cell wall by the eighteen-year-old girl waiting to be taken out and shot.

> *No, Mother, do not weep,*
> *Most chaste Queen of Heaven*
> *Protect me always.*

Images were coming thick and fast now . . . Goose-stepping jack-boots . . . Ghettoes . . . High walls with coils of barbed wire mortared into the top . . . Packs of ragged feral children . . . The images mimicked flickering black-and-white newsreel: scratched clips of old war footage, crudely spliced. Panning shots of puddles, peeling posters, blackened bridges. It was cold, terribly cold, I felt/knew that . . .

Again the scene dissolved, this time into a vast, ill-lit prison, with corridors extending in every direction. I could hear the clanging of cell doors, see (blurred, as though for some reason looking up from underwater) monstrously misshapen guards patrolling up and down the catwalks. I could hear them shouting to one another. I was in one of the cells, huddled on the floor. I had been tortured, my teeth were smashed, I was waiting to be shot.

Yet as I listened to Sofia Kilanowicz, I could feel myself being swept up by the power and beauty of her voice. Through all the horror an insane glory began to shine. This wasn't about pain and degradation any more, this was about redemption. About triumph. (In terms of Grof's model, presumably this would be where BPM 2 was ceding place to BPM 3.) I saw a vision, I saw crowds of people dressed in white singing together. They were working to create some kind of new universal religious ritual.

And lying on my bed in contemporary NW3, I found myself furiously trying to compose a cantata. I could sample the tramp of the marching boots, I thought excitedly; the slamming metal doors, the cries and screams. I was bursting with energy. I remembered a Klaus Schulze concert at the Royal Festival Hall I had gone to: toward the end Schulze had been stamping on the floor, bouncing up and down on his stool, and hammering the synthesizer keys with clenched fists. That was how I felt.

The Gorecki Third was conjuring up visions of the future: of a quite different conception of technology, one designed to process pain and turn it into wonder. Designed to . . . designed to transfigure. That's the whole purpose of art, I thought, to transmute the personal into the collective, because only on the collective level can individual pain be redeemed!

As the symphony drew toward its close, this trip, like the preceding one, tried to summarize its message in the simplest of symbols: virtually in cartoon.

Again there was a series of images, each one slowly dissolving into the next, only this time the images were crudely executed black-and-white drawings. Each depicted the successive stages of a grass seed germinating and forcing its way up from deep underground. And with perfect synchrony, the last image—a single blade of grass breaking though concrete into the sunlight—coincided with the last notes of the symphony.

After a while I removed the blindfold and earphones and got up from the bed. I stepped into the corridor, and to my amazement I saw that the whole apartment was bathed with light—with visionary, otherworldly pastels whose loveliness took my breath away. Perhaps the vision lasted four or five seconds, then melted away. Months were to pass before I put this together with Grof's thesis that BPM 4, the psychedelic archetype of spiritual rebirth, was frequently accompanied by rainbowlike spectra of color.

13

Session 8

Windle Hey

DURING THE FIRST MONTHS I was getting into tripping, the vivid recollections of childhood I mentioned earlier continued to occur. My mind appeared to be caught in an autobiographical undertow: more and more people, places, and events reappeared, and despite large gaps they were beginning to join up.

The earliest memory I had was of the sea breaking through barbed wire . . . Gran and I are on the beach at Crosby, and we've paddled out among the defenses against German invasion by sea. These are large concrete star-shaped structures, like giant toy jacks, designed to sink landing craft. Gran has her beret pulled down and a Craven A in her cigarette holder; with one hand she is holding up her skirt, with the other she is waving a tiny lace handkerchief at a ship far away on the horizon.

Going home we drive through Crosby itself. Merseyside got some of the worst of the Blitz, and there are bombsites everywhere: terraces full of gaps where houses had been. Just four squares of colored wallpaper to mark the rooms and a zigzag of bare brick for the stairs. Holes in the rubble leading to flooded cellars and air-raid shelters. But all this vanishes as we leave Crosby, then follow Moor Lane out of town and turn down the long drive to Windle Hey . . .

I am sketching in this background because, though I hadn't any inkling of it, my personal history was about to erupt in my trips . . . During the war my father had been stationed in Kashmir, and while he was away my mother fell in love with an American posted in England. In the domestic fracas that followed my father's return in 1945, I was dumped on my Gran, and most of the first ten years of my life were spent with her.

From the first she was more of an overgrown playmate than an adult. Another of my earliest memories is of her sitting on her chamber pot telling me how someone had "made a fortune" by buying up chamber pots on the cheap and color-printing Hitler's face on the bottom. We were sitting in front of the electric fire in her bedroom, her on the pot, me getting dressed and listening to her, wide-eyed. Outside the sea-fog swirled around Windle Hey.

Most of the money was long gone. Maudsley the gardener just about managed to stay on top of the huge garden. The tennis court had been dug up and fruit trees planted during the war. The wire mesh of the aviary was ripped, and the punt drawn up on the little beach in the woods had a hole in it. Whatever we may have lacked materially, however, was amply compensated by Gran's *folie de grandeur*.

She drove a 1930s maroon-colored Hillman sports car, once perhaps the height of fashion, but that now was falling to pieces. A tear in the hood grew larger until a bird found its way in and nested in the glove compartment; until the chicks were fledged we had to take the bus to Crosby. Another time, back from the cinema, Gran found she couldn't open the car door and, calling for Maudsley, had him fetch his felling ax and chop the door off its hinges. Ever afterward a rope stretched across the front from the door handle on my side to hold in the door on her side; on arriving at our destination I had to sit right back in my seat while she leaned over and unhitched the rope, which whipped across our laps, and the car door fell into the street. "It's Mrs. B—," she announced firmly as the bell tinkled and we entered Duckles the Grocer's (Mr. Duckles was the mayor of Crosby) as though this was sufficient explanation, as indeed it appeared to be.

I was to take these early lessons in surrealism only too well to heart. Doubtless they were driven home by the inordinate amount of time we spent at the pictures. Any afternoon too wet to play in the garden, or for us to go on one of our long walks through the fields, we'd drive to one of the many cinemas in Crosby. So far as I remember, we sat through an almost uninterrupted diet of Hollywood films noirs, a taste for which, like comic books, the departing U.S. Army had left in its wake. I remember Gran momentarily averting the smoking Craven A in its Dunhill holder to lean toward me in the dark and hiss conspiratorially, "What *ghastly* women!"

She insisted that, at the end of the performance, we stand for the National Anthem. This was played along with a Technicolor clip of the king sitting on horseback, in full military regalia, saluting endless troops marching past. Gran held the billowing Craven A behind her back so the king wouldn't see.

The session in which my personal story was to explode started in the same way as the others. Perhaps it was worse. Again I was twisting on the bed with the pressure building, until I thought I was going to burst. Never before had I seen nightmarish visions inside my head, but now I did: slithering, dark things; piles of wet coils, vicious eyes flicking this way and that, seeking me out. Tentacles whipped at my face, and instinctively my head jerked sideways . . . and a wash of watery blood, like something out of a horror movie, was spilling across the visual field behind the mask.

Then everything just popped. What it was all about was devastatingly clear. The journal entry I scribbled—and underlined—the following morning starts:

> The sense of inner pressure, which has been mounting steadily throughout the first part of all the trips I have taken, finally exploded yesterday.

Suddenly I saw what I have been repressing from the first . . . the most terrible sense of worthlessness.

Everything I have ever tried to do has been a complete failure. Subconsciously I am eaten away by self-hatred . . .

I stood in the middle of the bedroom, stunned.

Finally I got it together to lie down again, fumble the Gorecki Third into the Walkman, and put the mask and earphones back on. Almost immediately the music centered everything, and I lay there quietly for fifteen or twenty minutes, just listening; then as the first movement drew to its close, I received a kind of inner communication. Not exactly a spoken voice, yet something quite apart from normal thought.

Get the old photos out!

Instinctively I knew this meant the pile of photos and family albums I had in the back of the bedroom cupboard. Clutching the Walkman, and with Sofia launching into the second song, I fetched them out and dumped them on the duvet. Then I started to go through them.

Providentially, the key ones seemed to be all together at the top. First I found a large photo of my father in his World War Two uniform, looking absurdly young. Visibly the air between us began to darken, and quickly I laid the photograph aside. Next came an enlarged snapshot of my brother, Gilead, on a beach in Cornwall, one around Land's End where we used to spend our summer holidays; and after that I found the studio portrait of Mum I remembered so well from childhood. She looked as beautiful as I remembered her . . . but at the same time there was something terribly wrong. The angle she was holding her head made her look unnervingly like a snake getting ready to strike. There was something venomous about the rosebud mouth. There was a mad light in her eye. I wondered how I had never seen it before. Then there was one of me at five or six looking sweet, confused, and apprehensive . . . like a lamb to the middle-class slaughter, I reflected bitterly.

I worked down through the pile (the Gorecki still playing on the

Walkman) with a growing sense of impatience. I knew I was looking for something, but I didn't know what. At first I thought it must be a photo of Gran. Disconcertingly, there didn't seem to be any . . . and with one of those instant flashes you get on acid I knew there had been something badly wrong between her and my mother. Then I realized what I was looking for wasn't even so much a picture of Gran. What I was looking for was one of the gardens at Windle Hey.

There must be *something,* I thought, speeding through an entire album. The garden had been huge; there must be a glimpse of it somewhere. A woman friend who was also dumped as a young child once told me she had responded to abandonment by making nature her mother, and I think I had done something similar. Certainly the pain of losing that garden was as deep as that of any bereavement . . .

The ponds!

That was what I was looking for!

The acid was roaring in my ears as I went through the pile, faster and faster. I don't believe it, I thought, there isn't anything . . . until finally, almost at the very bottom, I found two large photos. Originally both had been framed and were still glued to their cardboard backing, old and very scuffed. The first was of the garden shortly after it had been laid out—it must have been from the late 1920s or early '30s— and showed the winding, iris-fringed path, which led to the island bed of azaleas and the little lead statue of Peter Pan on its pillar.

The photo had faded to the yellow/brown of really old photos, and on the acid it looked like a door to another time: like a path in a fairy tale, or the path you follow down into sleep, into the world of dreams. As I stared at it, it began to shift as though the focal depth was being readjusted, the center becoming clearer and clearer, which created a vertiginous sense of movement, as though it was getting bigger and sucking me in. Alarmed, I put it down again.

The other photo, and this was the one that went straight to my heart, was of the ducks on the last pond—the one deepest in the woods, where nobody but me ever went.

The ducks!

This photo too was charged with mojo. As I looked, it too appeared to be growing bigger . . . then I thought, No, it can't be doing that, it's more that the acid is magnifying bits if I concentrate on them. Yet the edges of the pond, where the trees came down to the water, were looking almost preternaturally real. With a start I remembered the mat of varied shocking pinks where tree roots were exposed underwater, and the shadowy amber world where the minnows and sticklebacks lived. As a young child I remember thinking that growing up meant that the world, not me, got bigger and bigger. I had imagined that I would be able to swim down into Gran's ponds, through the huge twigs and giant leaves and rays of underwater sunlight, silently like a frogman in a war movie.

What happened next had me staring incredulously!

First one then another of the mallards or moorhens seemed to wake up and start, jerkily at first, to move about, until they were all doing something. Around they went, pecking and waddling, the swimming moorhens making that prodding backward-and-forward movement with their heads. More bizarrely, some ducks in the background were ascending and descending almost vertically, like bees. The photo was like a laptop screen playing a flickering sepia documentary from the depths of my unconscious.

God, I thought, I'm seeing this the way a young child would see it. I am seeing what I once saw when I was very little.

Something broke—and the tears started to pour.

All of it had been taken away! My Gran and her magical world had been taken away! The grief throbbed like a wound that had just been inflicted . . . and suddenly I grasped the whole story of my life. Nothing had ever lived up to the promise of childhood. It was as simple as that. That was where the sense of failure came from; from that, and from the fact that somehow, though I still didn't know exactly what I'd done, I had been responsible for it. Somehow I had betrayed myself. I'd swapped everything I had—and it was everything; I'd had the whole world in my hands—for an adulthood that was worth nothing. Nothing at all. The awful simplicity of it took my breath away.

I was still trailing the headphone wires from the Walkman, the Gorecki had reached its climax, and the tears came in great sobbing waves. They would begin to subside, then I'd remember something else . . . the way frog spawn felt when you lifted it out of the water with both hands . . . the smell of caterpillars when you kept them in a jelly jar . . . my collection of birds' eggs (Gran said it was all right taking one so long as there were four or more, because birds could only count to three) . . . and I'd be sobbing my heart out again.

I hadn't cried like that since those days—not with that abandon, the way the tears welled promptly, unstoppably, like blood from a deep cut. And in and out of my grief flickered something of another quality altogether, a sense my personal sorrow was about to open into something still more profound, more general, the memory of some dim, holy place we had all once shared—shared and lost for reasons none of us could understand. But that was something I could only catch a quick glimpse of, out of the corner of my eye, as it were . . .

. . . Sometime later I put the photos back in the cupboard, washed my face, put a different CD on the Walkman, and slipped out of the apartment . . .

A fine rain was falling. I wandered off across the Heath, only this time not heading for the Vale of Health but for the woods around Kenwood. As I walked I could feel my step was lighter: the sense of relief was tangible. I don't know anything to compare with the way you can feel after a good trip, when there's been a breakthrough, catharsis, and then everything reconfigures on a more evolved level. I guess you feel the same sense of being unburdened, of freedom, when there's been a major breakthrough with conventional analysis—but with LSD psychotherapy there's that edge of magic, which seems almost the default setting of psychedelics.

Those ducks actually came back to life!

Finally I reached the woods at Kenwood, and it began to rain harder. I was playing Vivaldi on the Walkman, and there were fanfares of trumpets as I wandered through the dripping trees. That evening in the rain was the first time I knew for certain that I wasn't going to give up with the acid. I didn't give a damn what anybody said; I would trust it, and follow it wherever it led, and if I had to do it on my own, then so be it.

Ironically enough, wandering around Kenwood that transfigured evening, I didn't realize that those very woods were precisely where it was leading, and that so much was due to happen there. But all that was still a year in the future.

14

Session 9

Mum

THE PHOTOS WERE PAY DIRT—and I knew it. Sorting through the albums and boxes, I selected the few dozen that I thought had real edge. Of Gran and Windle Hey itself there were only two snapshots, so small I had missed them the first time around. These I had enlarged in a High Street print shop and put the blowups on top of a smaller, edited pile. And for the next session, a fortnight later, I repeated exactly the same formula: I waited until the acid started to come on full strength, then put the Gorecki on the Walkman, fetched the new selection of photos, and started to work my way slowly through them. Again I was in tears for most of the trip, in the throes of some of the most raw feelings I had ever known.

Among the first pictures I came to was the one of my brother, Gilead, taken on the beach in Cornwall. It was an enlargement of a holiday snapshot, which had been blown up to portrait size after his death. Looking at it, I realized he would have grown up to be a very good-looking young man; and, feeling sick to the gut, I knew my parents, though they might never have admitted this even to themselves, would have preferred me to have been the one to die. For that was the tragedy that had finally destroyed our family. Dysfunctional from the first, it was Gilead's death that pushed us over the edge.

When I was sixteen my father lost his well-paid executive job, and from middle-class affluence we were abruptly reduced to poverty. I was pulled out of public school, and my parents decided we should start a new life together in West Cornwall, where we went for our holidays every summer and which had always been the high point of our life as a family.

We rented a fisherman's cottage in Newlyn, down by the harbor front, and all went well for the first ten weeks we were there. Then one morning Gil woke with a headache, which grew steadily worse throughout the day. Light became intolerable to him, and the next morning he was rushed to the hospital in Penzance. The doctors diagnosed meningitis, most probably caught from playing in the harbor stream, but it was too late for them to do anything, and he died during the night.

God knows what pain he went through. Presents from his eleventh birthday were still all over the floor of his little attic room. My parents fell apart. My mother had always drunk too much, but after the funeral she set about drinking in earnest. Her behavior became increasingly erratic. Hospitalized briefly, she escaped in the middle of the night, climbing out a lavatory window, shinnying down a drainpipe, and walking back through Penzance in her dressing gown.

Several times she wandered off to my brother's grave with a bottle of gin. Once she disappeared in the middle of the night . . . it was the beginning of her descent into madness.

I had found another photo of Mum while I was going through the old albums, one that I didn't remember ever having seen before. She had been very young at the time, twelve or maybe thirteen; at any rate her hair was still in braids. Perhaps it was the acid, and I was projecting, but she looked as though she was about to burst into tears . . . and my heart went out to her.

On the last trip I had instinctively started talking out loud to the photos, and I tried to do it deliberately with this photo of Mum as a young girl. What had happened to her when she was a child? Why had she hated Windle Hey? What had driven her to the phenomenal amount of reading she had done as a teenager (for she was exceptionally well read by any standards)? What was the story of her American lover?

Again I was in tears.

After my brother's death she converted to Catholicism, which seemed to help; and the following summer when I left Newlyn and went up to London, she and my father had also left Cornwall and moved to a little village in the Cotswolds. There they found an Anne Hathaway cottage (thatched roof, blackened beams, and climbing roses) called Crooked Thatch and promptly bought it. My father had a new job by then, but it meant he had to be away from home sometimes for days on end, leaving Mum alone in the cottage. The village was predictably archconservative; she couldn't make any friends, and she started to crack up.

Her Catholicism buckled under the strain, and she went back to drinking heavily. On several occasions she got in the car and drove it straight through the fields, across pasture, through crops, until finally the car was embedded in a hedge so thick she couldn't accelerate through it; and then she'd uncap the dark green bottle of gin and drink herself unconscious. Another time she climbed out one of the cottage's dormer windows and scrambled up to the top of the thatched roof. She had brought a volume of Aquinas and a bottle of gin and, apparently happy for once, sat there all afternoon drinking, smoking, reading the *Summa Theologica,* and waving good-naturedly down at the occasional passerby.

By this time I had understood why I spent so much time at my Gran's: all along my mother had been much more unbalanced than anyone wanted me to know. Thinking back on my early childhood, I reckon she must have gone on benders and slashed her wrists even then, but now her self-hatred was out of control.

That Christmas Eve my father picked me up at the railway station, and we drove back to Crooked Thatch together, but when we arrived there the cottage was ominously silent and seemed deserted. There was blood all over the living-room floor. Splashes of it led across the carpet and up the stairs. Following the trail up to the bedroom I felt like someone in a horror movie, ascending stairs, which everyone in the audience knows is the very last thing they should be doing. I found her in bed, her wrists crudely self-bandaged. Looking up as I entered she started to thump them on the counterpane to get them bleeding again, roaring with laughter. The scene was straight from a slasher flick.

Two or three psychiatrists and several hospitalizations later my mother had ended up in . . . LSD psychotherapy.

During that time, the late 1950s, far more people than is realized today were being treated with LSD as a very promising if still controversial medical option. My mother checked in as a private patient at Guys Hospital at London Bridge, where they were using much the same approach as Grof was exploring in Prague, the use of a blindfold, the pre- and post-session interviews, and so forth. At Guys they even injected the drug intravenously (a practice later abandoned, as it failed to accelerate the drug's effects).

Each afternoon I used to visit her there, and she would tell me about her latest session. For the most part her sessions were symbolic, quasi-Jungian waking dreams; or at least that was all she told me about. One trip, however, I remember her recounting in detail, during which she lived through her brother John's death in the Second World War. Uncle John was the blue-eyed boy of the family. He had played cricket for Lancashire and was the one destined for great things. During the early days of the war he had enlisted in the Air Force, only to be killed on a training mission in an RAF bomber. On Mum's LSD trip she found herself in the plane's cabin with him during the last moments of his life: as the plane came in to land, the trainee pilot made some fatal miscalculation and the plane cartwheeled and exploded in a fireball. Mum said the force of the blast lifted her bodily off the hospital bed and tossed her on the floor.

She must have had a dozen or more sessions without showing any marked improvement, when, at the tail end of one of them, she was left unsupervised in her hospital room for a few minutes. Seizing the opportunity, she smashed one of the framed photos of my brother she had on her bedside locker (I was sure it was the very photo I had on the duvet before me, the blowup of Gil on the beach) and used the biggest shard of glass to slash her arms again. In the resulting fracas she either discharged herself or, as she insisted, was thrown out by the hospital as intractable. She checked into a hotel, and the next day she and I agreed to rent an apartment in London together.

But (and this was the bit that froze me with shame in the middle of my own trip so many years later) I had made one or another excuse and shortly afterward had fled to Paris. I had to confess, and this made me feel I was going to vomit. I had abandoned her and left her to her fate. I was nineteen; I just couldn't handle her insanity . . . Before this trip I had never admitted to myself that this was what I had done. As with my Gran's death, the emotion felt so raw I couldn't believe forty years had passed. Wherever such memories are stored, it is beyond time as we know it.

To everyone's surprise (possibly first and foremost her own), Mum's LSD psychotherapy turned out to have worked.

Whether she consciously integrated something she never told me about, or whether the shock of Guys throwing her out in the middle of the night broke a pattern of compulsive behavior, something basic shifted. She patched things up with my father, they sold the accursed Crooked Thatch, and they moved into Oxford. For the first time in her life, Mum got a straight job—at Blackwells, the university booksellers—made new friends, and wrote a book about her breakdown and treatment with LSD.

15

Underground Psychotherapy

WHILE I'D BEEN SORTING through the pile of photos of my childhood, I had also leafed through the albums of my own family life. Glancing at pictures of my ex, of our son, of the places we had lived together, I had wondered whether I couldn't use the same combination of photos and LSD to clean out and heal some of the remaining wounds left by what had been a protracted and painful breakup.

Flushed with success from the past two sessions, I couldn't see why not. And so, two or three weeks later, I was back sitting on my bed with several bulky albums of photos beside me on the duvet, waiting for the trip to come on. It seemed to take forever before I could feel that sudden tremulousness, that sense of impending mystery that LSD throws before itself like a shadow.

The bedroom was growing dim and beginning to fade—like the movies when the curtain finally parts, I thought excitedly. Only there wasn't any movie. All that happened was I started to cough.

I coughed, and I coughed.

I hadn't had a trace of a cough a moment before, but now I was gasping for breath. There's something wrong about this, I thought almost immediately. The sense of irritation wasn't located in any particular place, nor did coughing bring any release. Perhaps there's something caught in my throat, I thought, so I went into the bathroom to try to hawk it up . . . but no, there was nothing. Breathing was getting difficult and I was beginning to panic when, as abruptly as it had started, the coughing stopped.

What on Earth was that? I wondered, as I went back to the bedroom and sat down again with the albums. But what happened next was equally disconcerting.

The first photo I came to was one of Asha (that's my ex) taken when she was pregnant. I looked at it for a while . . . and found I didn't feel anything. Nonplussed, I looked at a second one . . . and found that was as lifeless as the first. A third was the same. I couldn't believe it, the vibrancy of my childhood photos—the poetry, their devastating poignancy—simply wasn't there.

Hurriedly I looked for one of our son . . . and, yes, that one worked. Taken when he had lost his front tooth, it went straight to my heart. I turned the pages of the album, and all the photos of him had the same sparkling, happy quality . . . though they didn't suck me into them almost bodily the way the childhood ones did. Looking at the photos of my son simply made me see how much I loved him.

But, returning to the photos of Asha, I drew the same blank. I turned over pages of her pregnancy, of pictures I'd taken of our son's blood-splattered birth, of the funky old North London houses where we had lived . . . and all of it had the emotional impact of a bus timetable.

Uh-uh, I thought, I don't like the look of this. There's something I'm deliberately refusing to feel here. I pushed the albums aside and leaned back against the wall. But what do you do when you run into massive resistance like this? Volatile as ever, the acid promptly turned against me, and I was flooded with doubts about everything I had been trying to do. Could you try to analyze yourself with no professional training of any sort? Didn't dissolving blocks like this call for considerable expertise? Or, I reflected after a moment, was I making a basic mistake with what I was trying to do? Could it be that acid simply didn't work with recent memories? That its forte was the distant past . . . particularly early childhood?

Not just for the rest of the session, but for several days afterward I was in that state of irritability and pervasive depression in which a dud or ill-resolved trip can leave you. I began to suspect I could not think my way through this alone. What I needed was someone to talk to. Probably just a few tips from a professional would be enough . . . but where could I find such a person?

I tried asking around, and I did hear rumors of one woman, an Osho sannyasin, who was said to be practicing clandestine LSD therapy in London. Would she do just a session or two to help me get unstuck? For obvious reasons she wasn't the easiest person to approach, and while I was still putting out feelers, something else happened. I was lent a recent book from the States, which, to my surprise, proved there was already an ongoing underground use of psychedelics in psychotherapy and had been since the late '60s.

The Secret Chief was a slim volume of tape-recorded interviews with an anonymous West Coast psychotherapist, code-named Jacob.

Jacob had worked as a psychotherapist most of his life and had started experimenting with psychedelics while they were still legal. So major a breakthrough did he believe them to be that after they were criminalized, he just went on using them clandestinely. This wasn't as hazardous as it sounds because most of his patients were referred to him privately by lifelong colleagues and friends.

What Jacob did was streamline an initiation. A single client-centered interview was enough for him to answer any practical questions, and for the two of them to work out exactly what the subject wanted to explore and establish an appropriate dose (plus a booster should such prove necessary). All Jacob asked of his clients was that they assemble a series of photographs of themselves and their family since their babyhood.

Trips were scheduled for the early morning, when Jacob would go around to his clients' homes and settle them in with the mandatory blindfold and earphones. During the first half of the trip he was completely nondirective, sitting beside his subjects in silence, merely holding hands should they wish to; or, should they go into deep regression, holding them bodily. Not until the peak was passed and the trip had started to plateau did Jacob remove the blindfold and bring out the collection of photos and a tape recorder.

> I take the first one and I hand it to them and I tell them, "Just look at it, just look at it and see what you experience. If you have anything to say, fine. Say it. If not, you don't have to say anything." One at a time I hand them the pictures. Some time around the age of six is a very significant picture for them. That's the point in life where we lose our naturalness. Frequently they get to that picture and they start to cry. And cry and cry and cry.

I was miffed to learn I hadn't been the first person to discover the potency of photos on LSD; but my appreciation of Jacob's use of a tape recorder (obvious though it was in retrospect) somewhat mollified me.

> I'm taping everything that's being said. They'll do a lot of talking and a lot of crying. And a lot of ruminating, and remembering. This talking is very important to them later on when they go back and listen to it. It reconnects them with their whole experience. I give them the tape. After we've gone through all the pictures we just sit around. Then maybe about four o'clock in the afternoon, say, I arrange to have the baby-sitter come by.[1]

If the subjects found the experience to be what they were looking for, then they could proceed to the second stage of Jacob's initiation. They were introduced to one of several ongoing groups.

Typically these met for a weekend once a month at an isolated country house. On Friday evening, about a dozen people would gather, socialize a bit, then form a circle and talk about what they wanted from the session. The next morning everyone would stake out a spot in the house or grounds that felt right to them and take their trip there. Though LSD remained the drug of choice, several other psychedelics were available, and experimenting with them was encouraged. Two or more helpers were present should there be any problems, but otherwise everyone was left very much to their own devices.

The group as a whole did not assemble again until the following morning, when the circle re-formed and everyone shared what had happened on their trip. This plenary session went on for several hours and was the climax of the weekend.

Jacob continued to expand this clandestine network throughout his sixties and seventies. By the end he estimated he had initiated some four thousand people, a large percentage of them psychotherapists and health care professionals, into the use of psychedelics—particularly, from the mid '80s onward, into Ecstasy. There was never a serious mishap. No psychotic episodes were triggered. No one informed on him, and Jacob continued "tripping" people, as he nicely phrased it, until his death in the '90s.

The Secret Chief, slight a book though it was, had a hugely demystifying effect on the way I saw LSD psychotherapy. Push comes to shove, I thought, I can work out this stuff for myself. Instinctively I had realized that the material that came up in a session needed to be worked through subsequently, and I was doing my best with the trip journal. Equally I had found out about the use of photos on my own, and whatever the block I had run into with them, I would find some way of solving it. Hadn't the first therapists taught themselves? And if they could, then why couldn't the rest of us?

In fact, if ordinary people didn't begin to educate themselves, I couldn't see that psychoanalysis had much of a future left. Clearly everyone's problems are uniquely individual, with roots stretching back to their earliest years, and unpacking them calls for one-to-one attention. But such a process is enormously labor intensive, and basically psychoanalysis had been forced to price itself out of the market—yet without such individual treatment, there wasn't going to be any alternative to state psychiatry blindly prescribing antidepressants to repress symptoms, and with no idea of what the long-term effects of such repression might be.

For the first time I understood what a terrible blow banning LSD from psychoanalysis had been. We've seen that therapists at the time had reckoned the drug could cut down the average duration of individual analysis by a magnitude of ten to one. This could have meant that psychoanalysis entered society as a mass healing force. Either such a huge potential breakthrough was going to have to be scrapped—or the professional mystique about analysis was going to have to be brushed aside, and many of us would have to start to learn the basics.

With acid we would have a head start. Whatever technical skills there were to this or that school of therapy we could rediscover for ourselves. All you really needed to begin was a good sitter—most obviously a lover or close friend—for surely nothing could match the healing power of someone who genuinely cared for you. And, in broader social terms, wouldn't this bring back to friendship and to sexual relationships much of the spiritual muscle that has been filched? "Love has to be reinvented," wrote the French poet Arthur Rimbaud, an observation whose edge time has done nothing to dull. Wouldn't LSD give friends and lovers a profound psychological adventure to share—at once reempowering intimacy, and bringing some magic back to interpersonal relationships, from which it is so cruelly absent?

16

Set, Setting, and History

BUT THE DECISIVE INFLUENCE on the way I saw LSD didn't come from the drug underground. It came from a drastic change to the whole political climate. In early September of 2001, two hijacked jumbo jets were flown into the twin towers of the World Trade Center in New York, and the event was instant history. The fireballs . . . the skyscrapers sliding in slow motion into billowing clouds of dust . . . the crowds fleeing in terror . . . these images recycled endlessly on TV have become part of our collective twenty-first-century psyche.

Was 9/11 really the work of Middle Eastern terrorists? Perhaps the people I know are particularly cynical, but the first thing most of us asked was, Do you think the U.S. government did it? Investigating any crime, surely the first thing you try to do is establish motive . . . and in this case the beneficiary was clearly U.S. corporate capitalism. Did the Bush government know some such terrorist coup was in the offing and turn a blind eye? Or was 9/11 an inside job from the first?

Looking back on it today, the answer doesn't seem to make that much difference. Either way, what 9/11 did was trash the last vestiges of middle-class society.

For decades—for most of the twentieth century, in fact—the

broad-based economic power of the middle classes had been steadily undermined, and by the end of the century it was a thing of the past. What became horribly clear as the U.S. military/corporate juggernaut rumbled into action was that even the pretense of democracy was gone too. Five hundred years of middle-class society, with its complex system of checks and balances, was over, and all that remained was to rescind civil liberties that had taken hundreds of years to win.

Henceforward the West was controlled by a few vast multinational corporations—a government not only unelected but also composed of individuals whose very identity was unknown. All that was clear was their agenda: the introduction of a kind of urbanized neofeudal order, and the creation of a single World State.

And almost immediately anticorporate, anti-imperial sentiment hitherto restricted to a politically educated minority began to spread.

The pitched battles at Seattle (1999) or Prague (2000) or the still wilder surreal riots at Genoa (July 2001) began to seem more than vehement but localized outbursts against the powers that be. They began to look like the first stirrings of a New Left. And, despite the horror of the carnage in Manhattan, it felt like a breath of fresh air was blowing through the world. The mighty U.S. imperium was no longer the unchallenged colossus straddling the planet. At least the truth, however awful, was out in the open—and it was exhilarating.

"Another world is possible" proclaimed the most famous political slogan of the decade; and, like a growing number of other people, for the first time in years I started going to demonstrations and political meetings again. Even on those early marches, and in the company of an admittedly motley crew of fellow demonstrators, I began to wonder whether there was any question of a new revolutionary opposition being born in the West. At first this was little more than idle speculation; but, as each march became more crowded than the preceding one, I started to take the possibility more seriously. Hostility to the status quo on this scale hadn't existed since the '60s.

What *had* caused the radical politics of the '60s and '70s to collapse? Why had "the Movement" caved in so ignominiously? Had the feminism, the psychotherapy, the attempts to explore religious psychology of the mid-1970s thrown any light on what went wrong? When the energy finally drained out of everything, say around 1980, the chaos and heartbreak were such that none of us had ever really tried to analyze what had happened. But now, years later, I returned to these questions, picking away at them in a way I had never done at the time.

Why, more generally, do revolutions always seem to go wrong? Why do they spawn hierarchies of their own every bit as corrupt as those of the society they originally opposed? Is it through some inherent corruption in human nature, as the chorus of conservatives everywhere assures us, or are there identifiable errors, things that could be done differently and put right?

Failure to solve the problem of hierarchy, was that at the bottom of it?

For all the song and dance we made about "participation" in the '60s, there had been the same old split between leaders and led. Was that what lay behind the endless infighting—the competitiveness, the dogmatism, the almost gratuitous sectarianism—that dogs the Left like a shadow? The hypocrisy? The way youthful idealism so often masks covert self-promotion? Were revolutionary movements always defeated in the end by their own internal contradictions?

Whatever the truth, one of the ideas I kept coming back to was that any future revolutionary movement, however you conceived it, must have some kind of psychotherapy at its heart: some basic analysis of the ego. This struck me as being just as important, if not far more so, than any purely political or economic strategy. What kind of psychotherapy? Obviously my own recent experiences, both of getting in touch with repressed emotions and of seeing how this could be organized clandestinely along the lines Jacob had been exploring, were uppermost in my mind. But when I tried to work out how this could be done on a large but decentralized scale, I was forced to admit that I hadn't a clue . . .

Several months later I was to find myself researching psychedelic history; and, oddly enough, one of the first things I ran across was an example of just what I had been trying to envision.

During the mid-1960s a young radical feminist had gone to Tim Leary's psychedelic center at Millbrook, New York, and taken LSD. On her return she introduced the rest of her sizable and tight-knit group of friends to the drug. Such was their enthusiasm, they started to take it regularly together and to turn on other people they knew. They were cautious and responsible, offering the drug only to friends, or close friends of friends. Books were passed around, and newcomers were welcome to attend group trips solely as observers.

Two main approaches to tripping grew out of this.

The first was what they called *work sessions*. These were healing oriented, consisting of small groups, generally not more than three or four people, and were devoted to helping one member explore a particular problem. The latter would spend several days preparing for the session and take a high dose, 250 to 500 micrograms, while the others took substantially less, something in the 100 to 150 range. This was so they could keep a foot in both worlds, acting as what they referred to as "mirrors" or a "bridge."

> There was very little verbal communication in this type of session, but psychic communication was felt to be very strong, so strong in fact that in one instance a member who was "going through hell" in one room caused the guide, who was in another room, to lose her identity altogether. Distressing as this was to both, the guide let it continue, feeling that the other had to "work [her problem] through or it would always be there."

Such work sessions were always at night and were followed by all participants going out for a celebratory breakfast.

The second approach they evolved—which they called *play sessions*—involved a much bigger group of people and was purely celebratory. Play sessions were psychedelic party-going, and if they had any agenda it was to explore the sensory or aesthetic level of LSD in its own right. At the time the article was written, the group was discussing whether the two approaches could be conflated, one member observing:

> Usually we find that we accomplish more in terms of psychological development and working through problems at a play session than we will on a work session. This is something that we've only recently discovered. . . . You know, you go after something and chances are you're going to miss it.

During their first flush of enthusiasm the group had stopped being exclusively feminist, and an almost equal number of men had been invited to join. Core members stayed in close contact, while there was a plenary session about once a month. I couldn't make out from the article the exact number of members involved at any one time, but my impression was that the core group was a little under a dozen, and the whole circle three or four times that.

All this evolved spontaneously, without even the guiding hand of a renegade therapist like Jacob. Yet, like Jacob's own network, during the several years the group had been in existence, nothing had ever gone wrong. The somewhat bemused academics who wrote the report observed, "All the members of the research team commented on the air of innocent gaiety that seemed to pervade the group." There appeared to be no question of them freezing up into a narcissistic, self-enclosed cult.

> Asked about a tendency to withdraw from the concerns of society as a result of taking the drug, one member replied: "On the contrary . . . the only thing it's done is make us more discriminating in our choice of friends."[1]

17

God as Light

BUT I AM RUNNING ahead of myself here. At the time of 9/11, I had been experimenting with LSD for less than six months, and what had been happening remained largely within the personal biographical sphere.

That September I was still trying to master using photos on trips, and for the next session (having managed to convince myself the last trip had inexplicably been a dud) once again lined up the photo albums of my life with Asha and our son. But as the trip started to come on and I began to leaf through one of the albums, exactly the same thing happened as the time before. I started to cough. Oh, no, I thought; I couldn't believe it. Only this time it didn't stop.

At first I was laughing in between spasms, as it seemed more absurd than anything else. But as the minutes went by and I still couldn't stop, I began to get worried. There wasn't anything stuck in my throat, I was sure of that. This was something the LSD was doing, but it was utterly different from anything I had ever associated with the effects of psychedelics. For a start, there was nothing remotely hallucinatory about it. Everything was just the way it always was—apart from the fact that I couldn't stop coughing.

I started to hear a roaring in my ears. Suppose this just goes on and on? I thought; and I began to lose my nerve. I remembered that pope, whichever one it was, who had died of hiccups, and how funny it had seemed at the time. Well, it didn't seem so funny any more. I had a few Valium 5s, and I thought of taking a couple . . . but realized I couldn't swallow, and even if I could I'd never be able to keep anything down. I thought of phoning my son who lives nearby, but to say what? "It's Dad. I'm on an acid trip, and I can't stop coughing. COUGH COUGH COUGH. *Aaargh* . . ."

I thought of going to the emergency room at the nearest hospital, which was Hampstead's Royal Free, but fortunately decided against the idea. Casualty on acid was the last thing I needed. Just as there were no hallucinations, I seemed able to think perfectly normally. You could see how young people in the '60s whose trips had suddenly gone weird—particularly if they went exclusively physical like this—could believe they had been poisoned, and how the myth about LSD being cut with strychnine had grown up. What else could you conclude?

Apart from a few short periods during which I just wheezed, the convulsive coughing continued for the whole trip. My throat was raw and my lungs throbbed. I thought I would start bleeding internally—but no, there didn't appear to be any physical damage. Indeed, though I was all but choking, there was a subtly incorporeal quality to the whole performance, almost as if (and I was getting warm here) I was being *haunted* . . .

Then as abruptly as it had started, between one paroxysm and the next, the heaving stopped.

I was back in the kitchen. Sunlight was pouring through the window. With my bare hands I was eating some ice cream I had found in the freezer, trying to soothe my throat.

Shit, I thought—what was that?

The seizure had burned the trip out. I pulled on my black down jacket, let myself out of the apartment, and went for a grateful if brain-stunned walk through the Vale and up to Whitestone Pond; it had been raining, and there was a wild loveliness to the trees and clouds and sky. I felt utterly drained.

Subsequently I asked one of the few friends with whom I could still discuss acid (this was someone who'd been an aficionado in their time) whether they had ever heard of anyone having an acid trip that consisted solely of coughing. They looked at me with so disturbing an expression I hastily changed the subject. I was flummoxed myself. For someone who claimed you could work through trips on your own, I have to admit I made a pig's ear of this one. Any therapist worth their salt would have noted the coincidence (whatever it may have signified) between my trying to confront my feelings about Asha and a hacking cough . . . though I suppose you would have needed a fair bit of hands-on experience to make much sense of it.

Nothing if not persistent, I did make one final attempt with the photos.

Once again, for what must have been my twelfth trip, I lined up the photo albums on the duvet, clicked the Gorecki Third into the Walkman, and sat on the bed, leaning against the wall. As I watched, the albums themselves started to change. They began to shimmer and morph into bulky, calf-bound folios, glowing on the scarlet silk the duvet had become. They looked like grimoires or ancient books of spells . . . certainly they had an air of meaning business. But when I started to turn the pages, nothing was any different: energetically they were still as flat as a pancake . . . and this time I had to admit defeat. Whatever I'd had going with photos was over.

Abruptly at a loose end, and with the acid starting to rush, my main concern was not spending another trip coughing convulsively.

My eyes fell on a CD I had borrowed from the public library, one of late medieval music, a recording of the music of St. Hildegard of Bingen. Quickly, before any cough had a chance to take hold, I replaced the Gorecki with St. Hildegard in the Walkman, drew the bedroom curtains, and lay down on the bed to listen. I had never heard St. Hildegard's music before; in fact, apart from some Gregorian chant, I had never heard any "early" Western music and had chosen the disc on impulse. To my surprise, the songs of the twelfth-century Christian saint sounded breathtakingly clear and lovely. She felt totally present, in an almost Zenlike way, only with a feminine rather than masculine energy. I listened, enchanted . . . yet nothing beyond aesthetic appreciation happened until the disc played out.

Poet, doctor, musician—what an extraordinary being, I was thinking as I sat up and drew back the curtains.

Suddenly the room was flooded with a rush of light so bright I could barely see.

Light!

As my eyes adjusted, I was amazed by what was revealed. I could see the light itself. I had always assumed it was merely a neutral medium through which sight was possible, but now I saw that I couldn't have been more mistaken.

Light was what everything was made of.

Light was the holy itself.

Screwing up my eyes, I stared through the dazzling window, through the bare branches of the elder, and directly into the sun as it set on a winter afternoon. Depth upon depth, radiance upon radiance, was revealed within it. Faintly I could see transparent geometric patterns, intricate as the structure of snowflakes, yellow, white, amber, moving slowly in and out of one another, instinctual with the sacred.

I found I had fallen to my knees. To my astonishment, I was pressing my palms together, in the Christian prayer position, something I hadn't done since chapel at school. The bedroom window was transformed into stained glass—but rather than the somber, rich colors of a church window, these were exquisite pale shades of gold and white, reflecting the brightness of snow or frost.

Soon after I went to my second public school I had lost the sense of beauty that, throughout childhood, had been my door to God. Now the years parted, and that simple sense of wonder, of inner silence, flooded back as though it had never gone away. This was my first explicitly religious trip, my first trip about God—and I mean proper, old-fashioned God, not some watery Buddhist approximation thereof. What was the phrase Aldous Huxley had used? *Mysterium tremendum,* that was it . . .

I don't know how long I knelt there, gazing rapt into the mystery of the Godhead the bedroom window had become. When I returned to myself, all the strength had drained from my limbs, and I lay down on my back on the bedroom floor. All I wanted was to melt into God and be gone. I lay there staring at the upside-down ceiling, which for reasons unknown was sparkling like mad. Okay, God, I thought at last, this is it. I paused a moment, then said aloud with a pomposity I blush to record, "I am ready to die."

God certainly knew a piece of bullshit when It heard one.

No sooner were the words out of my mouth than I was seized by blind panic. I couldn't breathe and started to gag. Only this time, rather than cough, my mouth filled with the taste of blood: quite a lot of blood. Alarmed, I rolled over onto my hands and knees and stood up. As I did so I could feel something slimy coming out of the corner of my mouth, which, as I lurched through the door, I was trying to brush away with the back of my hand. I made it to the bathroom and leaned over the toilet trying to spit the bloody saliva into the bowl . . . but there was nothing there.

Just ordinary transparent spit. I couldn't believe my eyes; that metallic taste had been unmistakable.

Badly rattled, the only thing I could think of doing was to have a bath. Perhaps the trip's leveling off, I thought as I watched the tub fill, added a liberal quantity of bubble bath, somehow got out of my clothes, and climbed in.

Leveling off? I must have been joking. No sooner did I lie back in the suds than I began to see apocalyptic visions. There was nothing religious about these. They were hardcore politics. Gritty visions of a society whose infrastructure has come apart, straight off TV News . . . Politically, this was the time of the anthrax scares in the United States, when anthrax bacteria were being sent to targeted individuals through the mail, and the packages added enormously to the hysteria about bioterrorism immediately prior to the invasion of Afghanistan. The postal services were close to collapse as the mail workers refused to handle any further letters and parcels . . . but in my visions that afternoon, this already critical situation had spiraled out of control.

Lying back amid mounds of insanely green foam, I saw Western metropolises turn into death traps.

What exactly had happened wasn't clear, but I saw crowds smashing and looting the supermarkets: overturned shopping carts, people shoving one another in the aisles. I had read somewhere that there is only enough food in a modern metropolis to last thirty-six hours . . . and increasingly savage violence broke out among the looters. Cars, then buildings, were burning, and the streets sparkled with shattered plate glass. The electricity dipped, staggered, and went off. Then the taps ran dry. By the first night, city centers had turned into hell. Cities were locked down and the army shot anyone trying to get through the highway blocks, but by then it was already too late. Country fields and lanes became a killing ground for maddened gangs of those who had managed to break through . . .

Like earlier series of visions, these ended with an elaborate, even formal flourish. The scenes of slaughter in the Home Counties dissolved, and the camera's eye returned to city centers. There were dreamy, almost elegiac tracking shots of streets full of the dead and the dying. Close-ups of friends cradling one another without moving, looking steadily into one another's eyes . . . hieratic in death.

"Bullets will be a luxury," a TV anchorman's voice assured me, with public-school crassness.

18

"I Saw a Man Cloathed with Raggs . . ."

READING THE FOLLOWING MORNING'S trip journal entry, it's difficult not to laugh. "This is preposterous," I had written—and the crusty epithet says it all. God as Light . . . ? Prayer . . . ? Armageddon . . . ? What on Earth had any of this got to do with me? All my life I had been an anarchist: church Christianity had always struck me as being primarily political ideology, and the church itself probably the most evil single institution the world has ever seen.

But the next trip turned out to be very much the same.

The early stages were dominated by identical physical symptoms . . . tremors in the legs . . . the hacking cough . . . the pungent taste of blood, like something out of a Victorian ghost story; and the second half was spent mostly in the bath, watching a rerun of the same apocalyptic visions. New diseases rioting in ruined immune systems . . . cities imploding . . . tracking shots of streets full of the dead. The only things missing were the fundamentalism and the role played by prayer.

What made this so off the wall was that I did have religious convictions of my own. I mentioned my involvement with Gurdjieff and Buddhism, and while I had failed miserably with my attempts to meditate, I had never stopped feeling that Gurdjieff's vision of everyone being asleep and trapped inside their own minds was a deadly accurate reflection of our lives.

Over the intervening years I had been surprised by the increasing number of people who were coming to feel the same way. Not only had Buddhism made steady inroads into Western culture, but so had the Indian tradition of Advaita Vedanta, of nondual philosophy. Probably Ramana Maharshi had been its most celebrated exponent in the twentieth century, and his teaching, like Gurdjieff's—or like Zen, for that matter—was simply to locate, from moment to moment, your own most intimate sense of yourself and to examine whether it is truly separate from everything else. The meaning of the Sanskrit word *advaita* is not just "one," it is something subtler than that. Literally *advaita* means "not-two"; and by the end of the twentieth century, a number of different contemporary religious philosophies were beginning to crystallize around the term.

What I found particularly striking about this process was the way it was happening outside any kind of previous "religious" context. Perhaps it's worth remembering that twentieth-century awareness of "sleep" and daydreams wasn't originally highlighted by a religious teacher at all, nor by a psychologist, nor even by a philosopher. On the contrary, they were first held in the spotlight by a creative artist, by a novelist—by James Joyce in Ulysses.

For Joyce, the central feature of twentieth-century psychology was the internal monologue. Subjectively, our daily lives are characterized by an inner running commentary on what we are feeling and thinking, the self-obsession of which is matched only by its vacuousness. Moment by moment we are separating ourselves from the world and one another, and the picture of twentieth-century life that emerges from Ulysses is frighteningly schizoid: inner and outer never meet. We are utterly alone: this is the central message of the most important work of fiction of the twentieth century; and while it may have seemed overstated when the book first came out, by the end of the century I suspect it had become the conscious daily reality of millions of people . . .

I am running ahead of myself again . . . but this was the background against which my trips started to go "religious," and in terms of which I dismissed them as not being authentically spiritual at all. I thought my unconscious had got its wires crossed. Consciously, what I wanted to do was to go on working with personal psychological material, with Grof's psychodynamic realm, in which I believed I still had much to learn.

No longer in my case, apparently. Far from it, prayer, in fact revivalism at its crudest, exploded still more wildly in the next session. Even the write-up in the journal is barely coherent. Scrawled across the page, it starts abruptly in the midst of the session. Mask and earphones gone, and my normally bland personality along with them, I was pacing around the apartment like a caged animal.

I was in despair at my unworthiness and the abyss separating me from God.

Exactly what had happened I couldn't remember. One moment I had been my habitual agnostic self, the next I was a Christian fundamentalist— and the trip saw me seesawing wildly between the two. One moment I was yearning passionately for God, convulsed by emotions that seemed torn from my very depths; the next I was standing there incredulously, appalled by the whole performance. I appeared to be experiencing the emotions of another person entirely. Never before had dual personality been a real phenomenon for me, but now I saw that being haunted, or even possessed, was a frighteningly real psychic possibility. I felt exactly as though I had been hijacked by a seventeenth-century Protestant, by the kind of religious bigot I had always steered well clear of.

"What must I do?" I repeated to myself aloud, *"what must I do?"* *

Talk about a divided self. On the one hand I was gripped by an all-but-uncontrollable urge to go down on my knees and pray . . . while on the other I resisted doing any such thing with the stubbornness of a mule.

The situation bordered on burlesque. Down I would go, feeling as though I was being flattened by an invisible giant hand, only to shoot up again like a jack-in-the-box, protesting vehemently, I-am-not-going-to-do-this-stupid-fucking-thing. Shoved back to my knees even more forcibly, I had no idea what to do down there. Almost malevolently I tried to mumble the Lord's Prayer. *Our Father, which art in heaven, hallowed be Thy name*—I was all but spitting the words out—*Thy will be done . . .* only to find I couldn't remember what came next . . . *trespass against us . . .* but there was a bit missing in the middle, and I couldn't remember what it was.

I felt hideously guilty; and up and off I went again, mooning around the apartment. I remember wringing my hands, something I had always taken to be a figure of speech. Not a bit of it, you can do just that.

Abruptly, almost with a pop, my mind cleared and I came back to myself. I was utterly calm and centered . . . ominously so. I felt I had acceded to a higher type of thought, something still in the process of evolution, and was thinking with a speed and urgency previously only known in moments of great physical danger. Back and forth I paced in the little living room, with tigerish theological intensity. Essentially

---

*For Protestant credentials, cf. John Bunyan: "I saw a Man cloathed with Raggs, standing in a certain place, with his face from his own House, a Book in his hand, and a great burden upon his back. I looked, and saw him open the Book, and Read therein; and as he Read, he wept and trembled: and not being able longer to contain, he brake out with a lamentable cry; saying, what shall I do?" (*The Pilgrim's Progress*, paragraph one, sentences two and three). Also, regarding doom and gloom in the bubble bath: "Moreover, I am for certain informed, that this our City will be burned with fire from Heaven, in which fearful overthrow, both my self, with thee, my Wife, and you my sweet babes, shall miserably come to ruine" (paragraph two).

three factors—God, the world, and the self—confront us. What we have to do is discover the true relation between them. Can the three coincide?

The power with which I could concentrate began to alarm me.

The acid was climaxing in huge, slow pulses, propelling me irresistibly into greater and greater intensity. Was direct revelation at hand? I remembered the Bible: *"It is a fearful thing to fall into the hands of the living God."*

Too late I recognized the symptoms, the sense that everything was decelerating, that objects were becoming heavier and increasingly dense. The pressure in the little room was building up alarmingly. Before I knew it I was overcome by apocalyptic terror once again. The whole was about to manifest in the part, and the universe be torn apart.

There was a whirring noise in my head, then a faint but horribly audible cracking sound. I was sitting up straight on the side of the bed, my knees pressed primly together: the very picture of the Foolish Virgin.

Don't think of God, I told myself.

Whatever you do, don't let the word cross your mind.

Writing the trip journal the next morning, I was well and truly angry. While I felt stuck with my inability to meditate, in fact to come to grips with the nature of my moment-by-moment consciousness at all, I felt I'd at least had a clear idea of the direction I wanted to follow. Of all the *advaitin* mystics I had read, the one I found most attractive was Nisargadatta Maharaj, the legendary "enlightened *beedi-wallah*" (which was disrespectful: he ran a proper, if humble, little cigarette shop in Bombay). Measure my last trips against his collection of talks, *I Am That,* and I was simply losing the plot.

Like Gurdjieff or Ramana Maharshi, Nisargadatta zeroes in on our unconsciousness in everyday life. We have to wake up, that's the first thing. We have to become aware of ourselves and our environment from moment to moment. Without this, nothing whatsoever is possible.

Just keep in mind the feeling "I am." Merge in it, till your mind and feeling become one. By repeated attempts you will stumble on the right balance of attention and affection and your mind will be firmly established in the thought-feeling "I am."

For Nisargadatta, if you can maintain this state of self-awareness for even short periods of time, your perception of yourself will change dramatically. Your sense of identity will become far more intense . . . yet simultaneously there will be no way you can describe it.

Once you are convinced that you cannot say truthfully about yourself anything except "I am," and that nothing that can be pointed at, can be your self, the need for the "I am" is over—you are no longer intent on verbalizing what you are. All you need is to get rid of the tendency to define your self. All definitions apply to your body only and to its expressions. Once this obsession with the body goes, you will revert to your natural state, spontaneously and effortlessly.[1]

To what natural state will we revert?

To the detached purely attentive consciousness, which has always registered everything we have ever experienced. To what Indian religion calls *the witness*—that is, the presence of consciousness itself in each individual. Pure consciousness, consciousness independent of, and prior to, any experience. Search the whole of our past, search the present moment itself, and we will find that this is the only thing we have always been. Always are, rather. The only constant in our experience . . . the sole element that has never changed, and that is in some sense a substance, one out of which everything is made. "I am not a person," as the old *beedi* shop owner assured his visitors affably, as he ushered them in. "I was never born."

19
Resistance

WHAT "THE ACID" (as I was coming to think of it) had done was to blow my so-called spiritual trip out of the water. I saw that Advaita philosophy had become just a way of coasting along, vaguely assuring myself that I was consciousness itself from time to time. It had no transformative power over my being. If I was honest, I would have to admit that it was just a bandage over a wound that refused to heal. Spiritually I was in denial . . . and had been for years. Scratch the surface and there was a sense of being little more than a zombie. My life was a blur. Briefly I would wake up, look around in momentary wonder, then without even noticing it, be back on autopilot again. Horribly, I appeared to wake up for only long enough to know I was asleep, and then I was asleep again. Yet, almost perversely, I refused to commit myself heart and soul to trying to do something about it.

Why then, when such spiritual despair was so close to the surface—barely repressed at all—why did acid confront me with this clowning around and melodrama about Christianity?

There seemed to me two possible interpretations. First, there wasn't anything particularly personal about these trips: they were going deeper into the collective unconscious, which was now opening up and revealing, as surely it must, a massive amount of Christian material. Perhaps you could add that personally, for whatever reasons, I had intense resistance to Christianity, which somehow warped the emergence of this data, allowing it through—like repressed material in dreams—only in censored and, in this case, virtually self-parodying forms?

That sounded plausible enough—but at the same time there were elements that didn't appear to be censored at all, but to be truly heartfelt. The sense of loss, the call of beauty, the longing for God—these seemed sincere, even unmistakably urgent . . . Then was there (along with features of a travesty, and a malevolent one at that) a genuine call to reexamine Western Christianity? A sense that there was a *moral dimension to true religion, which my dabbling in nondual philosophy failed to address? That prayer, rather than awareness practice, was more appropriate? That, overall, truly religious life was driven far more by the heart than the head?*

Increasingly I came to feel that these trips—again, like dreams— called for interpretation, but I didn't know where to begin. What I needed was an overview, and I turned back to Grof's Realms of the Human Unconscious, rereading several of the sections dealing with his division of psychedelic experience into three major stages:

the psychodynamic: the realm of biographical, highly charged emotional memory.

the perinatal: the realm of birth and any other trauma encoded deep in the physical body.

the transpersonal: the realm beyond the confines of the individual self, beyond space and time as we know them, where the collective unconscious begins to disclose itself.

What had been happening did approximate this model. Given that the psychodynamic stage had stopped rather abruptly, many of the features of these last three sessions could well be seen as an interplay between perinatal and transpersonal themes, between quite brutal (and, on the hallucinatory level at least, bloody) somatic phenomena intershot with glimpses of what did appear to be the collective mind . . . and, more rarely, flashes of something authentically "spiritual."

No, as I reread his book a third time, the misgivings I began to have were more about where it was all heading. For Grof insisted there was no way of stably accessing the transpersonal without living through the full implications of the perinatal—implications that climaxed in a convulsive death/rebirth crisis. And, frankly, I wasn't sure how much I was up for this. I double-checked by reading another of his early books, *LSD Psychotherapy*, which is very much the professional, hands-on manual; and, spelled out in greater clinical detail, the final paroxysms of the perinatal make chilling reading.

In a section titled "Critical Situations in LSD Sessions," he wrote:

> For some it can contain certain physical conditions, such as a high degree of suffocation, agonizing physical pain, blacking out, or violent seizure-like activity. Others have to face a situation which is psychologically utterly unacceptable to them, and surrender to it. The most frequent of these are vomiting, losing control of the bladder or bowels; sexually unacceptable behavior; confusion and disorientation; making various inhuman sounds, and humiliation or loss of prestige. A very difficult and important experience that occurs in the context of the ego death is the expectation of a catastrophe of enormous dimensions. Subjects face agonizing tension increasing to fantastic proportions and develop a conviction that they will explode and the entire world will be destroyed.[1]

Decidedly I was getting into a lot more than I had bargained for a few months earlier. Wetting my pants, making inhuman sounds, and losing my prestige I felt I could handle (by the time you are sixty they're pretty much par for the course). What had me on edge was the cosmic terror. At my most paranoid I feared there was something worse than physical pain out there, something really bad—a pitch of horror only known from childhood nightmares, of, to use a word I never thought I'd use, evil . . .

But then, didn't Grof also say that reliving the birth trauma did not necessarily involve reliving the full physical agony? The crisis could also play itself out in symbolic or even purely philosophical terms. Was I going to back out from cowardice—back out from the first thing that had fired my imagination in years? Without even trying?

I've got to get a handle on this, I thought. I've got to find some other, firsthand accounts of ongoing self-experiment with LSD. I can't be the only person who has done this. There must be others; surely someone has left a written record?

Dr. Grof, I thought, I want a second opinion; and I settled down to do some more sustained serious reading than I had done in years.

20

Psychedelics Since the Sixties

I HAD BEEN OUT of touch with the drug scene for a long time, and I was in for several surprises. The first was discovering that LSD was no longer the model psychedelic it had been for my generation. Over the intervening years, the only contact I'd had with psychedelics had been with Ecstasy, and I had imagined that, if anywhere, it was to MDMA that the lineage had passed.

By the time I had read a couple of books and looked through some underground magazines, I realized that this was far from being the case. Both LSD and MDMA had been eclipsed by the plant hallucinogens, in particular by magic mushrooms and dimethyltryptamine. A large proportion of the books I looked at were focused on ayahuasca and South American shamanism.

At first I thought that this could be traced back to Carlos Castaneda. *The Teachings of Don Juan,* first published in 1968, has, after *The Doors of Perception,* probably been the most widely read book on psychedelics ever written. But according to recent psychedelic literature, *The Teachings of Don Juan* wasn't the pioneer in the field of plant hallucinogens I had imagined. In 1957, more than a decade before Castaneda, there had been a striking, not to say sensational, article in the mass-circulation *Life* magazine called "Seeking the Magic Mushroom," and if there was any single text to which the new orientation in psychedelic studies could be traced, this was it.

A true-life adventure story, the article recounted the journey of a wealthy New York banker, R. Gordon Wasson, and his wife, Valentina, deep into the mountains of Mexico in an attempt to track down rumors of an ecstatic mushroom cult of great antiquity that still survived there. Finally, led to the remote mountain town of Huautla da Jimenez in the state of Oaxaca, the couple were introduced to a local *curandera,* a diminutive, middle-aged Mazatec woman called Maria Sabina.

This meeting between Gordon Wasson and Maria Sabina was to prove as iconic as Hofmann's bicycle ride more than a decade before. Without further ado, Maria Sabina invited Wasson and another man in his party to a *velada,* or mushroom ceremony, that very night, and within an hour of eating the sacred mushrooms Wasson was in the thick of visionary experience.

> The visions came whether our eyes were open or closed. . . . They were in vivid color, always harmonious. They began with art motifs, angular such as might decorate carpets or textiles or wallpaper or the drawing board of an architect. Then they evolved into palaces with courts, arcades, gardens—resplendent palaces all laid over with semi-precious stones. Then I saw a mythological beast drawing a regal chariot.

All the lights had been extinguished, and Maria Sabina danced and sang in the dark. At times she chanted, such extemporary poetry being seen, as Wasson was to learn, as the speech of the mushrooms themselves. At other times she clapped, or thumped her body rhythmically, apparently employing some kind of ventriloquism, for the sounds seemed to issue from different corners of the room. In the gloom Wasson thought he could glimpse her taking hits from an *aguardiente* bottle. At the height of the mushrooms' action, however, the room disappeared.

There I was, poised in space, a disembodied eye, invisible, incorporeal, seeing but not seen. The visions were not blurred or uncertain. They were sharply focused, the lines and colors being so sharp that they seemed more real to me than anything I had ever seen with my own eyes. I felt that I was now seeing plain, whereas ordinary vision gives us an imperfect view; I was seeing the archetypes, the Platonic ideas that underlie the imperfect images of everyday life. The thought crossed my mind: could the divine mushrooms be the secret that lay behind the ancient Mysteries? Could the miraculous mobility that I was now enjoying be the explanation for the flying witches that played so important a part in the folklore and fairy tales of northern Europe?[1]

Such speculations were to run through the two-volume *Mushrooms, Russia and History,* which the Wassons published on their return from Mexico. Their book, or so the story goes, had started life as a cookbook of mushroom recipes. As the couple researched their subject, however, they were struck by the vehemence of the taboo against eating wild mushrooms, the overwhelming majority of which are well known to be harmless, with the few poisonous ones being easily identifiable. This taboo extended over large geographical areas, and as the Wassons began to trace back cultural references to fungi, they found an association with the supernatural to be widespread in folklore. Etymologically, there were repeated links to the infernal. Why such a widespread yet manifestly irrational attitude?

The Wassons put forward the hypothesis of a prehistoric religion stretching across most of Europe and northern Eurasia, one in which psychoactive mushrooms had played a sacramental role. The religion was suppressed by Christian missionaries (hence the demonization), but vestiges of it had survived until comparatively recently, most notably in Siberia. As eucharist, the Wassons proposed the most charismatic of all fungi, the *Amanita muscaria,* or fly agaric, the archetypal red-and-white-capped mushroom, stock in trade of countless fairy tales.

That, however, was only the first part of their hypothesis. Bolder still, the second was the suggestion that hallucinogenic mushrooms could have played a decisive role in human evolution. Eaten by prehistoric hunters and gatherers, magic mushrooms could have opened an entirely new dimension to primitive awareness. They could even, or so the Wassons suggested, have provided the initial impetus toward religion itself.

> Our divine mushrooms, along with the secondary vegetable hallucinogens, may have played a role in the origins of human culture. . . . Our divine mushrooms must have unlimbered the imagination of those first men who ate them, stirred their curiosity and speculative faculties. Our mushrooms could have sparked in them the very idea of God.[2]

The next book I set about reading was Mircea Eliade's *Shamanism: Archaic Techniques of Ecstasy,* which proved to be an inspired choice.

Mircea Eliade's groundbreaking research had been published only a few years before the Wassons', and in many respects their books dovetailed. Like the Wassons, Eliade believed that the primitive, virtually archaic tribal societies stretching in an arc from Scandinavia to Indonesia all evidenced traces of a vast pre-Christian religion. But whereas the Wassons thought they had discovered the sacraments at the heart of such a religion, Eliade believed he had identified its priesthood.

For the spiritual life of all the tribes Eliade studied revolved around a single maverick figure—at once doctor, magician, and poet—for whom Eliade used the Siberian term *shaman*. Anything further from the Christian priest would be hard to imagine. At best chronic misfits, at worst shamans appeared downright insane. They could be either men or women; in fact, they were often sexually ambivalent and crossdressed. Shamans were neither hereditary nor elected, but were individuals who assumed the role on their own initiative. Their right to do so came from having survived a mental breakdown or life-threatening illness (frequently epilepsy) during their childhood or adolescence.

Their initiatory experiences themselves always revolved around a descent to the underworld, where they died and were reborn. The following from the Siberian Yakut is typical of the many cases Eliade cites.

> The candidate's limbs are removed and disjointed with an iron hook; the bones are cleaned, the flesh scraped, the body fluids thrown away, and the eyes torn from their sockets. . . . The ceremony of dismemberment lasts from three to seven days; during all that time the candidate remains like a dead man, scarcely breathing, in a solitary space.[3]

Only after this experience of death and resurrection were they apprenticed to an established shaman. The teaching they received was substantially the same over a vast geographical area—that they were not their physical body, but were capable of sidestepping time and space. For this world was not the only one. There were two adjacent worlds: a world beneath us, which was the underworld; and a world above us, which was the heaven realm. What the sorcerer's apprentice learned from his or her mentor was how to navigate these three worlds: the "archaic techniques of ecstasy," which compose the central practice of shamanism, and which Eliade refers to as *magical flight*.

> The essential schema is always to be seen, even after the numerous influences to which it has been subjected; there are three great cosmic regions, which can be successively traversed because they are linked together by a central axis. This axis, of course, passes through an "opening," a "hole"; it is through this hole that the gods descend to earth and the dead to the subterranean regions; it is through the same hole that the soul of the shaman in ecstasy can fly up or down in the course of his celestial or infernal journeys.[4]

This was the point at which Eliade's and the Wassons' version of archaic religion diverged sharply. Angrily, Eliade repudiated any suggestion that psychoactive plants could have fueled magical flight—dismissing such substances as "narcotics," which hardly indicates familiarity with the subject. Vigils, trance-dancing, vision quests, these Eliade could accept—but reliance on psychoactive plants was a sure sign the shaman belonged to an increasingly degenerate tradition.

The dispute was to be resolved from an entirely different quarter: from the fieldwork of the Harvard botanist Richard Evans Schultes.

Richard Schultes was the last of the great explorer/botanists of an earlier age. As a graduate student he had researched the peyote cult in the American Southwest. Moving to Mexico, he collected the first specimens of *teonanactl*, the legendary Aztec psychoactive mushrooms (it was this research of Schultes that had first directed the Wassons to Huautla). Next he identified *ololiuqui*, another long-lost Aztec psychedelic, one said to have been used for divination, as the seeds of one of the morning glories. These, when he sent them to Albert Hofmann for analysis, turned out to contain lysergic acid, which was the first time LSD had been discovered in a natural form.

It was the Amazon basin during the 1940s and early '50s, however, that was to prove the theater of Schultes's truly revolutionary research. Traveling on his own, or with a single native companion, he paddled his canoe deeper and deeper into the northwestern Amazon of Colombia, into jungle no one but local tribes had ever penetrated. Mapping uncharted rivers, collecting three hundred new species of plants, Schultes threw open the Pandora's box of natural hallucinogens. With his work, "ethnobotany" ceased to be an adventurous hobby and became a fledgling science . . . and one of the first things it revealed was the extent to which psychoactive plants were spread across the earth and the central role they had played in many archaic cultures.*

---

*For an introduction to the most potent plants of the 150-odd species known to be employed for their hallucinatory alkaloids, see the popularization Schultes coauthored with Albert Hofmann, *Plants of the Gods* (1979). For an account of Schultes's life, travels, and ethnobotanical discoveries, see Wade Davis's *One River* (1996).

In particular, Schultes put the ayahuasca brew in its commanding position on the South American cultural map and started to unpick the complex chemistry involved.

Before Schultes, no one had understood that the decisive ingredient of ayahuasca wasn't the giant *Banisteriopsis caapi* vine so much as the various dimethyltryptamine-rich admixture plants that also went into the brew. The visions came, or came largely, from the DMT. What the *Banisteriopsis caapi* was doing was something subtler. Normally DMT has to be either smoked or injected, because if it is taken orally it is instantly neutralized by a stomach enzyme, monoamine oxidase; but *Banisteriopsis* contains alkaloids that can temporarily neutralize the monoamine oxidase itself (hence referred to as MAO-inhibitors) and allow the DMT to be digested gradually in the stomach. This results in a much longer and steadier exposure to the world's most potent hallucinogen than the few timeless, action-packed minutes you get if you smoke it.

Mircea Eliade, to do him justice, is said to have been about to change his attitude toward psychedelics just before his death. How could he not have been? No way can the chemistry involved in the ayahuasca brew be described as "degenerate." On the contrary, it is highly sophisticated. Indeed, the far-reaching question Schultes's fieldwork raises is how the local tribes could possibly have worked it out. Trial and error, in a jungle containing some eighty thousand different species of plant, hardly seems credible. The case of curare, the paralyzing arrow poison (the chemistry of which Schultes also cracked) is even more enigmatic. In *The Cosmic Serpent*, Jeremy Narby writes:

> There are forty types of curares in the Amazon, made from seventy plant species. The kind used in modern medicine comes from the Western Amazon. To produce it, it is necessary to combine several plants and boil them for seventy-two hours, while avoiding the fragrant but mortal vapors emitted by the broth. The final product is a paste that is inactive unless injected under the skin.

If swallowed it has no effect. It is difficult to see how anybody could have stumbled on this recipe by chance experimentation.[5]

So how did these "primitive" tribes acquire such botanical and chemical knowledge? The Indians, Narby reports, all say either (a) that the gods told their ancestors how to do it at the dawn of time, or (b) that they were taught by the plants themselves, particularly when the plants were taken in conjunction with ayahuasca, which showcases the properties of any given plant. Such explanations have, needless to say, left most Western scientists speechless with indignation.

21

Resistance

(continued)

WELL, I WASN'T GOING to get my second opinion, that much was evident.

Grof's work was the only systematic attempt to analyze LSD anyone had undertaken, and it had been suppressed by the U.S. authorities. What had replaced it was largely academic study of the "ethnobotanical" role played by psychedelics in previous societies, which, while it is undeniably fascinating—and has proved psychedelics to have a pedigree as old as human culture itself—has done nothing to explore their relevance to our own lives.

Neither Wasson, nor Eliade, nor Schultes—nor, for that matter, Carlos Castaneda, nor Wasson's disciple Terence McKenna—none of these great trailblazers of shamanism have paid much attention to what is clearly its primary feature. *Shamanism is about healing,* about curing pain, and (just like LSD) the complex interplay between healing and reconnecting with information we have lost. While there are Westerners who have studied to become *ayahuasceros,* I couldn't find any account of their training, nor how they thought their experience could relate to the contemporary West.

My earlier decisiveness about acid began to falter. Was I going to continue with trips that were becoming steadily crazier, and with the only person who had ever studied LSD in depth saying that they were about to become considerably more so? Misgivings I had brushed aside started to return. Another of the books I had been reading was Terence McKenna's wonderfully subversive *The Archaic Revival,* but his banging on endlessly about DMT and psilocybin being the true model psychedelics had further undermined my confidence. Was I way off beam, following an approach everyone else had long abandoned? Much of my old negativity about LSD resurfaced. I was right about this drug when I was young, I thought. Admittedly it can do things that border on the miraculous, but at best it's a hit-or-miss affair.

Also, on a more mundane level, I was running out of acid.

When I went to see the only dealer I knew, he said he was sorry but there wasn't any around at the moment. Then, seeing my disappointment, he relented and said, "Come on, I've got some of my own, and you can have a bit of that." Getting a small bottle and dropper from the fridge, he laid out several lines of 50 microgram drops on a sheet of blotting paper. "Organic paper," he said over his shoulder. Unbleached I am sure it was, but it wasn't very absorbent, and when the baby started to cry he just tucked the sheet up in some kitchen foil before all the drops were fully dry. Then, refusing to hear of taking any money, he shooed me off.

I'm still not sure what happened. Perhaps the acid was a higher concentration than he thought; or perhaps a substantial amount was never soaked up by the blotting paper but dried on the foil, and when I came to unpack it I got some on my fingers and absorbed it through the skin. I don't know; but I had decided to up my dose from 200 to 250 micrograms in an attempt to break free of whatever loop I was caught in, and cutting out five of the irregular pale-brown splodges seemed to take forever.

Finally, I washed them down with a wineglass of water and repacked the rest in the foil. I had barely stashed it away when the trip started to come on. I had never known a trip to kick in so fast or with such violence. I could just about ride the first surges, but then a huge wave smashed into me. It bowled me over, and I blacked out.

. . . I came to in the bath. The water was up to my chin. An alarm bell, clear but very small and far away, was ringing. Something about drowning. Irritatingly, I couldn't remember precisely what drowning consisted of. Something about either going up or going down, but I couldn't recall which . . . nor on further reflection could I work out which direction was up and which was down.

In fact, I seemed to have lost all capacity to distinguish one thing from the next. So I did what seemed the most intelligent (if that's the word we are looking for) thing to do and just froze. I had run out of decent bubble bath and had only some cheap green goop from Sainsburys; during the blackout, I appeared to have poured ill-considered quantities into the water. So I lay there without moving a muscle, balefully surveying mountains of suds, a neon-lit and exceptionally vile shade of green. There was no time. Talk about no-exit situations. This was pure Dante.

Another blackout supervened . . .

When I came to I was standing beside the bath, with no recollection of how I had managed to get there. Nor did I have any idea what to do next. Drying myself proved impossible because I couldn't figure out what was me and what was not. Perhaps hell has its own *unio mystica*. The same applied to my underpants; I could not get into them because I could not work out what was inside and what was out. My underpants and I were, as mystics promise, "not-two," but by no stretch of the imagination could the experience be described as blissful or illuminating. Moreover, they were sopping wet, as I seemed, like an infant, to have splashed enormous quantities of bathwater. For the rest of the trip I just wore my black down jacket, which I had found somewhere or other—but which, even more unaccountably, was also soaking wet.

All that was quite merry, in a psychopathic sort of a way, compared with the next trip. So far as I can make out from the trip journal, I still hadn't caught on that I could be getting an overdose from the foil, through my fingertips; but this turned out to be a candidate for my scariest trip ever.

Everything got off to a promising start. Again I found myself capable of what seemed preternaturally clear thought. I was standing in the middle of the living room, rehearsing the steps of some argument or other, then thoughtfully went and sat down at the table.

After a moment I looked at my watch. I froze in amazement. *According to the watch two hours had passed since I sat down.* That's impossible, I thought. I double-, triple-checked the watch—but no, I had made no mistake. Two hours had passed. Suddenly I felt I was going to throw up.

What had happened?

I couldn't remember anything at all.

Had I left the apartment?

Oh, my God, I thought, *have I gone and done something dreadful? Something dreadful and blacked it out?*

My back was slick with sweat as I tried to remember. Fragmentary images of the Heath started to form in my mind. Images of a bright and frosty afternoon, like today. I could see legs in beat-up black Levis like mine striding down a path through bare winter woods . . . but I was still very high, with my imagination working at white heat, and I couldn't tell whether these were real memories or just images I was conjuring up. This was the first time I had ever experienced my skin crawl. Like wringing your hands, the expression is literal. Your skin can do just that . . .

The next morning I still felt dislocated and physically in shock.

What had happened? I'd had experiences of overload before, brief episodes from trips I couldn't recollect . . . but never total blackout for hours on end. Were the official warnings I dismissed with such indifference all too accurate, and LSD could well trigger psychotic breaks? For the first time in my tripping career I started to get really scared.

Then I remembered that Grof had listed blackouts in the passage from *LSD Psychotherapy* I quoted a couple of chapters back. I reread that section, "Critical Situations in LSD Sessions," more closely and found another paragraph that was equally chilling.

Ego death involves an experience of the destruction of everything that the subject is, possesses, or is attached to. Its essential characteristics are a sense of total annihilation on all imaginable levels, loss of all systems of relation and reference, and destruction of the objective world. As it is approached in different directions and on different levels, the process requires more and more psychological sacrifice. In the final stages, subjects have to face and confront experiences, situations, and circumstances that are unacceptable or even unimaginable to them.

Even after I had calmed down a bit (and, truth to tell, furtively combed the local paper for corpses on the Heath), something had snapped inside me.

What the fuck do you think you are doing? I thought. You are risking psychosis, without even so much as a sitter. True, you started off with some very positive experiences. Acid dissolved a state of chronic depression, and those trips about childhood and adolescence changed the way you saw your whole life—but these recent escapades are totally out of order. All that lunacy about Christianity. You are doing exactly what everyone else did with acid in the '60s—and that's take far too much. Don't be a fool. What's happening now is a clear message to stop.

What did happen with those two trips? Was I overdosing? Can you absorb LSD transdermally, through your fingertips? That's widely held to be what happened to Albert Hofmann when he first discovered the psychoactivity of LSD . . . but then I've heard other people deny that any such thing is possible.

More generally, what I'd suggest was involved was . . . resistance.

Resistance is an analytic concept you don't hear much about in relation to psychedelic drugs, as though they were so potent that blocking them was out of the question. Such hasn't been my experience. My first dose of mescaline I managed to stop dead in its tracks, and I wonder whether a lot of recreational acid trips don't owe their remarkable shallowness to the same subconscious fear of losing control.

So what was I resisting?

Something personal? Some long-buried trauma? That could be the case, since later I was to unearth a massive physical and emotional wound in early childhood . . . but somehow I don't think that was what it was. Rather, looking back on it today, I'd suspect there is a qualitative break involved in leaving the aesthetic and psychodynamic realms behind and beginning to penetrate the deeper, transpersonal levels of mind. Perhaps we weren't meant to do any such thing. Perhaps there's a Promethean, heaven-storming quality to acid that arouses deep-seated, almost biological levels of resistance. Perhaps all the fear we have been denying suddenly explodes in our faces.

I just don't know. All I can say for sure is that serial tripping may well run into phenomena that will not make sense unless you factor in resistance. Failing to do so—which was what happened to me—led me to try to abandon the whole project.

I didn't do so without a fight.

Almost defiantly, I tried a last few trips. I reduced the dose, back down to 200 micrograms, which did blunt the psychotic edge—but only at the price of returning to the Protestant fundamentalism, the same drunken blur, out of which emerged the hacking cough, the phantom taste of blood, and the apocalypticism. By now my mind was beginning to feel like damp clothes flopping around and around in a spin dryer.

I began to question my entire involvement with psychedelics. Was the truth that I was faced with a real spiritual crisis, one brought on by old age and the certainty of death . . . and that rather than using acid to explore this, I was using it to distract myself? To distract myself from what I should be doing, which was commit myself wholeheartedly to prayer and to meditation? To put staying in the present moment above everything else in the world . . . which, deep down, I knew was the only way it was going to work?

Finally, the morning after the last of these trips, I decided that it was all over. Brusquely I got up from the table where I had been trying to express my frustration in the trip journal and stuck the notebook in the back of the living-room cupboard.

The hell with this, I thought, I don't want to have anything more to do with it.

22

Anna and
A Cappella

I BELABOR THIS, BECAUSE it was while I thought I had abandoned acid for good that my real trust was to form. What started to happen over the following weeks, then months, was without any pharmacological presence of the drug in my system. Not until the very end did I imagine there was any connection between the following events and LSD.

The first thing was the role my friend Anna started to play in my life.

Anna was the old friend from India, the one diagnosed with cancer, for whom I had wept during my first trip. During the previous winter she had experienced what she believed to be two minor epileptic-type seizures. She had been left with no more than a slight limp, but subsequent hospital tests had revealed that the problem wasn't epilepsy but the presence of a tumor on her brain. Further tests had shown the tumor to be metastasis of lung cancer. Treated with radiation, the tumor had shrunk in size, but the consultant warned her that the effects of the treatment would be only temporary. The cancer was inoperable, and she was given six months to live.

Anna appeared her normal self, if a little weak, for the summer and autumn, but by the early winter she was bedridden. Her best girl-friend, who proved extraordinarily loyal throughout, organized her move to a local hospice. Spiritually, Anna had the same background in Gurdjieff and Buddhism as I had, and she believed her cancer was an eleventh-hour wake-up call. She talked of "dying consciously," and had her girlfriend and me buy a four-by-two-foot mirror and hang it at the foot of her bed. With this Gurdjieffian gesture she was always faced by her death. I was touched by her bravery, for her dying wasn't a pretty sight.

Anna was from Sweden and had been strikingly beautiful in her youth. During her teens she had worked as a model in Paris, and even when I first met her (driving around Goa on a battered Harley-Davidson with her English boyfriend, who made false-bottomed suitcases for the drug smugglers in Anjuna), she had retained the ice-princess quality, the coolness and audacity. Just a few years before she had trekked through the Himalayas on her own, walking for weeks on end through the mountains of Garhwal: from Mussoorie to Jamunotri, with no guide, no map, and precious little money, staying with shepherds and sadhus she met along the way.

Now, in her early fifties, she was paralyzed from below the waist. Her legs were useless appendages, knobbly sticks like the legs of inmates in the Nazi death camps. Chronically constipated, for the last months of her life she was fitted with a catheter and wore pale-green government nappies; nurses had to come around and wash her bottom as if she was a baby. Her hair fell out from the single radiation treatment, so did a front tooth, while the steroids with which it was followed pumped her up and made her skin angry red and blotchy.

That was what the mirror saw; and I think Anna hoped the shock would anchor her in the here and now. She was holding out for awakening at death's door; and if she saw anything in the way, she thought it would be physical pain . . . which didn't turn out to be the case. She was prescribed one of the new fentanyls in a transdermal patch, which effectively neutralized the worst of it.

Her hospice was not far from where I lived, and I began to spend more and more time with her.

Hanging out with Anna as she died was the first thing. The second was the music.

During the trip when I caught my first glimpse of the sacred, I had been listening to a CD of Hildegard of Bingen. The music must have touched me more deeply than I realized, because when I returned the CD to the library I borrowed two further discs of late medieval/early Renaissance music. I took them home and listened, though more dutifully than anything else, for they lacked the pristine clarity of St. Hildegard; and, if anything, sounded predictably churchy.

However, one evening I'd had a smoke before I started to cook supper, and I put one of the discs, Ockeghem's fifteenth-century *Requiem,* on the stereo as background music. I was doing something at the stove *when all of a sudden I heard it. It was as though my ears had been unblocked.* I took the pan off the gas and walked back into the living room to listen. At first I was just amazed by the intricacy and richness of the counterpoint, the aesthetics of the voices dancing in and out of one another; then as I continued to listen, I became increasingly fascinated by the nature of the emotion the music was expressing. I couldn't find any adjective to describe it . . . but whatever it was, the lugubrious ecclesiastical quality had vanished.

Abstruse liner notes sketched in some background. Historically Ockeghem was considered the first true master of Western polyphony. Early in the Renaissance the old medieval plainsong (where everybody sang in unison, and which I'd always called Gregorian) began to give way to new approaches to sacred music. A small number of voices, generally between four and eight, sang individual parts in counterpoint. Instruments were never used, just voices, a style that became known as *a cappella*. Despite the Italian, such sacred music had not originated in Italy, but in Northern Europe, in the old Low Countries, most of its first masters being Dutch, French, or Belgian.

All this was news to me. For years, apart from some minimalism,

I had hardly ever listened to Western classical music, but now I began to borrow more and more CDs of early Renaissance music from the library. At first most of them were like the Ockeghem, and I simply couldn't hear them; then suddenly, as though my ears had popped, I would be listening wonderstruck. A smoke usually did the trick. But I still couldn't pin down the nature of the emotion inspiring this music. Faith? Celebration? Rapture? Whatever it was, the complexity and need for split-second timing produced an exhilarating sense of purity, speed, and elation—qualities I'd certainly never associated with the church. Sometimes as I listened my body seemed to be melting or dissolving; and there was a marked sensation of soaring . . . of ascension, virtually of flight.

I settled into a rhythm of spending almost every evening at Anna's hospice. I had never been present at a deathbed before and had no idea what you were supposed to do. Anna spent her days drawing and painting in bed, like a child, and in the evening she, her friend, and I would sit and chat, or we'd read to her, or meditate together for a while. Often one or another friend would drop in, and in a funny way the three of us started to really enjoy our evenings together.

It was during this time of abstention from acid that I first saw the drug was having an ongoing effect.

Had I not been living such a placid and outwardly uneventful life, I doubt that I would have noticed, but the personal, biographical material, which I believed those last trips had put an end to, was on the contrary continuing to flow. If anything it had quickened. Childhood and boyhood memories continued to surface in the same abrupt manner, but I could understand the story they were telling now. A sort of spontaneous self-analysis was taking place. Piece by piece I put together the truth that I had been an unwanted child, one who had responded by overcompensating wildly. I had set myself impossibly high goals, because (and I'm sure this is all too typical a story) the only way I had been able to cope was by believing I was special. Suddenly it was as though I was learning to read the story of my own life. One thing that had changed was the period the memories related to. Rather than just relating to childhood, they were also about the two boarding schools to which I had been sent. To my surprise, for I had always believed I had detested public school, I saw that a lot of the time I had been very happy there. I saw my prep school again—the lake, the woods, the path through the dog roses to the old chapel with its tumbled box tombs— and felt a shocking pang of longing. I saw the faces of my friends there, one by one, and saw how beautiful each one was, perfect like the faces of animals. I saw my second public school, not the grand if dilapidated eighteenth-century manor the first had been, but a bleak, barnlike affair in the Welsh borders; but I saw that there, too, contrary to what I had believed all these years, much of the time I had felt very fulfilled, with some of the best friends I ever made.

All my life I had flaunted being a public school dropout, but now I saw that there was part of me that had wanted to go to university and to have lived a successful academic life. It was as though I had to think all the things about my life I had never allowed myself to think before. What made me so angry was that the overcompensation had meant I could never see myself objectively. Imperceptibly, life had maneuvered me into stupidity. That was what really pissed me off. I had been forced to be a fool.

Somehow the acid had catalyzed a process that continued without further chemical action. Gradually this ongoing life-review began to bring about an increasing sense of dissociation from the self I had so blindly identified with. My life seemed to become ever more objective, something "out there" in the world. Something no longer subjective . . . even, in a sense, no longer "mine" at all. Needless to say, this happened almost imperceptibly, over a period of months; it was just that I first began to notice it at this time.

23

Anna's Death

DURING THE LAST WEEKS before Anna died, the a cappella became obsessive. The winter was ending, but the weather was still stormy and bitterly cold, and as I went back and forth from the hospice I was always playing the Walkman. I had exhausted the small stock of Renaissance music at the library (Josquin des Pres, then Lassus and Tallis, then Palestrina and compilation discs of lesser masters, finally doubling back to the roots in Dunstaple and Dufay), and by now if I wanted anything new I had to take the tube to the West End. I hadn't been so involved with music since the early days of rock and roll. Indeed, I wasn't far short of a lovesick teenager as I wandered through the night and rain, playing and replaying Lassus's *Infelix Ego*. With its dark ecstatic surges, surely the motet is one of the most haunting pieces of all Renaissance music . . . though finally I was beginning to ask myself, How come you just cannot stop playing it?

The dark and cold seemed to have lasted forever, when overnight it was spring. The wind dropped, the sun came out, and like magic the cherries were all in blossom. Perfect spring day followed perfect spring day, and instinctively Anna's friend and I knew this was what Anna had been hanging on for. She had us open the window as wide as it would go and push the hospice bed until it was almost sticking out: the ensemble of bed, potted polyanthus, and huge Gurdjieffian mirror like something from the heyday of Surrealist art.

Afternoon after afternoon Anna lay there, staring quietly into the sky.

But it was the end. Deep inside she turned to face the wall. During her last days she became increasingly confused, babbled Swedish to the nurses, and could never get comfortable. Before, I had never known what was meant by the "agitation" of the dying, but during the very last day of her life, though she was unconscious, she tossed and turned on the bed, throwing herself this way and that.

By late afternoon the staff had pumped her full of enough diamorphine to sedate her, and as the light began to fail the nurse brought in two armchairs and some blankets for us. Then she attached a small machine to Anna's arm, which administered regular shots of morphine with a whirring clockwork sound; it seemed to be doing it awfully often.

During the early evening her breathing became increasingly labored. Each outbreath sounded like it was the last; but each time the lungs rallied and started to inhale again. You could hear liquid. I remembered being told that when you died of emphysema what happened was that the lungs flooded, and you could not breathe. *"Is she going to drown?"* I whispered to Anna's friend, in horror.

But by late evening Anna's breathing had stabilized again; and we were nodding in our chairs when abruptly we realized how quiet the room had become.

Midnight had passed: it was the witching hour. Anna's head was slightly to one side on the pillow, and for a moment I thought she was making funny faces at her friend. Very slowly and very, very deliberately she seemed to be blowing raspberries. Her mouth was making a perfect bud shape, more exact than anything you could choose to do deliberately: more like the purely natural working of an internal organ. Each time a precise measure of air was released; then there would be a long pause, and finally another kiss blown. Very clearly I remember thinking you could not say she was either conscious or unconscious, she was something else altogether. As though she was around herself. Unmistakably, the hospice room was highly charged—but with what?

The pauses grew longer and longer; there was one final little *moue* . . . but there was no more air for it to release.

I think it must have been ten days or a fortnight after Anna's cremation—it was an afternoon, I remember—when abruptly I understood what had been happening. In a flash I saw that all of it was an ongoing form of the opening to religion, to Christianity in particular, that I had been struggling to deny during my last acid trips.

Several times already I had suspected there was more than the call of friendship involved in my desire to help Anna: an unconscious need to be exposed to the reality of death, which I, in common with our whole culture, had spent a lifetime denying. While I had been able to repress religious feeling during those last trips themselves, the acid had outflanked my defenses and started to operate directly on my daily life. A cappella was part and parcel of the same thing. First and foremost, it hadn't been about music but about getting me to acknowledge the reality of prayer and devotion. Aesthetically I was open in ways that I was not intellectually. Sacred music allowed me to surrender to an inner melting—to an ecstatic thrust into disembodiment—that otherwise I would have continued to deny.

My conditioning had been sidestepped, elegantly and very effectively: though once I saw it, it was staring me in the face. Sung mass and the deathbed—I mean, how much more hardcore can you get?

Over the following days the remaining pieces fell into place. Underpinning my resistance to acid had been the most common of all objections to psychedelics: that while experiences on trips could be electrifying, within a matter of hours the substance appeared to lose any power to transform, even influence, you any further. Acid could sweep you off your feet, no two ways about it . . . only to dump you back again in exactly the same position.

During my reading spree I had run across an essay by Houston

Smith titled "Do Drugs Have Religious Import?" The text was well known and had been one of the most widely reprinted of all papers on psychedelics in the '60s. Despite being in many ways unusually positive for an academic, Houston Smith had felt bound to draw a line under psychedelics, and his tentative conclusion had become all but axiomatic in psychedelic studies.

> Drugs appear to be able to induce religious experiences; it is less evident that they can produce religious lives.

While I was still tripping I would, however ruefully, have agreed. But since I'd stopped tripping I had observed, as I just mentioned, a process of self-analysis at work, which was continuing without any further doses of the drug. Acid appeared to have kick-started a process that in itself was spontaneous. Trips were not "just a drug" at all. Aldous Huxley's original image of mescaline bypassing a reducing valve in the brain, however simplistic in terms of brain chemistry, was substantially correct. Something repressed was being freed.

Only it was being freed for much longer than Huxley imagined. And not only that, while activated, it was capable of responding to different individuals with very great flexibility. Blocked intellectually or emotionally, it was capable of shifting tack and expressing itself through aspects of our nature as varied as friendship or our taste in music—capable, in fact, of communicating directly through apparently outer events.

No doubt it was reprehensibly primitive thinking, but I was beginning to find it difficult not to see acid as something akin to an intelligent entity, capable of autonomous action. Jung's concept of "the Self" was as close to making this intellectually acceptable as I could get . . . though in my present mood I would happily have inserted "Higher" in front of the term, and have done with it. For these insights left me with a glowing sense of melting into a more comprehensive identity. Into something, somewhere, that was looking out for me.

No, Houston Smith's dictum struck me as being highly debatable. I felt that he, in common with many of us at the time, thought that you could go straight to "mystical" experience, whereas now it was beginning to seem that you had to pass through a preliminary stage of healing and moral change. You couldn't vault over self-understanding, which was precisely the missing link between religious experiences and a truly religious life.

24

Session 21

Being Two People Simultaneously

AS THOUGH ON CUE, my new friend the dealer phoned, inviting me over. When I arrived at his apartment, he said he'd finally got some LSD again, both as sheets of blotter and as bottles. Which would I prefer?

Momentarily I was fazed, for in the old days I dread to think what a whole bottle might have meant. (Enough to take out Wolverhampton, I thought wildly.) To my relief, he explained that a bottle was one hundred 100-microgram doses. Purity, he added, he was happy about; however, he did have a suspicion that somewhere along the line the acid had been watered down a bit. One drop from the dropper, which should have been 100 mikes, was probably closer to 80. But all he was asking for a bottle was £150, which, considering the risks everyone concerned was running, was positively Utopian, and I bought one forthwith.

Back at my apartment, I removed the bottle from of its mini–Ziploc bag. Standing it upright on the living room table, I sat down and stared at it. An old-time, little brown bottle with a dropper, the picture of innocence until you wondered why there was no label . . . and it brought back all the romance of drugs with a surge of affection.

Dreamily I unscrewed the cap, sucked some acid into the dropper and held it up to the light. The liquid was pale-tea-colored; the dealer said brandy had been used as a solvent . . .

Despite my enthusiasm I thought I should test the bottle. I hadn't had a trip in four months, and I wanted to make sure it was a memorable one. So a couple of afternoons later I put two drops in a wineglass of water, which, according to the dealer, should have been about 160 micrograms . . . well, if it was, it seemed distinctly weak. The trip was agitated and never settled down to focus on anything. So much so that the first of my entries in my brand-new trip journal, volume two, reads like a passage from *Dr. Jekyll and Mr. Hyde.*

> Is the new bottle slightly off? Was there something about the first batch that was stronger or purer? Or do you build up a resistance over a period of time? Do the effects get progressively weaker— then just start to fizzle out?

Perhaps, ten days later, these misgivings made my promised big trip get off on the wrong foot.

Despite three full drops this time—which should have been 240 micrograms, to all intents and purposes the hippie benchmark dose of 250—the trip still seemed watery and amorphous. An hour passed, and nothing had happened; the second hour started to go by, and still nothing, apart from feeling restless and on edge. I lay on the bed, half-heartedly listening to a Josquin mass on the Walkman, until the beginning of the third hour, by which time the drug's effects should have been approaching their climax.

Shit, I thought: I've bought a lemon. I looked through the window at the sunny afternoon outside and felt really pissed off. Abruptly I thought, The hell with this! I'm going for a walk on the Heath.

One of my ground rules had been never to leave the flat until well after the trip had plateaued, and this was the first time I had ever ventured out while it was still full on . . . or meant to be. In fact, this was the oldest story in the book, the one about the acid trip that doesn't work. I was lucky I didn't do what other people had done in the past and drop a second one, then have them both come on simultaneously. Though what was about to happen was so weird I can't see how it could have been doubly so.

I slipped down the stairwell, then took the first street heading toward the Heath.

The street was empty.

The sun was shining, the birds were singing, and it was a glorious afternoon in early summer . . . apart from the fact that the trip was a dud. There was just one bizarre impression nagging at me as I walked down the street. *Somehow everything was more normal than it usually was.* There was no one else around, and I had walked some fifty yards or so when a figure turned the corner in front of me, heading down the pavement toward me.

The pedestrian was a man, and about my own build, but I didn't look at him directly until we were only a few paces apart. Then our eyes met—and I recoiled as though slapped in the face.

It was me looking out of his eyes.

It was me!

The recognition was as instantaneous and self-evident as seeing oneself in a mirror.

He was me!

I was him!

Never in my life had I been so freaked. Mechanically, I turned the corner and kept on walking down the street. So stunned was I that for once my mind was silent. My pulse was racing, true, but otherwise I seemed to be functioning perfectly normally . . . while everything else retained its unnerving quality of being über-normal.

I walked under a couple of old plane trees, continuing on my way toward the Heath. Then, out of the blue, I remembered that years and years before a girlfriend had told me exactly the same story. In the middle of a big acid trip, she had turned into the person she was talking to. She had been both of them simultaneously: she had been equally present at both ends of the conversation. Nothing else changed; I remembered her saying that too. Despite her vehemence, I had politely dismissed, then promptly forgotten all about her story. Until this very moment.

There were no further passersby until I came to the crossroads. There is a pub on the other side of the road there, and four or five people were dotted around the respective pavements. As I walked toward the scattered group, one looked my way . . . and again the afternoon went insane.

As our eyes met, I saw that we too were one.

Not that he looked like me or resembled me in any way. Nothing like that. He *was* me, and I *was* him. Just the way you know you are you, I knew I was him. It was self-evident.

And as I looked at each person there, the same thing happened. I became each one of them individually, and then we all became one collectively, forming a joint star-shaped field of being stretching perhaps thirty feet in several directions. While an integral part of this field, I had no specific sense of bilocation. I didn't see things through the eyes of the others, nothing like that, though there were waves of something that felt like seasickness. It was ontological. I was the mother and her baby sprawling in the stroller. I was the worried middle-aged man crossing the street. I was the pretty young girl by the railings. I was all of them: and all of them were me.

I hadn't a clue what to do, so I just crossed the street with what I hoped was a poker face, then continued to walk on down the pavement through the dappled sun and shade. But inside I was enormously elated. In fact I was manic. This is vintage science fiction, I thought. Like *Invasion of the Body Snatchers*—and I have landed the star role! I get to be space monster!

I don't know where everyone was that afternoon, for again the street was empty. Nor were there any cars on the road as I crossed over onto the Heath. Still no one, and I could feel the wave of wild excitement beginning to ebb as I walked toward the Vale of Health pond. Finally I did cross a group of foreign tourists taking in the Heath; but when I made eye contact with one of them, nothing untoward happened.

My utter madness seemed to have burned the trip out, and I wandered around the pond in an increasingly desultory fashion, finally lying down beside the little silver birch grove where the *Amanita muscaria* grow in autumn.

For the next hour or so I just lay there in the grass, propped up on my elbow, watching the breeze play in the treetops on the far bank of the pond. I had never observed how complex air currents were, how one set of leaves would shimmer in one direction, while those a few inches away would be rippling in another. You could see how each little gust of wind was incorporated into the movement of the whole. Each tree responded to the wind in its own unique way, some sedate, some rippling passionately, yet at the same time all of them were moving in unison, as an organic whole.

Strange that such in-your-face hallucination could be followed by such a profound sense of peace! For this, I realized, was the first occasion I had ever felt truly meditative on a trip. The acid hadn't been played out at all. The same sense of boundaries dissolving, which had allowed me to become one with people on the street, was granting this gentler, sweeter sense of empathy with wind and water and trees. I felt I could lie there watching them forever.

Why was something normally so difficult now so effortless?

All at once my attempt to introvert acid with mask and earphones seemed to be crudely manipulative. I needed to open up, not contract still further. I needed to let go. Was that what my sessions of several months before—trips I had brushed aside—had been trying to tell me? That my approach was far too intellectual and needed to become more heartfelt? More passionate? More prayerful? Patently that had been the message of the first of the group of trips, the one when I had been listening to St. Hildegard.

That I needed to let go . . . but I needed to let go into something. I needed to let go into beauty, into natural beauty. That was my way.

I should start tripping on the Heath, I thought, as I finally rose to my feet. I should find a quiet corner of the woods and see what happens if I just sit quietly and don't try to control things at all.

25

The Transpersonal

THE NEXT MORNING I opened my copy of *Realms of the Human Unconscious*, laughing aloud at myself as I did so. Really, this is getting to be too much, I thought, thumbing through the pages . . . but there it was! *Dual unity*, Grof calls such moments, and they figure largely among the transpersonal phenomena that compose the final category of psychedelic experience.

> The subject experiences various degrees of loosening and losing of his ego boundaries and merging with another person into a state of unity and oneness. In spite of feeling totally fused with the interpersonal partner, the individual always retains simultaneously the awareness of his own identity. In LSD sessions, this state of dual unity can be experienced with the therapist, sitter, family members, or other participating persons.[1]

The concluding chapters of *Realms* are the truly mind-blowing ones. For Grof, while transpersonal phenomena can appear sporadically in early sessions, they only begin to occur regularly in the measure that the death/rebirth crisis is lived through. What is the "transpersonal"? Perhaps the term *boundary loss* is more graphic. In *The Doors of Perception*, Huxley quoted the English philosopher C. D. Broad, and so powerful is the passage I'd like to repeat it here.

> The function of the brain and nervous system and sense organs is in the main eliminative and not productive. Each person is at each moment capable of remembering all that has ever happened to him and of perceiving everything that is happening everywhere in the universe.

Over the top as this is sounds, psychedelic experience does appear to bear out its possibility. Something resembling Huxley's Mind At Large does start to bleed through; and with it glimpses of the whole side of life that left-brain, industrialized society has done all it can to deny, everything it has consigned to the ragbag of the occult or the esoteric or the paranormal. Only, unfortunately, none of it appears in a coherent form. Magic manifests piecemeal—anarchically—in bursts that defy reproduction in laboratory conditions.

Grof struggles to classify what seems the chronically miscellaneous nature of such material under three broad headings: first as what he calls "expansion of the temporal dimension of consciousness"; next as a corresponding "expansion of the spatial dimension of consciousness"; and last as "experiential extension beyond the framework of objective reality" itself.

temporal expansion of consciousness

The first cases of transpersonal experience he encountered came from subjects who had regressed beyond the birth trauma, initially as fragmentary memories of life in the womb; then, more disturbingly, as what appeared to be things their parents remembered. Where verification was possible, these flashes tallied with their parents' recollections (details of specific instances are given in *Realms*). Next came images of what were seemingly "past lives"; then, and again more disturbingly, flashes of ancestral or racial experience. But not only did the past begin to open up, so did the future. Instances of what appeared to be precognition also occurred.

spatial expansion of consciousness

This second category was that of boundary loss between subject and object. All episodes of "dual unity" were not only with other people, as mine had been, but with animals, with plants, with inorganic matter, and even with the planet itself. Subjects experienced a corresponding change in their sense of identity, and cases of out-of-the-body experience, including traveling clairvoyance and clairaudience, were reported.

experiential extension beyond the framework of "objective reality"

Grof's final category is, if possible, still more of an affront to reason. Out of the body, out of the mind experience becomes central. An entirely different universe, inhabited by qualitatively different beings, begins to appear. I'll just give some of Grof's subheadings: "Spiritistic and mediumistic experiences"; "Experiences of encounters with suprahuman spiritual entities"; "Archetypal experiences and complex mythological sequences"; "Intuitive understanding of universal symbols"; "Activation of the chakras"; "Consciousness of the universal mind"; "The supracosmic and metacosmic Void."

For me personally, my experience of turning in to the passerby on the street initiated a cycle of boundary-loss experiences, marking a qualitative break with everything that had come before. My earlier trips seemed like fumbling with a radio dial and getting bursts of this or that station: but from the time of that first trip on the street, I felt I had tuned in to one station loud and clear. Everything became coherent, and session after session went deeper into the same themes.

At the same time as the themes became more consistent, however, they became more alarming; and at this point I'd like to quote several other people's experiences, basically just to illustrate how extreme psychedelic experience can be—and how great a threat to normal accounts of reality it poses—and to show that it's not just me who is off my head . . . I'll stay with Grof's three categories but not quote his own case histories, as I don't want to strain his personal credibility either, but merely show that such phenomena have been reported independently by a large number and wide variety of other people.*

First a case of expansion of consciousness in terms of space.

The following is a relatively straightforward example of boundary loss and empathic identity with the object of perception. It is from the prologue to Paul Devereux's *The Long Trip* and is an account of his own first trip. After a fairly grueling death experience, Devereux awoke to a transfigured world. The first thing he noticed was "a dull glow of color" around a friend's shoulder.

> I looked closer and focused on the effect. I saw bands of very soft, almost ethereal color surrounding the person's head and shoulders. I could easily see the wallpaper pattern through this delicate, slowly shifting rainbow atmosphere. It suddenly dawned on me that I was looking at the human aura, the stock-in-trade of clairvoyants and other occult practitioners. "Jesus! The aura is a real thing!" I thought in amazement. I knew then, as I remain convinced, that this was a true observation.

Next, sitting down at a table, his attention was drawn to a single daffodil in a vase. At first he was fascinated by the way the flower seemed to breathe, but as he looked more closely he noted something else.

---

*The '60s and '70s high tide of firsthand reports is a thing of the past. Today the only popular compilation in print is Charles Hayes' *Tripping: An Anthology of True-Life Psychedelic Adventures* (2000). Despite patchiness, the fifty accounts make gripping reading. While I was finishing this manuscript, Grof himself brought out a new book, *When the Impossible Happens* (2006), which contains a large and varied number of cases of transpersonal experience from his own files.

I was horrified to see tiny bugs crawling up the flower's stem. I looked more closely. They were not bugs, but very small droplets of moisture moving by capillary action up the inside of the stem. I realized with shock that I could only be seeing this because I had X-ray vision. Is it possible for the visual cortex to process energy outside the visible spectrum? While I struggled to understand how this could happen, I lost the novel visual ability and the daffodil became just a daffodil once more.

But interaction between myself and the flower wasn't yet over. Some time later, I entered into a most curious empathic relationship with it. There was no visual component; it was strictly an emotional link. Without losing my own (admittedly by now somewhat bruised and fragile) sense of identity, I found my awareness slipping inside that of the daffodil. While still being conscious of sitting in a chair, I could also sense my petals! Then an exquisite sensation cascaded through me, and I knew I was experiencing light falling on those petals. It was virtually orgasmic, the haptic equivalent of an angelic choir. At every moment I felt, repeatedly, as if I were receiving the first ray of sunshine on the first morning in Eden. The world was unutterably new and innocent.[2]

Obviously if you wanted to pooh-pooh this, you would say that it was just imagination . . . imagination wrought to an extraordinary pitch of intensity, without doubt, but just imagination for all that. Nor, in a sense, would you be wrong. The more you study the transpersonal, the more intimately it appears to be involved with the imagination. Which in its turn leads to the bigger question: What is imagination? Is it just a bastard form of reason, as conventional wisdom would have us believe? Or does it have another, altogether different ontological status of its own—one beyond the antinomy of real and unreal, for instance?

Next, let me quote a case of expansion of consciousness in terms of time. This example is particularly interesting since it deals with the relation between time and timelessness—not merely with expanding one's perception of time, but with transcending it altogether.

During the mid-1950s Christopher Mayhew, former journalist and author (and at the time a member of Parliament), took mescaline under the supervision of Humphry Osmond, the same Osmond who had been responsible for Aldous Huxley's first trip. The entire session was filmed by a BBC film crew for television. Those were the days. Later, trying to summarize his experience, Mayhew was to write:

> On many occasions that afternoon I existed outside time. I don't mean this metaphorically, but literally. I mean that the essential part of me . . . had an existence, quite conscious of itself . . . in a timeless order of reality outside the world as we know it.

The first symptom induced by the drug was a sense of disembodiment. "I felt completely detached from my body and the world, and was aware of my eyes seeing, my ears hearing, and my mouth speaking as though at some distance below me." Next Mayhew realized that his perception of time was warping dramatically. He was starting to perceive things in the wrong order. *He had become unstuck in time.*

> I was experiencing the events of 3:30 before the events of 3:00; the events of 2:00 after the events of 2:45, and so on. Several events I experienced with an equal degree of reality more than once . . . I was aware of my eyes seeing the tea being poured out after I was aware of my throat swallowing it . . . In films, "flashbacks" transpose us backwards and forwards in time. We find events of 1956 being suddenly interrupted by events of 1939. In the same way I found later events in our drawing room—events in which I myself was participating at the bodily level—being interrupted by earlier events and vice versa.

This continued throughout the trip, only being interrupted by a second—and so far as I understand the word, genuinely mystical—

experience, during which time ceased and he experienced eternity.

At irregular intervals—perhaps twice every five minutes at the peak of the experiment—I would become unaware of my surroundings, and enjoy an existence conscious of myself, in a state of breathless wonderment and complete bliss, for a period of time, which—for me—simply did not end at all. It did not last for minutes or hours but apparently for years. During this period I would be aware of a pervasive bright, pure light, like a kind of invisible sunlit snow. For several days afterwards, I remembered the afternoon of December 2, not as so many hours spent in my drawing room interrupted by these strange "excursions," but as countless years of complete bliss interrupted by short spells in the drawing room . . . On the first occasion when I "came back" in this way from an excursion I assumed that a vast period of time had elapsed and exclaimed, in astonishment, to the film team: "Are you still there?" Their patience in waiting seemed extraordinary; but in fact, of course, no time had elapsed, and they had not been waiting at all.

All that announced that the session was drawing to a close were the increasingly frequent appearances and disappearances of the afternoon tea-trolley (which "in the real world" was wheeled in only once, at the very end of the experiment). The trolley, along with cups of tea and biscuits, came and went more and more often, until it finally solidified and Mayhew realized that he was back in normal time once more.

Several months later, trying to make some coherent metaphysical sense of the afternoon, he was to write:

A rational explanation is possible if we make one revolutionary assumption. This assumption is that from my peculiar disembodied standpoint, all the events in my drawing room between one-thirty and four o'clock existed together at the same time. This is, of course, a terribly difficult idea to grasp: but it is not, despite appearances, self-contradictory. When we take off from an airport at night, we are aware of individual runway lights flashing past in succession. But when we look down a little later, we see them all existing together motionless. It is not self-contradictory to say that the lights flashed past in succession and also that they exist together motionless. Everything depends on the standpoint of the observer.[3]

To illustrate Grof's third and final category—"experiential extension beyond the framework of objective reality"—I'll give a case of a young man meeting seemingly more highly evolved spiritual beings. The story is from Charles Hayes' *Tripping,* and the subject, who was called Jason and in his early twenties, had taken two high-dose trips to make sure he really got off. And that he did. After several insights as to the primacy of consciousness over matter, the trip started to come on full.

I felt I was ascending and passing into a new dimension. . . . I started to hear celestial sounds (not coming from the turntable) like little synthesizer riffs. . . . I became aware of energy forms descending from higher up. It didn't matter if my eyes were open or closed. I could feel another reality superimposed. Consistent with my expanded consciousness was an extended field of vision. I seemed to have 360-degree wraparound vision, as though my eyesight were liberated from the confines of its socket-based axis and could now behold all of ocular space as a dome. There was a humming sound as the forms from on high descended. I immediately intuited that they were beings. I could sense another consciousness coming into contact with me, an assembly of minds. I strained to see these forms, which at first were just indistinct blobs of light and energy. Then they took on vaguely humanoid outlines, like glowing silhouettes of yogis in the lotus posture. . . . I realized that these were higher beings, angelic hosts from a spiritual dimension that I had now accessed. They were enlightened beings working for the good of creation, blessing me with a visitation. They were calling to me telepathically, linking me with their consciousness. I could distinguish individual voices. . . . They were touching my mind, beaming thoughts at me in an ecstatic chorus, saying, "Jason, it's beautiful. Come join us. Be one with us." I reached up to touch them, not with my physical but my astral-form arms. All of their hands reached down and touched my hands, clutching them as their voices repeated, "It's beautiful. You're one with us." Tears were streaming down my face. It was the peak moment of my life. It wasn't like communion with another human being, where you wonder where you're really situated in the other person's mind. There was no question here. Our souls were touching. . . . I stayed in this state as long as I could, but slowly the angelic hosts began to pull away. I redoubled my efforts to contact them, but they were fading. "No, no, no. Don't go! Don't go!" I was receding out of the astral dimension and it was becoming darker. I couldn't hold on. I fought against it, but faded from this radiant plane.[4]

Again, and even more derisively, the materialist stance would be that this is pure imagination. And again I wouldn't contest this, so much as to reply that such so-called explanations merely beg the question. What is imagination? Surely that is the question. Why is it so disparaged? One of the most fundamental features of tripping is that *the experience is more real than normal reality.* "We imagine the truth," said Osho, summing up the idealist position in a phrase.

Philosophically, the implications of this would take us back to the very roots of Western culture, specifically to Neoplatonism and Plato's theory of archetypes. But while Plato argued that (a) the only sane society would be one where everyone was a philosopher, but that

(b) this was impossible and that therefore (c) the only thing to do was to breed and educate a philosopher-king, we would retort that ritual use of psychedelics could make apprehension of a far more essential world informing this one available to everyone. And a passionate imagination could prove a very much more powerful tool than logic in any such undertaking.

26

Tripping
on the Heath

FINDING SOMEWHERE TO MEDITATE on the Heath was a lot easier than trying to get my head around such idealist metaphysics, and I spent several afternoons exploring the area between the Vale of Health and Kenwood.

I narrowed the search down to the woods just south of Kenwood House and spent a further afternoon clambering over fences and wading through bracken but still unable to find exactly the right spot. I was getting warm, though, I could feel that; and I was struck by how much the mixed woodland reminded me of my prep school, the rundown Georgian manor in Derbyshire.

Blundering through the bushes, I finally discovered an old beech tree surrounded by a small glade thickly carpeted with leaf mold. Though a fallen and half-rotten tree trunk made the spot invisible, it was not that far from a little-used path, and very occasionally you could hear voices as people passed . . . but instinctively I wanted to be in the woods, and it was the best I could do.

Kenwood woods are all but deserted on weekdays, and so the following Friday morning at noon I put three drops from my little bottle of acid into a wineglass of water and drank it down. I stuck a few things in a daypack, locked the apartment, and headed for the Heath.

I arrived at the clearing well before the drug had time to take effect, spread a shawl at the foot of the beech, and sat down. Blindfold I had dispensed with; I was just going to close my eyes when I felt like it, but I had brought the Walkman and a couple of Josquin CDs.

During the past few days I had picked up *The Secret Chief* again, and I had memorized part of the seventeenth-century prayer that had been Jacob's preferred "set" for psychedelic work.

> *Lord, I know not what I ought to ask of Thee . . .*
> *I am silent; I offer myself in sacrifice;*
> *I yield myself to Thee; I would have no*
> *other desire than to accomplish Thy will.*
> *Teach me to pray.*
> *Pray Thyself in me.*
> *Amen.*

As I sat there listening to the Josquin, the trees began to look not just similar, but the very same as the woods around my prep school. From its eighteenth- and early-nineteenth-century grandeur, the house and estate had fallen on hard times. During the Second World War it had been requisitioned by the Army as an officers' training center, and by the time it reopened as a school, the woods weren't dotted only with ruined Georgian walks and arbors but with scattered Quonset huts. There was a boathouse with a partly caved-in roof and a sinister icehouse dug into the side of a hill. Behind the blazers and school caps we had lived a life straight out of *Lord of the Flies,* both violent and, in those days before television, much more creative as to the mischief we got up to . . . and I had loved it.

So spellbound was I by the procession of images, I failed to notice that insidiously my self-hatred was resurfacing, the sense of paradise lost . . . of having staked everything on doomed romantic politics . . . of chronic spiritual indecision. Then the images began to cohere around one particular summer afternoon during my last term.

A group of us were lying in the long grass at the edge of the cricket pitch. All of us were sitting our exams and due to leave at the end of term, and we were boasting about what we were going to do with our lives. My head was stuffed with adventure stories, with *The Black Arrow* and *She* and *The Scarlet Pimpernel:* the extent to which the school library was bulging with anarchism and the surreal never ceases to surprise me . . .

I could remember the long blades of grass we were chewing, the distant clunk of ball and bat, the scattered and ironic ripples of applause . . .

My sense of despair deepened.

By now it must have been more than two hours into the trip, and I was slumped against the beech looking upward into the tree canopy, idly watching the midges darting to and fro in the shafts of sunlight. How much energy they put into something so futile! There's no real difference between my life and theirs, I thought morosely, watching them with sudden sympathy . . . and, without a moment's warning, everything turned inside out.

For an instant I became one with the midges. I knew the thrill of hurtling through the rays of light, the knack of being able to turn in midair on a dime. Wow, I thought, and sat up, enthralled. And as I did so, the leaves and branches above my head shimmered, as though a ripple was passing through them, and when they refocused it was as something incredibly beautiful—cosmic, yet elfin in its delicacy, the leaves the subtlest palette of pale greens picked out in gold.

There was magic in the air.

A frond of bracken arched to one side of the shawl where I was sitting, and as I watched a midge approached one of its still uncurled tips. The creature was perfect. You could see its tiny head and body, while all around its wings made a rainbow blur. The midge hovered there, checking out the tip of the frond.

"No," I breathed, peering in amazement. *It's got a face!*

For a moment I saw into the mind of God. Everything was equal—that was the secret. All creation was of a piece. Problems, and this was as clear as a bell, can never be solved, they can only be transcended. All you can do is step back into a larger and more inclusive frame; and in that bigger frame things are perfect just the way they are.

It was a flawless June afternoon and I lay back, looking up through the leaves and shafts of sunlight, briefly free of my Furies. Deep down, the acid must have eaten through to a further level of reality, though it did it gently, almost imperceptibly, for all I knew was that I was back with my friends in the long grass at the edge of the cricket pitch. Everything looked the same . . . but I could feel a strange sensation, as it were of meaning being turned about, like scenery shifted silently behind darkened wings. The tableau of boys about to lose their childhood and their innocence no longer seemed tragic, but curiously at peace. I felt as though I had reconnected with my younger self, and a dialogue had begun between that sunburned, high-strung schoolboy and the person I had become.

I stayed leaning against the bole of the beech until late in the afternoon. Finally I rose to my feet, stuffed the shawl, water bottle, and CDs into the daypack, and slowly made my way back through the woods. This trip was the first time I had any inkling of what could be meant by the "redemption" of past time.

27

The Purple Flowers

THE SECOND TRIP IN the woods could not have been more different. Far from being the sunlit summer-of-love paradise of last time, the glade was overcast, damp, and almost foggy; the ferns stood out more prominently, lending the clearing a misty New Zealand forest quality. There were sprinklings of rain.

Despite this, the session started in the same way.

Again I found I was sinking deeper and deeper into a trancelike state of depression, and again I did my best to let go into it. But this time the series of images as they began to unfold reflected something quite different from personal despair. They reflected . . . death.

The starting point was a memory from Anna's hospice. One evening I had watched a group of relatives in the main ward sitting silently around the bed of someone who was dying. All were wearing black, and they hadn't even taken off their hats and coats. They were perched there like a row of vultures, and I had thought, God, don't let me die like that. Then I saw myself being wheeled on a gurney, in nappies like Anna, with a tube leading from my arm to a drip-feed bottle on a rod. Horribly, the staff trundling the gurney all appeared to be children. I saw them whisk the tacky plastic curtains around the bed at the end; I could even hear the clatter of the curtain hooks. Dying smacked-out in a public ward with the TV blaring—it seemed such an awful way to end it all.

I leaned back against the tree and tried to relax. Let go, I told myself. Let go, and let it take you where it wants . . . the trouble was, I liked the look of where it wanted to take me less and less.

There was growing pressure on my chest, and I was finding it hard to breathe. Then I seemed to catch sight of something inside myself that made me freeze with incredulity. *I saw that I wanted to die. Deep down, I didn't want to live at all.* No, no, I thought. That can't be so. That doesn't make any kind of sense. Then I remembered Freud's concept of the death instinct, and I wondered whether there could be some truth in that after all. Hadn't Freud called it "the Nirvana Principle" at first? That would have quite different connotations. Returning to a state neither living nor dead . . . returning to the changeless, the unmanifest.

Suddenly death was all around.

At the same moment purple flowers, startling in their clarity, appeared in the air before me.

I recoiled in shock. The flowers were a full-blown hallucination. They were in silhouette, in groups of three and four, and looked like a sort of stylized tulip, only the head was slightly inclined. When I tried to make them disappear by closing my eyes they were still there, just a darker shade of purple and against a violet background.

On that first occasion the flowers appeared, there was nothing threatening about them. If anything, they looked like flowers on rather tasteless old-fashioned wallpaper—yet intuitively I was certain that such purple flowers were associated with death or the underworld in classical antiquity.

For a moment everything froze. I stood up dumbfounded, and the flowers remained stationary in the air—then, equally to my surprise, I felt the intensity begin to drain from the situation. The rush, which had felt like a wave towering above my head, started to falter and withdraw. The purple flowers phased in and out, and then disappeared; and the wave sank back, collapsing into itself.

I tried to sit down again, but massive bursts of energy were still gusting through me. I got back to my feet and started to pace up and down in the clearing . . . The trip journal says not only was I freaked out by not knowing whether I had seen Freud's death instinct, but I had also remembered that in the early days of LSD research there had been reports the drug could work as a diagnostic agent of surprising accuracy, so I was now paranoid that this had been a premonition that I was seriously ill myself. Could the hepatitis C be much worse than I had imagined?

At least I still had sufficient wits to recognize that the trip was over, and that the awful sense of cosmic shoddiness I was feeling had characterized resistance on earlier trips. Finally there was nothing to do but gather my things from beneath the beech and wend a jumpy, ill-natured way back home through the woods.

The cycle of trips that was to take place in the glade all showed marked features of "bad trips," particularly in the early stages of each session; and they confronted me once more with the question of how some people appear never to have scary, or self-confrontational, or even plain grueling acid trips (or so they swear), while others have them in spades.

"It's too early for a science," as Terence McKenna already observed. "What we need now are the diaries of explorers." And until we have more of such firsthand reports it is foolish to generalize. Perhaps, though, it is worth noting that something similar has run through the history of world religion. Christianity is divided into its *via positiva* and its *via negativa*: the theology of the first being based on the praise of God, as opposed to that of the *via negativa,* which asserts that no finite attributes of any sort can be applied to That Which Is. On the one hand, St. Francis, on the other St. John of the Cross. Much the same distinction is made, though perhaps more sturdily, by the early Buddhist division of humanity into "greed" and "hate" types: into those who always want more experience, and those who always want less.

Are we faced with some basic difference between human beings here? Something comparable to the distinction between extroverts and introverts? Frankly, I just don't know. The best I can do is speculate that both poles could be part of a single overarching process and point to a vision as mainline as that of Dante for support. In the *Divine Comedy,* Paradise is reached through traversing Hell and Purgatory; and though there may be faster, more direct ways to the presence of God (that of Beatrice most famously), only completing the full journey, with all its terrors and ecstasies, sets so high a premium on understanding and compassion.

Some such perspective has been touched upon in recent psychedelic studies.

During that summer in the glade I read Christopher Bache's *Dark Night, Early Dawn,* which had just come out and remains the outstanding attempt to get LSD studies on the road again. For a large part of his self-experimentation Bache had a series of horrendous trips. At the most agonizing point of each one, however, when he felt he could truly bear no more, the trip went through a 180-degree turn, and he found himself swept up by new insight and joy.

From this experience he suggests that the dynamics of a fully resolved trip fall into two opposed halves, which are related dialectically.

In the first, which he calls the *provocative,* the subject is flooded, and not infrequently submerged, by unconscious material. In the second, which he calls the *integrative,* the new material is digested in a more balanced, more highly evolved whole. While the provocative stage can indeed be dire, the integrative almost always tends to be joyous. In this sense the only truly "bad" trip is the one in which the process isn't fully completed, and material that has not been integrated can linger and cause distress for days or weeks to come. Which perhaps could be seen as corroborating the old hippie street wisdom that a high dose of psychedelics is in fact much "safer" than a low one.

Gradually I was reading more and more religious material, and the most satisfying overview I found was the model proposed by Evelyn Underhill in her *Mysticism.* In this classic work she breaks down Christian spirituality into five major stages, the first three of which are:

Conversion

Purgation

Illumination

These speak for themselves, and applied to psychedelics, the majority of trips fall into the Purgation/Illumination bracket. In practice, the intensity and duration of either stage varies with the individual, but commonly (Underhill clearly mirroring Chris Bache here) Purgation coexists and interrelates closely with Illumination.

These three stages form the substance of a sane and spiritually fulfilled life in the world. Ultimately, however, they constitute no more than what Underhill refers to as "the first religious life," and she proceeds to describe two further stages, which form a "second" and truly mystical religious life. These two more advanced stages are: Dark Night of the Soul (which is something qualitatively more devastating than Purgation) and only after this, at the very end, Unity with God.

I found Evelyn Underhill's simple map to offer a very helpful overview of spiritual experience. To an extent it informs or at least colors much of what follows, and I will come back to it in more detail later.

28

"Ecstatic Journey of the Living into the Realm of the Dead . . ."

THE NEXT TRIP WAS the truly dreadful one.

Once again I sank deeper and deeper into depression. It was like being in an elevator and just going down . . . down . . . down . . . through states of emotional negativity I had never even known existed. Never had I felt such disgust with my own life. Early in the session the purple flowers reappeared—but now they were openly hostile—aggressive, throbbing, in shades of purple I had never before seen. There was none of the dull, leaden quality of ordinary depression: this was electric with self-hatred. I remember banging my body against the trunk of the beech, physical pain offering momentary relief from psychic agony.

Yet in the midst of this there were moments of total detachment and lucidity.

How come, I asked, you are so disgusted with yourself when you can't even remember who you are? True, I had long forgotten who I was; let alone why I was so despicable. *In a flash I understood that this was no longer my own pain. I had sunk through the bottom of personal suffering and was drowning in an ocean of anonymous, collective pain.**

At one point I remember thinking: I am personally responsible for the failure of everything Western civilization has aimed at since the Renaissance. Presumably you get sanctioned for thinking considerably less . . . yet, of what would true morality consist if not of making each one of us personally—repeat, personally—feel responsible for everyone and everything else? I believe I was catching a glimpse of the world from a genuinely post-individual, in fact almost post-human, point of view . . .

At its most intense, the pain lost any specific characteristics. It was all emotions in one, wrought to an intolerable degree of poignancy. I thought it was going to kill me. I was reeling around the glade like a drunk. Bursts of the purple flowers exploded in the air like fireworks. Somehow they fused seediness and the psychopathic in a way I found uniquely scary. (So much so that I found I had peed myself . . . well, a bit, at any rate. Dr. Grof would be pleased, I thought glumly.)

In one particularly operatic transport, I threw myself to the ground.

It was the last thing I was expecting, but everything seemed much better down there. With my cheek pressing into the leaf mold, my focus shifted, and just in front of me I saw a tiny frond of bracken emerging from the earth . . . and without missing a beat, hell turned into heaven. The frond was perhaps two, two-and-a-half inches high, and the sweetest shade of green. Just a single sprout, Platonic in its simplicity, still unpacked and curled around itself. If the purple flowers were from the underworld, the frond was from the heaven realms.

Straight from Eden.

---

*Bache's visions in *Dark Night, Early Dawn*: "Waves of increasingly intense pain—multidimensional anguish, elemental and on a vast social scale. . . . The forms of the horror were so many that there is no way to describe it. Disembowelings by the score, the mauling of lives, deaths in the thousands. . . . War, savagery, destruction, killing, anguish. Trying to articulate it I am reminded of Dante's Inferno but sped up incredibly fast and overlaid many times." (Christopher Bache, *Dark Night, Early Dawn* [New York: SUNY Press, 2000], chapter 3, "Expanding the Concept of the Perinatal.")

I was so moved that I sat up straight and tried to dust the worst of the leaf mold off my clothes. Then I crossed my legs and started, a bit shyly at first, to talk to it.

As I warmed to the subject, I lost my inhibitions and tried to explain to the plant that it was so happy because it was part of everything else. I brushed some of the leaf mold away from its stem (the mold rich and cool in my hand, the minuscule pieces all jostling like mad) and showed the little creature how it could be traced back to a more extensive, woodier root.

"You see," I confided, leaning back affably and talking out loud by now, "you've got roots. My problem is that I don't have any."

I was positively avuncular.

At which point I decided I would like to go for a walk through the woods. I felt perfectly capable of handling this; in fact I appeared to have come down and be functioning quite normally again. Unbeknownst to me, a new phenomenon had appeared in my sessions: one referred to in the clinical literature as, ominously, "illusory sobering up." This is when, in the middle of a trip, you suddenly feel you have come right down, and the trip is now over. This, and the point needs stressing, is emphatically not the case.

My only misgiving was that I had lost all sense of time. In itself this wasn't particularly uncommon. To counter it, I had made a habit of always taking my dose at exactly twelve noon: twelve o'clock I could always remember, and I had only to look at my watch to tell my whereabouts in the drug's trajectory. The first hour it was still coming on; the second it was going deeper fast; and in the third it climaxed. During this particular trip I even found a note printed in capitals I had written to myself and propped up against the water bottle. "PEAK DURING THIRD HOUR," it read. Unfortunately I could no longer work out exactly what this meant.

Twelve to one, I thought, that's one hour. One to two, that's two hours (I was counting this out on my fingers, as ponderously as a Neanderthal); two to three, that's three. But what I couldn't work out was whether the note meant that the climax came in the hour leading up to three, or in the hour following it. I squatted under the tree, staring at my three mute fingers. God, I thought, I'm like one of Gran's birds. In fact, Gran's birds had the edge on me, because they could count to three while I could only get to two. Like any tyro mystic, I was, if I say so myself, a dab hand with one and two . . . but when it got to three I became hopelessly confused and had to go back to the beginning again.

Nothing daunted, I waded off through the bracken, climbed over the wooden fence, and soon found myself on the main track leading from Kenwood to the Vale of Health. During this early part of the walk I did, in fact, seem to have sobered up, and it was only when I reached the point where the trail descends for thirty yards or so and then ascends steeply to the fields above the Vale of Health that the trip exploded in my face again.

I got down to the bottom of the slope all right, but halfway up the other side all strength suddenly drained from my body. I could barely lift one foot and put it after the other. I felt quite horribly ill. A cold sweat broke out on my back, everything started to go smaller and further away, and abruptly, with sickening conviction, I knew that I was about to die. I looked up at the gnarled and ancient oak at the top of the slope. Silhouetted against a sky boiling like molten lead, it looked like a logo for The Last Judgment.

Oh, God, I thought—it's now.

How to convey the overwhelming conviction tripping conveys? It's not that you can't see consensual reality, it's that you are in the grip of something immeasurably more real . . .

Somehow I did manage to keep putting one foot after the other, however slowly, and what seemed an eternity later reached the top of the slope and tottered out of the trees. Before me lay a sunlit meadow full of long grass and mockingly beautiful wildflowers. My last flowers, I thought, and found a place in the long grass to lie down to die. I was surprised how easy, almost pleasurable, it was when it came to it. The sun was shining, and I lay on my back looking up at the great golden clouds as they moved across the summer sky. They were indescribably lovely, and I felt such gratitude for having been born and died.

I could hear children's voices nearby, their laughter literally pealing like little silver bells. With a pedantry that in extremis seems native to me, I recalled the last minutes of Tangerine Dream's "Phaedra," where all you can hear is children at play in the distance, and very, very slowly as Phaedra dies, their laughter and cries get fainter and fainter and farther and farther away . . . only in my case, they failed to do so, because there wasn't anything the matter with me.

After a while my strength returned, and feeling a complete dickhead, I got back to my feet. I even looked around to see whether anyone had been watching. Then, shouldering the daypack, I headed for the spire of Christchurch rising above the trees.

Praying I'd not bump into any of the other tenants, I ducked back into my apartment block (looming ominously overhead, a blackened Dickensian skyscraper) and finally made it up the stairs.

But no sooner had I pulled the door shut behind me than the sea of collective pain—which had disappeared without a trace since my meeting the bracken frond—exploded again, if anything even more savagely than it had been in the woods. There was nowhere I could turn. Everything I thought hurt my mind. I've read that the brain cannot feel physical pain, but that wasn't my experience. Again, head-banging or slashing my wrists felt like the one way I could override the horror.

This is the very worst of the worst, I remember thinking—when, lunging unannounced like the other insane emotional swings of the afternoon, the pain just vanished into thin air.

I found myself gazing around the apartment as though it were the very heart of the Mystery.

There was no thought. I was both alone and simultaneously an integral part of everything. I was pure wonder . . . but as against any state of meditation I had known in the past, this lacked any sense of fragility or precariousness. This was solid. Substantial. Tentatively I took a few steps around the living room, then, with the glee of a child, jumped up and down on the floor to see if that dislodged it. Nothing shifted a fraction of an inch. Faintly I could sense the fine-material disturbance of what could have become thoughts, but spirit checked them effortlessly, the way your body corrects its balance when you are riding a bike.

In such stable absence of mental activity, any Tom, Dick, or Harry could see what the Buddha saw: that the one place, the only place, where there is no confusion or suffering is the immediate present moment.

Perceived thus, every instant is potentially sacramental.

29

"Ecstatic Journey . . ."

(continued)

EACH TRIP IN THE woods started off, like episodes in a serial, at the point the last one left off . . . which, in the present case, was the point of death.

The journal entry is another of those scribbled under pressure, starting with me already in the glade, in the midst of the rush. In between bouts of coughing and choking, I was down on my hands and knees in the leaf mould trying to vomit.

Suddenly my lungs seized up and I could not breathe. I went into blind panic. As though a dam had blown out, I was hit by a lifetime's denial of death. Literally, I was petrified, frozen like a deer blinded by the headlights of a truck barreling down on it at seventy miles an hour. Caught in that glare, this was the very last second of my life, and time was arrested there . . .

My legs gave way and I fell heavily to the ground.

Once more, to my surprise, I found that total let-go worked; and after a moment I rolled over onto my back and lay there gazing quietly into the upside-down trees.

I felt curiously at peace. Everything that had separated me from other people in life was draining away in death. This was the death everyone who had ever lived had died, the death everyone who still hadn't even been born would inevitably die in his or her turn; and fear no longer seemed even relevant as a response. The sky, though it was still only early afternoon, began to dim, but it was with a detached, almost scientific, curiosity that I watched as a sort of delicate filament began to stretch between the treetops, then reach down to the lower branches, extending until it had become as complex and symmetrical as a huge spider's web spanning the clearing.

The filaments caught the light. Nacre—with brief flashes of the purple flowers, though these were smaller and in the mid-distance now, eerily pretty in their way, almost festive . . . like Christmas in the underworld, I thought. Was this a personal memory of childhood Christmas trees glittering with lights and tinsel? Or were Christmas trees themselves a race memory of something much more ancient—of primitive celebrations when entire forests had sparkled with vision? [*1]

The phrase "the vast company of the dead" crossed my mind, and it expressed very well the way I was looking at things. I had become generic. The eyes that saw the branches come together and join, and everything grow quiet and dark, were collective ones. Idly I wondered how many other people had died in this same spot over the centuries. Hundreds? Thousands? How many, on dull overcast afternoons like this, had watched as everything they had ever known started to thin out and disappear? There must be an even greater throng of animals, I reflected: thousands and thousands of years of them. If you piled them all on top of one another, how high would the pile go? Up to the first big branches? Up to the treetops?

No! No! Not that!

Not to be torn apart by wild animals!

---

*The phrase "ecstatic journey of the living into the realm of the dead" is from Carlo Ginzburg's study of witchcraft, *Ecstasies: Deciphering the Witches' Sabbath*. The passage in full reads: "The night flights to the diabolical gatherings echoed, in a distorted and unrecognizable form, a very ancient theme: the ecstatic journey of the living into the realm of the dead. The folkloric nucleus of the stereotype of the Sabbath is here."

Not while you were still alive!

There was just enough time to scrabble back onto my hands and knees before I was retching and trying to throw up . . .

When my mind cleared I was sitting quietly, leaning up against the beech trunk, thinking about death. Gurdjieff used to speak of two higher "centers" in us, a higher emotional center and a higher intellectual one; and I know that on several trips I have touched on a qualitatively more highly evolved type of thought, something far more focused, swifter, and more incisive than the sluggish mulling over of things I normally call thinking.

So it was now. Far from being a taboo from which my thoughts inevitably skittered away, death had become a subject of compelling interest; and what I was trying to understand was the extent to which we have lost our freedom through our culture-wide denial of death.

For once you know, really know, that you are going to die, there is no way you can take this world with the same deadly humorlessness. A crack runs through your identification with your own life. You start to see the forever disappearing, evanescent, insubstantial nature of all objects and events. You start to intuit that the only truly solid thing is the very thing that seemed the least substantial of all: consciousness itself.

Surely, I reasoned, that's why mystics are forever banging on about being aware of death. "Die before you die . . ." "Live every day as though it were your last . . ." Only living in the light of death can bring you entirely into the present moment—into your utter ignorance of what life really is—and the uselessness of the mind in even trying to approach this problem.

How then can you approach it? How? From my own experience in the past, I couldn't see that meditation did it. However much you said you were open, or surrendered, to the present moment, the ego was still there subtly orchestrating it all. So far as I could see, you had to lose control for real.

Perhaps I went off at a tangent here, but I began to think about

war: about genuinely life-threatening situations. I had just been reading, for the first time ever, *The Iliad,* and been struck by the spiritual
dimension that is tacit in all the great epics, the way aristocratic cultures since the dawn of time have been predicated on risking your life.
Was the way of the warrior, however hideous the carnage, more authentic than the self-manipulation of the contemplative? (God, I could use
a cigarette, I thought.) You didn't have to be that culturally upmarket
about it, either. The only period of their lives my parents had ever spoken about with any real warmth had been the war. My mother, so far
as I could understand, had been mixed up with a Gurdjieff group in
London and went to live there during the Blitz, for the sheer intensity
of it. "War groupies" we had called the hippies in Vietnam when we'd
first been in India . . .

Oh, shut the fuck up, I thought merrily to myself, as the rush of
mental energy began to slacken; and I laughed at myself with genuine humor. In fact, I found myself in an exceptionally good mood as I
left the glade, enjoying every detail of the walk. I was already halfway
toward Hampstead when I remembered I had to get something from
the supermarket. Clipping a favorite Lassus mass into the Walkman, I
took another path and set off for Belsize Park, via South End Green.

Once again, I thought the trip had more or less played itself out,
until I turned the corner and saw South End Green.

To my horror, I saw that there had been a huge accident. Cars were
gridlocked, at crazy angles, their horns blaring. Pedestrians were running. The air was thick with fumes, and I wondered whether a car
was burning. I was craning my neck to try to see over the heads of the
crowd, when suddenly I thought: Hang on a moment, there are too
many people involved for a pileup . . .

God, it's the rush hour, I realized.

A deep hole yawned in the middle of the road, and sections of the
pavement were overturned. Makeshift traffic lights were dotted here
and there, and boards with red arrows pointed in directions I couldn't
make any sense of. If you'd had an unlimited budget and a work force

of millions, you couldn't have created a more hellish scene. I was swept along the pavement past the news agents (with *Evening Standard* headlines about murdered children), past the Royal Free Hospital, and up onto Rosslyn Hill, where crowds were streaming up from Belsize Park Tube.

Outside the Kentucky Fried Chicken a street-crazy with a Mohawk, naked apart from an orange Indian dhoti tucked around his waist, was going through the trashcan. Such was the venom with which he was hurling sodden packets of food and empty soft drink cans to the pavement that instinctively the crowd parted around him, though otherwise no one seemed alarmed or even interested. The Lassus mass, now fully into its stride, provided a dimension of unnerving cosmic jollity.

I stood back to watch the crowds, and as I looked, I felt sick to the gut. These weren't the shabby middle-aged people I had assumed. They were all young men and women, in what should have been the pride of youth—falling in love, wanting to hitch around South America, afire with new ideas—and here they were shuffling along like tired old people, with the last bit of fight long kicked out of them.

Had they really known that all of them, every single one, was going to die, they would have woken up as though sluiced with a bucket of cold water. They would have told their bosses to shove their stupid jobs. They would have started to talk to one another from their hearts, because nothing could be worse than to go on living like this. Standing there outside the Kentucky Fried Chicken, I saw that I had not been so wide of the mark in the woods. Ultimately, fear of death is the cement of slave society—that's at the root of our fear of freedom, and we'll never get out of this mess until we have integrated both life and death in a higher unity. Because it's awareness of death alone that can wake us up: death alone that can make us kind and gay.

30

Terrible Beauty

FINALLY I FELT THAT I was beginning to understand how acid worked. On the one hand, I could appreciate what Grof had meant in the passage quoted earlier. "Ego death involves an experience of the destruction of everything that the subject is, possesses or is attached to," he had written. "In the final stages, subjects have to face and confront experiences, situations and circumstances that are unacceptable or even unimaginable to them." That, in my experience, was true; but however scary or grueling this was, it was worth it. If Purgation was the price of Illumination, so be it. I had come to trust the process.

Perhaps because I was also beginning to see how ancient it was. More and more clearly these trips in the woods were reenacting features of immemorial shamanic initiation. Earlier I also quoted the Siberian Yakut's account of the shaman-to-be's mandatory descent into the underworld:

The candidate's limbs are removed and disjointed with an iron hook; the bones are cleaned, the flesh scraped, the body fluids thrown away, and the eyes torn from their sockets . . . all that time the candidate remains like a dead man, scarcely breathing, in a solitary space.

Yep—sounded like Friday afternoon at Kenwood to me. Perhaps I was even beginning to feel I knew how to control the drug, which, on the contrary, was a major error. Loss of control—complete discontinuity with the past—seems to be essential to vision.

The next trip, which was to prove the climactic one in the cycle, started in a way unlike any of the others. I was sitting down, leaning against the beech, looking at the bracken, which was already beginning to turn golden, when a small area (about the size the beam of a pocket torch would illuminate at night) abruptly became colorless. The patch went black and white, like an old movie, then with a jerk began to move around the glade, turning whatever it touched monochromatic, color returning only as the spot traveled further, moving drunkenly, again very much like the beam of a torch.

Uh-oh, I thought, here it comes; and braced myself against the tree trunk. I closed my eyes and saw straight into a writhing mass of snakes and worms directly behind my eyes. Big sluggish snakes intertwined with others more like large earthworms, only they were crimson and lashing furiously, like the ones you get when you're making compost.

I jerked bolt upright and kept my eyes wide open. Once more I was on the verge of panic. Snakes had always scared me, and here I was sitting in this clearing flickering between Technicolor and black and white ("eyes torn from their sockets," as the Yakut shaman had said) with a nest of serpents in my brain. Suppose I saw them outside, and they started to crush and smother me? To be buried under snakes, that was a death I could never surrender to.

I was saved by a phenomenon I have never experienced before or since, by a full-blown auditory hallucination. A voice spoke out of the air with, of all things, a Cockney accent.

"Two big farts!" it announced cheerily, in the tone of a pantomime of Cheeky Chappie.*

"Two big farts—and you're gone!"

---

*[Cheeky Chappie refers to Max Miller, Britain's top comedian from the 1930s to the 1950s. —*Ed.*]

I started laughing so much I fell over sideways.

What was even more bizarre was that by the time I had stopped laughing and sat up again, what the voice had predicted turned out to be true.

Even sans farts, I was gone.

The glade had turned into something holy and enchanted. The sickening light show was gone and the color had become exquisite. The trees were shining with an otherworldly light. When I looked at them, their bark didn't seem to be made of wood any more, but of some crystal or mineral I'd never seen before.

The world had shrunk to this small clearing in the woods. The manifestation of the whole in the part, the prospect of which had so frightened me in the past, had taken place in the most lovely and deeply peaceful way. There was only the here and now. The rest was a silky black sea of nothingness, against which the glade hung, glowing like a single magic tree.

I stood motionless in the clearing as the vision slowly dimmed and faded away.

My mind cleared. Everything began to return to normal, and I thought that had been the climax of the trip. When I wrote this up the following morning I dismissed what happened next as merely a further instance of "illusory sobering up," but now I wonder whether such apparent detoxification couldn't itself be part of a larger process, one that precedes the real explosion of vision—as though the mind reaches such a pitch of hallucinatory excess it simply cannot function at all any more: its normal processes jam and grind to a halt.*

Whatever the dynamics involved, I was well into my illusory

---

*There's definitely a parallel with the French poet and visionary Arthur Rimbaud here. Rimbaud's basic hypothesis was that through a "systematic derangement of all the senses" it becomes possible to be a seer. "I forced myself to hallucinate," he wrote. "I saw a mosque where there had been a factory, a class of angels learning to play drums, a coach and horses on a road in the sky, a front parlor at the bottom of a lake." Overload cognition to the point where it seizes up, and a higher faculty of perception can take over. The visionary learns to see through the world like an X-ray.

sobering-up routine. Time for a walk, I thought and, apparently compos mentis, gathered my few things together, packed them with care, then picked my way through the bushes and bracken, climbed over the wooden fence, and jumped down onto the path.

Perhaps the impact did it.

I was the wood.

I was everything.

There was only me!

As I write this, true recall of what I felt, the existential suchness of it, has gone. But like the other no-boundary states that summer, what I do remember perfectly is its overwhelming self-evidence. *I was everything.* It was as simple as that. Nor was this something I had just become, I always had been everything. What was really difficult to understand was how I could ever have thought I was anything else.

There was a roaring in my ears, and I was trembling with the energy pouring through me. Way back in my mind I could hear a voice as distant as it was shrill. *Wait! Wait! You are saying you have become God! This is classic psychosis!*

Effortlessly sweeping that aside, the revelation surged back a second time.

There is only me.

Whatever I perceive I am.

What else could I be?

Though, gazing around, I had to admit I had never seen anything remotely resembling these woods. Again the trees seemed to be made of some kind of quartz or mineral, but compared to this, the vision in the glade had been mere prettiness. Magic had been eclipsed by mysticism. The intensity of is-ness these woods radiated was not to be endured. Their beauty was appalling. This was meltdown in God.

I thought I was going to black out. Providentially, there was a bench under a small holly tree (or under what had once been a holly tree), and I sank down. The revelation came in waves, and I just had time to catch my breath before it flooded through me a third time.

It is all me!

I am this wood!

I am sitting in myself!

But that was the last of the great surges of it . . . and over the next few minutes I could feel the intensity begin to ebb, gradually at first, then faster, and it was gone.

Far from falling to my knees in gratitude and awe, which surely would have been the appropriate response, my identification with my mind began to reinsinuate itself immediately.

Surely that couldn't be what it had so self-evidently seemed to be? The Presence of God? The direct proof that religion was true? You're kidding yourself, I said. You're off your face on drugs.

Fortunately I still had enough wits about me to wonder at my own vehemence: at why I felt so threatened by the thought that God was real and could be known directly. Why was even the possibility of this so . . . so *taboo?*

Something was nagging at the edge of my memory . . . then suddenly it was there. Hadn't the Advaita teacher Suzanne Segal described something very similar toward the end of her *Collision with the Infinite?* Just before her final awakening, she was driving her car through a snowy winter landscape when suddenly she had become one with everything. *She had realized she was driving through herself.* I was sure those were the exact words she had used, and it was the very phrase I had just used to describe my sitting under the holly.

I was sitting in myself . . .

Finally I felt strong enough to walk, and I got up from the bench. I felt far from steady on my feet, and manic energy continued to gust through me as I meandered off through the woods.

Definitely I was still in shock. Never in my life had I known such a powerful experience . . . and yet something felt subtly amiss. I couldn't get it straight in my mind. Had that been a moment of shattering mystical insight—or had it been something else?

And if so, what?

31

"Not the true samadhi . . ."

I LOOKED UP THE passage, the one I had remembered under the holly, from Suzanne Segal's *Collision with the Infinite:*

> In the midst of a particularly eventful week, I was driving north to meet some friends when I suddenly became aware that I was driving through myself. For years there had been no self at all, yet here on this road, everything was myself, and I was driving through me to arrive where I already was. In essence, I was going nowhere because I was everywhere already. The infinite emptiness I knew myself to be was now apparent as the infinite substance of everything I saw.

Collision with the Infinite was one of the most widely acclaimed accounts of awakening to appear at the end of the twentieth century. The "years there had been no self at all" to which Segal refers had been the key experience of her life. Out of the blue (in the middle, in fact, of boarding a bus) she had lost all sense of who she was. All her subsequent life had been spent in a state of ego-free dissociation in which she found, to her surprise, that she could function perfectly well. The passage quoted above was the beginning of her finding a new and far more profound sense of identity.

A second, even deeper satori followed on the heels of the first. Again it was while driving, on her way to a meditation retreat.

> As I drove through the wintry landscape on my way there, every-thing seemed more fluid. The mountains, trees, rocks, birds, sky were all losing their differences. As I gazed about, what I saw first was how they were one; then, as a second wave of perception, I saw the distinctions. But the perception of the substance they were all made of did not occur through the physical body. Rather, the vastness was perceiving itself out of itself at every point in itself. A lovely calm pervaded everything—no ecstasy, no bliss, just calm . . .
>
> From that day forth I have had the constant experience of both moving through and being made of the "substance" of everything.[1]

As best I can understand it, this sounds like the real thing. However unusual the way she had arrived there, the state she describes bears the stamp of awakening as described by Hindu and Buddhist nondual phi-losophy over the centuries. Put *Collision with the Infinite* alongside a work as mainline as Nisargadatta Maharaj's *I Am That,* and the simi-larities jump off the page. Repeatedly Nisargadatta's *satsangs* testify to fusion with the very source of life. One such passage, chosen from among many:

> I am the world, the world is me, I am at home in the world, the world is my own. Every existence is my existence, every conscious-ness is my consciousness, every sorrow is my sorrow and every joy is my joy.

Equally what had just happened to me in the woods resembles the experience described by both Segal and Nisargadatta. Yet it didn't leave me exhilarated and inspired in the way I'd always imagined a "mystical experience" would do. Or that's not exactly true, it did leave me enormously excited . . . but simultaneously prey to marked mistrust. I felt pulled in two opposed directions. For despite basic features in common, what had happened to me was no carbon copy of Suzanne Segal's experience.

"A lovely calm pervaded everything," she wrote. Well, that definitely hadn't been the case for me. Those woods were a roaring vortex. I'm sure my eyes were out on stalks. In any case, how can you take a vision that a saint or contemplative has worked toward for years and say that it is the "same" as one produced by dropping a dose of a drug? In the first place, the revelation, which has crowned years of effort, remains and transfigures your life and understanding, while one of the most unnerving features of acid is the speed with which its impact fades. While personally I am sure that acid can transform your life, it just doesn't work in the same way.

In which case, how to explain the undeniable parallels?

During the '60s, when the debate as to whether psychedelics afforded an authentic mystical experience was at its height, there had appeared to be only one solution: to find someone who had experienced both states and could affirm or deny their identity.

The only person who had managed to pull the scoop off was Ram Dass, when he gave his newly found Indian guru Neem Karoli Baba two hefty doses of LSD. These, or so the popular version of the tale went, had no observable effect on Neem Karoli, who merely made a disparaging comment to the effect that LSD did not produce "true" samadhi.

The story was well known at the time, but when I came to read Ram Dass's own account of what happened, as he records it in *The Only Dance There Is,* I found something considerably more ambiguous . . . and considerably more interesting.

Ram Dass (the name itself came from Neem Karoli) used to be

the Richard Alpert who was Tim Leary's right-hand man during the crusade to legalize LSD of the early and mid-1960s; but by the end of the decade, Alpert had realized that the psychedelic scene was spiraling out of control and went to India looking for a guru. Thus the background to the story is that Alpert/Ram Dass wanted to get away from the drug counterculture and yet was still not very familiar with Hindu philosophy.

What happened was that during one of his first visits to Neem Karoli, the guru had casually asked Ram Dass whether he had any LSD. Ram Dass did, and on Neem Karoli's insistence had given him some 900 micrograms, which indeed had no visible effect. Again, on a subsequent visit, Neem Karoli had asked him if he had any more and promptly downed the remainder of Ram Dass's stash of 1,500 mikes. This, Ram Dass assured him, would take effect within the hour.

> At the end of the hour he says, "You got anything stronger?" I said no. "Oh." And he said these substances were known about in the Kulu Valley, long ago, but all that knowledge is lost now. Then he said, "It's useful, it's useful, not the true samadhi, not the true samadhi, but it's useful."

What he said after this Ram Dass does not quote but paraphrases:

> He said it will allow you to come in and have the visit—the darshan—of a saint, of a higher being of a higher space—higher consciousness is how you can translate it. But he says you can't stay there—after a couple of hours you gotta come back. He said, you know, it would be much better to become the saint, rather than to go and have his visit; but having his visit is nice. He said it strengthens your faith in the possibility that such beings exist.[2]

Neem Karoli's rudimentary English and Ram Dass's unfamiliarity with Hindu terminology give a somewhat misleading picture here.

Darshan, literally the sight of a holy object or enlightened being, is a highly charged concept for Hinduism, not far from the Western idea of Grace. No way can it be translated as "visit." What Neem Karoli was saying is that LSD is an authentic opening to spirit, though certainly not identifiable with self-realization. "It's useful." This he repeats to Ram Dass three times in one sentence . . . but what Ram Dass heard was a blanket dismissal of acid.

Reading the story today, it seems a great loss that anyone who had been as involved with psychedelic research as Ram Dass could meet an awakened being who was happy to take LSD and discuss its effects firsthand, and yet fail to make the most of this unique opportunity. In another context he says that after his second "trip" Neem Karoli had even volunteered the information that psychedelics should be used in conjunction with fasting and yoga; Ram Dass, however, failed to rise to this obvious attempt to draw him out.

So if a traditional master as widely respected as Neem Karoli was saying that LSD was very, very useful—though not for true samadhi—then what was it so useful for?

32
Session 27
Last Trip in the Woods

BY NOW IT WAS October; the winter was drawing in, and already it was looking like the last time I would be able to trip in the woods that year. I remember sitting under my tree, the bracken all golden in the late autumn sun, and the trip coming on so slowly and gently I didn't realize it had come on at all . . .

Birds had never been much in evidence in the clearing, but this afternoon a growing number of them began to appear. First one, then another, then small groups of two or three started to perch high in the trees above my head. Could they be migrating? I wondered. But surely, if they were flying south, there would be more of them than this? When I craned my neck to try to see them more clearly, I found that the sky had become so bright as to be colorless; squinting into the glare, I couldn't tell from their silhouettes what kind of birds they were.

The trees too were becoming equally difficult to identify. They seemed to have drawn closer together and become more exotic, while the undergrowth was growing denser. Several times the word *Mayan* came into my mind, but I couldn't remember what it meant. Something to do with temples, I thought. I peered around suspiciously. Was I seeing creepers hanging down from the trees . . . or just thinking I could?

If this was Rimbaud's "derangement of all the senses," then what I began to *see* shocked me to the core.

The birds, the trees, the fierce and colorless sky, all began to knit together and form a single colossal presence.

Everything was solidifying, as though something I had long understood intellectually could now be perceived directly: that, however distant in space or time, everything in the world was interconnected. Ultimately everything came down to being but one thing, an incomprehensibly vast functioning whole, a single all-encompassing entity of which my body and mind were an integral part . . . *and from which I as consciousness was shearing wildly apart . . .*

Instinctively I knew I had to allow this to happen. I had to let go, to let go of everything if I was to find my true nature. To relinquish any trace of form or shape. Everything, every thought, every perception, was out there, part of the world, not of my real I . . .

But it was all starting to happen so fast I got confused, then lost my nerve. It was the same blind panic I was coming to know so well— the sense that my feet shot out from under me, and that as I fell backward time stopped . . .

The great wave drew back.

For a moment I recovered my wits.

This was what I had to go through, to let go of everything. For me this was the whole point of taking acid. Cursing myself for a coward, I tried to cross my legs and sit up straight. *"There's a mudra,"* something was repeating in my head, *"there's a mudra."* Never mind the fucking mudra, I thought, I can't even work out which leg is which and get them crossed . . .

But it was already too late. The wave smashed into me, and I just couldn't let go. Desperately I hung on, like someone in a hurricane. Too vast, it was too vast. Perhaps I should have screamed—screamed, and screamed—perhaps that would have done it . . .

The glade was heaving. I lurched to my feet and put out a hand to steady myself against the tree . . . then remembered what I was trying to do and sat down again.

The same vast inbreath of the Void took place for a third, and what I knew instinctively to be the final time—but even before it started I knew it was no good. I just couldn't surrender. Not to that. I don't know whether I ever had any choice . . .

Suddenly the glade was empty. I went on sitting there, but I knew the trip was over. I had blown it.

I felt dreadful, the way I had on my second trip there, early in the summer, the one when the purple flowers first appeared. Enormous waves of energy were still racing through me, and I couldn't focus properly. I wandered around the clearing as though in a fever, trying to concentrate on getting my things together and packing them up. Finally I strode off through the woods, at random as far as I can remember. I couldn't think clearly about anything, and the rest of the afternoon was drunken and confused.

Apart from one episode.

I found myself—literally, as though I had just woken up—in the middle of Hampstead Village. I was standing in front of Christchurch, and in the forecourt of the church was a nursery school. The children were little more than toddlers, mostly two or three years old. They were all pottering around in their rapt, elated way, falling over and picking themselves up again, when to my amazement I saw that silver light was streaming off them. It was subtle, but perfectly distinct. I moved around to look at them from another angle, and it was still there. The children were all radiating silver light.

They weren't doing anything in particular, just staring at things in wonder and spacing out. *They are sane!* I said to myself. *They are acting the way we are all meant to act!* I wanted to climb over the gate, sit down at their feet, and learn the proper way to be . . . but, fortunately, I saw how gross and alarming I must appear. I had to turn my eyes aside from what was effectively a small group of angels I had bumped into and lurch on my way—lost, befuddled, and desperate.

Again I found a luminously clear reflection of what had happened in Nisargadatta Maharaj. Consciousness coming apart from its identification with matter plays a crucial role in *I Am That.* Speaking of meditation, Nisargadatta says:

> When the mind is quiet, we come to know ourselves as the pure witness. We withdraw from the experience and its experiencer and stand apart in pure awareness, which is between and beyond the two. The personality, based on self-identification, on imagining oneself to be something: "I am this, I am that," continues, but only as a part of the objective world. Its identification with the witness snaps.

That described it perfectly . . . aside from "snaps" seeming a somewhat understated way of describing being torn in two. To "stand apart in pure awareness" you have to let go of absolutely everything. To all intents and purposes you have to die; and the terror I felt at dying was what kept blocking me.

This, so far as I remember, was the first time I tried to think through the idea of developing a new approach to meditation, one working in tandem with psychedelics. Could acid be used to blast apart the almost solid masses of conditioning—while some more-sedate practice was used to digest what happened and familiarize oneself with its implications?

For Nisargadatta himself appears to have lived stably, indeed ecstatically, in this state for most of his long life. Having exasperated one of his visitors to the point of exclaiming, "But you are living in the world!" Maharaj replied:

> That's what you say! I know there is a world, which includes this body and this mind, but I do not consider them to be more "mine" than other minds and bodies. They are there, in time and space, but I am timeless and spaceless . . .

QUESTION: I am asking you a question. You are answering. Are you conscious of the question and the answer?

MAHARAJ: In reality I am neither hearing nor answering. In the world of events the question happens and the answer happens. Nothing happens to me. Everything just happens.

Acid had brought me to the point of understanding this from the inside. So far as my last trip went I had panicked . . . but I had slipped through that door before, and I was sure I could do so again. Over the following fortnight I imagined my next session would see the disappearance of whatever resistance, whatever primal fear was paralyzing me—just as it had in the glade at the beginning of summer.

33

Demonstrations, Ecstasy, Advaita

ONCE AGAIN, THE NEXT trip started at the point the last one ended. As it came on I found myself back in the condition of half-delirious confusion to which I had been reduced in the glade . . . only it didn't go anywhere from there. The session passed in a state more like physical illness than anything else: very like a flu. This continued for the whole afternoon, only draining away with the dusk and leaving me tired, irritable, and hungover.

Worse—the one after that was just the same.

I'd never had a trip anything like this, let alone having two in a row. What on Earth was happening?

By now the winter was well set in; the days were cold and wet, and I was back in the apartment. Was it leaving the woods and returning to the cramped little bedroom? Or was I becoming casual, disrespectful even, in the way I approached the drug? For the third session I went back to using the blindfold and the Walkman, and I made a point of lying down for most of the trip; but that didn't make any difference either. As I tossed and turned on the bed, the session passed in a high fever, leaving me with little more than scrambled recollections of the afternoon.

Seemingly I was involved in a new cycle of trips. They weren't like any previous ones: first and foremost because each one was the same, something that had never happened before. There was no beauty . . . no terror . . . no madcap humor. All that remained from earlier sessions were the bizarre somatic symptoms I had always dismissed as side effects. Now these took center stage. While my legs had always trembled, never before had they vibrated with such violence. First one would start, then the other, then both together, the heels drumming wildly on the bed: when I raised the blindfold to look, they were literally a blur of action. The hacking cough returned, now so harsh I was frightened I was going to damage my lungs. There were waves of nausea. The eerie taste of blood came and went.

All along I had been in denial of this purely physical dimension to acid. Shaking in the legs I had dismissed as some form of bioenergy being discharged; while the coughing I conjectured, in an even more woolly minded manner, could be related to birth: perhaps to choking on the first breaths. This, as I said before, was one of the areas where my do-it-yourself psychoanalysis fell flat on its face. Any professional would have zeroed in on these symptoms, while all I did was try to pretend they weren't happening.

Session three became session four, and session four became session five, and still nothing changed. I had no idea what to do, so I just went on taking a trip once every three weeks or so, hoping that sooner or later there would be a breakthrough. After all the amazing trips I'd been having during the summer, I felt, to say the least of it, bitterly disappointed.

At first, abruptly disconnected from what had been an obsession for months on end, I didn't know what to do with myself. During the summer I'd spent tripping in the woods, however, I had continued to go down to the marches and political meetings in the West End, finding nothing contradictory in the two concerns—far from it, they seemed deeply compatible—and now I allowed myself to be swept up by the antiwar movement. This had been growing by leaps and bounds.

No sooner had Afghanistan been invaded than the antiwar and the antiglobalization factions of the Left had fused, creating a movement bringing together all the elements of a hitherto balkanized opposition; and this in its turn began to act as a beacon for those whose anger at society took forms not conventionally considered political. Corporate capital had made the one mistake tyrannies should never make: it had drawn a line where people could put their foot down. Already there was more than a whiff of Vietnam in the air.

My first demonstration had seen twinkly eyed Afghans gravely distributing free *maajun* in Trafalgar Square—which definitely hit a new note. All the young people there were noticeably more truculent than their so-called leaders. Perhaps they still couldn't put together a polished critique of contemporary society—but one thing for sure was that they weren't going to approach it in terms of the trade unionism and issue politics of the old Left. The Left itself, with its drabness, its earnest self-righteousness, was far more part of the problem than the solution. If the teenagers and people in their twenties on those first marches were taking anything as a yardstick, it was Ecstasy and the dance culture: you could see it in their determination to get bands on the marches, to emphasize the quality of carnival, to experiment with dance as a tactic of nonviolent direct action . . .

It's a long time ago now, but the runaway success of the first warehouse parties in the 1980s had seemed to promise a fresh cultural and political breakthrough. Since those days Ecstasy has been so commercialized that it's hard to recapture the excitement that greeted its first appearance in Thatcher's England of the Living Dead. Here at last was a psychedelic that was workable, a psychedelic that could excise the ego with surgical precision, but without the experience ever becoming overwhelming the way it does on acid. A psychedelic that could be used safely by anyone, however inexperienced, for MDMA simply switched off psychological fear—disconnecting it at the socket, so to speak. No longer was there any need to defend oneself, for rapport with others was revealed as the very substance of social life . . . and yet the experience could go very deep. For me at least, it was the first time that the mystics' assertion the world is made of love—literally so—made self-evident sense.

At that time, during the late '80s, my whole concept of revolution had broadened out, opening on perspectives in which Ecstasy could well play a significant part. I had just run across the work of Arnold Toynbee, who (prior to what it is difficult not to describe as his repression) had been the mid-twentieth-century's most famous historian, with his massive *Study of History* being widely regarded as the most creative contribution to our understanding of society made by anyone since Marx. Despite the overwhelming quality of *Study*—I believe there were ten volumes to the original edition—what Toynbee was trying to do was something very simple: to examine every civilization on Earth of which we have any record (some twenty-eight by his reckoning) with the goal of analyzing the factors responsible for the four major stages all reflected: their genesis, their growth, their breakdown, and finally their disintegration.

Predictably enough, surrounded by yuppies honking to get their faces still further into the swill bucket, I had turned first to the sections dealing with the breakdown and disintegration of civilizations— and what I found there was an electrifyingly contemporary vision of social change.

For Toynbee's first point about the breakdown of civilizations was that it always takes place when the civilization is apparently at the height of its power. And it always takes the same form, the ruling elite's psychopathic need to control absolutely everything—on the level of everyday life, every pettifogging little detail; and, expressed on the level of economy and politics, the obsessive need to construct a "universal" or single World State. This, according to Toynbee, inevitably sets the scene for the doom of the dominant civilization.

In his *Decline and Fall of the Roman Empire,* Gibbon declared famously that Rome was destroyed by Christianity and the barbarians; and Toynbee's analysis could be seen as an extended commentary on the thesis. For him, as for Gibbon, the untold millions of people enslaved by the dominant civilization break down into two huge groups, into what Toynbee refers to as two distinct "proletariats" (insisting on using Marx's term and, one imagines, courting his own subsequent academic doom by doing so). First, an *internal proletariat,* which consists of almost everybody living within the dominant society: frustrated and, if you probe to any depth, basically desperate, with only the thinnest veneer of ideology masking the fact that they have no real control over their lives at all.

Not that their existence is not luxury itself compared with that of the second, or *external proletariat.* This is formed by all those living beyond the increasingly militarized borders of the dominant civilization: those who bear the brunt of the exploitation and brute labor, and live and die lives little better than those of draft animals. Humiliated and treated with open contempt, this external proletariat finally explodes in violence. Fighting as terrorists and guerillas, they exhibit a ferocity and intelligence the mercenary troops of the imperium can never match.

The two proletariats come together in a pincer movement, which defines the last days of the disintegrating civilization. For, on its part, the internal proletariat also revolts. Toynbee's analyses of the various forms such resistance takes are too complex to do more than touch upon here—initially workers tend to be conservative and merely want to return to an earlier, less dehumanized stage of society; only as such Utopianism proves impossible do they turn to violent insurrection— and only after repeated failures on both fronts do a substantial number begin to see that there is only one way in which they can effectively secede: by what Toynbee, and I think he was one of the first Westerners to use the phrase, calls "being in the world, but not of it."*

---

*[This has been a common phrase in Christianity for quite a long time, derived from John 17:15–16: "My prayer is not that you take [those who believe in me] out of the world but that you protect them from the evil one. They are not of the world, even as I am not of it." —*Ed.*]

This process—which he further characterizes as being one of *detachment and transfiguration*—forms the matrix of a new "higher" or universal religion. Such a religion is predicated on the equality of all beings, spiritual brother- and sisterhood eclipsing the concern for personal salvation, which dominated the same civilization's earlier and less successful attempts at renewing spiritual awareness. Toynbee points to early Christianity or Mahayana Buddhism as being prime examples of such religions produced by vast civilizations in their agony. This is the only way the parent civilization can redeem and preserve any true values it may still possess; and, in my reading of him, at any rate, Toynbee is inferring that this is the process in which we are all involved today.

Obviously what I was wondering at the time was: Could Ecstasy play the role of sacrament in such a process? I don't think there can be much doubt about the drug's quality of being a sacrament in search of a religion. Not that the religious issues reflected in Toynbee's scenario are exclusively sacramental. In a more general sense, he had also observed that new universal religions tend initially to crystallize around an exotic cult, a philosophy profoundly alien to the parent civilization, commonly drawn from the depths of the external proletariat—and here Advaita fit the bill perfectly. During the early '90s, Osho's last teaching in Poona and Harilal Poonja's streamlining of the Hindu concept of *satsang* as consciousness-raising marked the first true popularization of the primarily "Eastern" twentieth-century spiritual counterculture stretching back to its roots in Gurdjieff and Ramana Maharshi. By the middle of the decade it looked as if Advaita was to become the prototype of a new nondenominational revivalism.*

With hindsight, Ecstasy and Advaita seem remarkably complementary. Both were rooted in understanding that the isolation and inability to relate imposed by this society have reached intolerable proportions.

---

*Such hybridization of East and West appears to have worked, even vigorously so. See, for instance, Tony Parsons, *The Open Secret* (1995); Suzanne Segal, *Collision with the Infinite* (1996); Satyam Nadeen, *From Onions to Pearls* (1996); and Eckhart Tolle, *The Power of Now* (1997). Tolle's book has even come surprisingly close to best-sellerdom.

Both were bent on dissolving boundaries, passionately. Both were effectively banned: the raves, like witchcraft, to the fields at night; Advaita *satsangs* to tacky rented halls. The main distinction between the two was that Ecstasy and the raves were approaching the problem from an emotional angle, while Advaita was coming from an intellectual and spiritual one. One from the heart, the other from the head.

But both, in their respective ways, hit a far more consistently radical note than anything produced by '60s and '70s counterculture. *"Where there are two, there is fear,"* says the Brihadaranyaka Upanishad—in what must be one of the most trenchant analyses of the human condition ever made. Yet both Ecstasy and Advaita can be measured up against this and not found wanting. The Ecstasy vision is not just that you are love . . . *it is that you always have been love.* Equally, the Advaita vision is not just that you are awareness itself . . . *it is that you always have been awareness.* This engenders a highly explosive spiritual atmosphere, one characterized in religious terms by the renewed vitality of the abrupt or sudden "path" where a single flash of insight can bring about definitive inner transformation. Many did in fact declare themselves fully "enlightened"—certainly, as Zen masters would have observed, they uniformly stank of it—only to come down a few weeks or months or years later, and to feel that they had made prize fools of themselves. In a sense they had; in a sense they hadn't. The old psyche is rotten to the core: all it would take is one good shove . . .

By the early winter of 2002–03, Western society itself seemed to be catching up with the extremism of such ideas. The antiwar movement was warping and beginning to tilt the orbit of the entire society: dissent was no longer merely nationwide, it was becoming international. By November or December of 2003, the possibility of truly worldwide dissent—something on a scale that left Vietnam far behind—was on the horizon.

34

Return of
the Repressed

I HAD ALL BUT given up hope of a breakthrough when, apparently out of the blue, the block vanished. After weeks and weeks of identical sessions—coughing, gagging, shaking—it just melted away. The trip journal reads:

> It took twenty, twenty-five minutes from putting on the earphones and blindfold before the legs began to quiver; then the coughing, the feverishness, and the nausea kicked in. I'm not sure how long this continued, I just kept my eyes tightly shut and lay as still as I could. The CD played out, so it must have been the best part of an hour—then abruptly several disparate pieces of information jigsawed themselves together.
>
> Suddenly I knew that I had been very seriously ill as a young child when I was living at Windle Hey. Perhaps it was bronchitis, though I was sure I could remember Mum telling me I had nearly died of whooping cough during the war. How old would I have been then? Two? Three?
>
> Equally, I was certain that the cough which has haunted so many of my trips was the ghost of this illness; and that such

physical trauma could be just as devastating, if not more so, as any purely emotional shock. Not only would I have felt that I was choking to death, I would have felt abandoned, interpreting my mother and my Gran's inability to do anything to help me as wanton if not malign indifference.

Furthermore, it seemed perfectly plausible that such pain going on for weeks on end could form a "matrix," an original template for all my later chronic mistrust of life. I saw exactly why the coughing would have first erupted during a trip when I was trying to focus on the deep feelings underlying my break-up with Asha. The unconscious spotlit the root trauma suffusing all my feelings of abandonment and despair, and which would have to be confronted before any later distress could be drained of its irrational affective content.

Not until several days had passed did I get a chance to go to the public library and check whooping cough in the Merck *Manual of Medical Information*.

Pertussis, to give whooping cough its medical name, is notoriously the worst of all infantile diseases. Normally striking children under the age of four, the first symptoms resemble flu, but paroxysms of uncontrollable coughing quickly develop. The "whoop" is the hurried deep intake of breath after a prolonged bout of coughing, which sounds eerily like the high-pitched wail of a child. Episodes of near asphyxiation, heightened by panic, can continue for weeks. Now, listen to this. Substantial quantities of mucus are coughed up (the "cobwebby stuff" trailing out of my mouth), while the brutality of the coughing can rupture small blood vessels in the lungs and throat (the "taste of blood"). If the child is young enough, pertussis can kill. Duration is between four to ten weeks, though the trademark hacking cough can continue much longer.

Yet again I was amazed at the drug's flexibility. All last summer I had been going deeper and deeper into boundary- and ego-loss states, and when finally I panicked at the depth to which surrender was being demanded, the acid had doubled back on itself to concentrate exclusively on digging out a trauma that appears to have been at the root of much of my difficulty in trusting, letting go, and surrendering to experience. This, so it seemed, had to be unearthed before the deconditioning process could proceed any further.

For proceed further it did. While the hacking cough disappeared almost entirely from my trips from this date, the high fever and the trembling in the lower body continued unabated. In fact, vibration in the legs became the central feature of the sessions. For five trips in a row, very little else happened. My legs vibrated, period; that was the trip. It was like a kind of spontaneous physiotherapy, as impersonal as an electric current being transmitted through the lower body. For long periods even the feverishness disappeared: I could have lain there reading a novel . . . notwithstanding which at the end of the session the backs of my legs throbbed as though I had tramped twenty miles.

Belatedly, I saw the full extent of what Grof had meant by "perinatal" experience: not just what I, and I suspect many other people who read his early books, tend to reduce exclusively to the birth trauma, but all the other shocks inflicted upon and recorded by the physical body.

I couldn't honestly say, since what happened to me didn't free anything resembling verifiable "memories" to consciousness. What did happen, however, was that more typically psychedelic material started to reappear in the later sessions of the series. During one session the white bentwood chair in the bedroom turned into something so elfin, so exquisite, I could not believe my eyes; during another, a set of shelves was bathed in a rainbow of the subtlest pastels. Another entry, intact from the trip journal:

> I found myself staring in amazement at a square of sunlight falling on the yellow wall of the bedroom. Sacred was the only word for it. Staring into that light, the nature of the world became luminously clear: the moment was contained within a much

wider context, a higher order invisible to us, which was divine. If only we could stand back and see the broader picture we would know everything was flooded with God.

Intuitively I was quite sure that I was recovering traces of pristine childhood perception: of the way I had seen the world before conditioning had robbed it of its magic. Not that I had once seen shelves bathed in rainbow colors, but that I had once, as had we all, lived in a world the keynote of our perception of which was wonder—though Wordsworth's revolutionary *Ode: Intimations of Immortality from Recollections of Early Childhood,* which I reread at this time, would favor a more literal interpretation.

> *There was a time when meadow, grove, and stream,*
> *The earth, and every common sight,*
> *To me did seem*
> *Apparelled in celestial light,*
> *The glory and the freshness of a dream.*

Of the later sessions in this series, the journal records only two instances of anything that could be described as true insight into the nature of early childhood perception. Both, incidentally, like my memory of my mother having said I'd had whooping cough, were things I had vaguely remembered all my life but which abruptly became charged with significance in the midst of a trip. The first, and I must have been four or five at the time, was a conversation with my father, who had been trying to make some point or another. "You'll see when you grow up," he concluded lamely; and I distinctly remembered looking inside to see how what I was could ever grow up . . . and so far as I could tell, there was no possibility whatsoever that what I was could ever grow "up," or indeed change in any way. Tripping, I recalled this moment graphically; as it was the only time I remember consciously trying to introspect as a young child.

I believe this was an accurate insight into the way I perceived as a child. Gurdjieff says somewhere that we are all born self-remembering, it is our birthright: spontaneously self-aware consciousness unites us with the universe—something corroborated by the way young children instinctively tend to talk about themselves in the third person: "Sam is doing this, Sam is doing that." They know that what they truly are is not this body-mind "out there" in the world.

The second memory was of the crux of our entire human tragedy: I remembered the moment of the Fall . . . At my first boarding school there were never any lessons on Saturday afternoons, and after lunch we were all free to goof off and play in the woods. But on that particular afternoon—I must have been eleven or twelve—I found my mind kept reverting obsessively to some prep I was supposed to have done and had forgotten all about. I had never felt anything like this before. I remembered my indignation, and finally my conclusion that I must somehow be ill. As indeed I was: for hitherto no-mind had always been my baseline reality. If I didn't want to think about something, I could simply shut up. *But that afternoon, for the first time in my life, I found I could not stop thinking; and it's never stopped since . . .*

Before they ceased there were to be twelve of these "perinatal"—or "bioenergetic," or whatever you want to call them—sessions, stretching in an unbroken row from session 28 to session 39, and constituting the most protracted and, in a sense, most taxing series of trips I was to have.

The coding of trauma in the physical body is an enormous subject; and the two cents' worth of personal understanding I have of it comes down to a hunch that the convulsive body tremors are of key importance. At the time of these sessions the only analogy I had was from the work of Wilhelm Reich. Among the most widely used techniques in the bodywork drawn from Reich's experiments are the "grounding" exercises developed by Reich's student Alexander Lowen. In these, the trembling brought about by standing still in stress-inducing postures is used to loosen what Reich referred to as "muscular armor," which he understood to be the chronic rigidity of groups of muscles originating in repression of unacceptable feelings: feelings, which, so far as he was concerned, could far more easily be reexperienced by dissolving the muscular armor than by conventional verbal analysis.

Not until this book was virtually complete did I first run into the Taoist discipline of Chi Kung.

In Chi Kung such tremors in the body, whether fine or gross, are seen as activation of what Taoists call the *dantian* or primal energy center and prize as the key to the healing of disease and rejuvenatory power in general. Indeed, thinking back, I recalled that body tremors had been the first symptom of the first acid trip I'd had, and, phenomenologically speaking, had been the most frequently repeated feature of all my sessions. Was this just personal idiosyncrasy—or was it possible that LSD accesses, at least in part, the same energetic powerhouse as is explored by Far Eastern, specifically Taoist, medical traditions?

This, once again, is something that can only be checked out when more of us have made comparable experiments and pooled our findings. Not, truth to tell, that it bothered me unduly at the time. Feeling reenergized and reinspired was more than enough. I was out leafleting a local tube station, humming merrily to myself and chatting to all and sundry, on the eve of the vast international antiwar demonstrations of February 2003.

35

"Another World Is Possible"

I DON'T THINK ANY of us could believe our eyes as we poured out of Marble Arch Tube. The sea of placards and banners and flags stretched on . . . and on . . . and on. Even after all the years I had spent in India, I had never seen a crowd a fraction of this size. The day was bitterly cold, but that had merely strengthened people's resolve to be there. People of every age, of every race, and of every class: silver-haired businessmen in pinstriped suits jostling skinny black kids with baggy pants about to fall off their asses . . .

Some two million people were there that afternoon, which makes it, hands down, by far the biggest political protest ever to have taken place in English history. But reducing it to numbers, however vast, misses something far more important: there was a qualitative difference here—most obviously, because this was middle England. This was the sleeping giant. The overwhelming majority of these people had never dreamed of going on a demonstration before; yet here they were, despite all their self-consciousness, defiantly brandishing their placards.

Second, and of far more profound significance, the atmosphere was heartfelt rather than political. Here were two million people suddenly trying to be kind, not only to one another, but to people everywhere.

189

Overall, if the demonstration resembled anything, it was a gigantic drug-free rave. Whoever was there that day, however tongue-tied and English they may get about it, ends by saying the same thing. This was about love.

Late in the afternoon, as darkness fell, there was a point when Hyde Park Corner, Green Park, and Piccadilly were totally overrun. Demonstrators had climbed over everything, the balustrades, the staircases, the pompous bourgeois statuary—all of it flickering in the light of the fires burning in the streets. The scene was straight from the Russian Revolution, arctic cold and all. Nothing, no police, no army, could have stopped us that night. We could have flowed down through Piccadilly Circus, through Trafalgar Square and Whitehall, dragged the sewer rat Blair out of his lair, and swept on to torch Parliament as the monument to ruling-class hypocrisy it always has been. But no—everyone went home quietly, with the same affection, indeed gaiety, as had marked the whole day.

What started to happen over the following weeks, then months—long after war had been declared on Iraq—is even less comprehensible without reference to something like mass *agape*.

For with the spring weather, "antiwar demonstrations" became a regular event in Hyde Park. Impromptu bands played, flags flew, people laughed and danced and flirted on the marches. PEACE IS SEXY, as someone's placard announced, summing up the ethos. Clubs and raves were advertised, self-published literature distributed gratis; and pouring into the park, the columns broke into smaller groups, with friends wandering off together to stake out a spot. Fires were lit, free kitchens assembled; demonstrators rolled joints, guitars and drums were passed around. Teenagers climbed trees and sat chatting in the branches. I had never seen so many children on a demonstration before. In fact, I had never seen anything remotely like any of it since the late '60s. I remember watching a pair of rookie cops (all freckles and big ears, barely out of their teens) listening to a speech by veteran left-winger Tony Benn. Their eyes were popping out of their heads. I'd never have thought you could talk about police being beautiful, but those two would have melted a heart of stone.

Most of the vast crowd sat in the grass around the central stage and PA system. Whoever you were, you got the same two or three minutes on the mike; young children, pensioners, refugees who barely spoke English, all were treated with the same courtesy as the big names. Never mind the '60s, this was something I had never seen in my life. A spontaneous Peoples' Parliament was forming before my eyes.

And from the kaleidoscope of contributions, a crude but effective analysis not only of the invasion of the Middle East, but of the political situation of England and Europe as a whole was spreading through hundreds of thousands of people: The various European governments couldn't give a flying fuck what their electorates wanted. The democratic system had long since been meaningless; Europe-wide there was only one political party, had only been one political party for decades, and the various purportedly national media had been in its pocket all along. Nobody but idiots voted. If you wanted to be emotional about it, you could say that the Third Reich had never been defeated; on the contrary, it had been installed universally and was functioning—functioning far better, in fact—as an economic system than it ever had as a political one.

So far as a more restrained, and specifically British, analysis went, the most influential book going round the park (certainly the one I saw the most dog-eared copies of) was George Monbiot's *Captive State.* It's a harrowing picture of contemporary Britain that Monbiot's left-wing best seller paints, of a country eaten up from within by giant capitalist corporations: corporations interlocking more and more tightly as the months went by, eliminating every trace of quality, variety, and intelligence as they did so. Who was behind big business? Not only were the key executives of the transnationals unelected, nobody even knew their identities.

Who were the new ruling classes, then—and what on Earth did

they think they were doing? Were they the bungling totalitarian incompetents they seemed to be? Or were they some truly nasty, ice-cold folk who were playing a game all their own? If so, how far had they penetrated into space? What were they doing there? Were they in touch with other life forms? Perhaps it had ceased to matter, because in either case they had set off a planetary chain reaction that had clearly escaped their control and threatened to kill billions . . .

Paradoxically, it was the very diffusion of increasingly radical ideas that pulled the antiwar movement up short.

For the issues that started to surface were so vast, so unwieldy, as to be almost unthinkable. *"Revolution! Revolution!"* chanted the university students on the marches; and it did everyone's hearts good to hear them . . . but that was about all the good it did. How, with the best will in the world, could nineteenth-century models be applied to a vastly different, globalized early twenty-first century? Everything was going to have to be rethought from the ground up.

I remember wandering through the park those glorious spring afternoons, through what looked like the camp of a rebel army pitched in the heart of London—flags fluttering in the breeze, lovers hand in hand, groups of people talking with real animation for once . . . but despite the high tide of energy, the hesitation quivering in the sunlit air was all but visible. "Time after time," Karl Marx had written, "proletarian revolutions recoil, appalled by the monstrous indeterminacy of their own goals." *Monstrous indeterminacy* . . . the phrase had lost none of its bite. Years before, I had seen the same paralysis strike as my own generation lost its nerve and caved in; and already you could see the same shadow stretching over those appar-ently omnipotent gatherings in Hyde Park.

Later that year George Monbiot was to bring out *The Age of Consent,* the sequel to his success with *Captive State.* In it he tries to trace all economic and political problems back to a single source, lack of communication. Faithfully reflecting the spirit of the gatherings in the park, he suggests that ultimately the only solution is radical reform of the electoral system worldwide and the creation of a truly democratic World Parliament.

Could something like an authentic—radically revised—United Nations be created? If so, how could delegates remain accountable? How could such a parliament exert effective power without becoming a tyranny in its turn? How could it retain economic independence? The sense and sincerity with which Monbiot tries to answer these questions are hard to fault, and I couldn't understand why I was feeling increasingly restless . . . until I came to the following passage:

> If you respond with horror to the idea of a world parliament, as many do, I would invite you to examine your reaction carefully. Is it because you believe that such a body might become remote and excessively powerful? Or is it really because you can not bear the idea that a resident of Brussels would have no greater voice in world affairs than a resident of Kinshasa? That the people of Mexico would, collectively, become two and a half times as powerful as the people of Spain, while the Indians would cast seventeen times as many votes as the inhabitants of the United Kingdom? That, in other words, the flow of power established when a few nations ruled the world would be reversed? Are you afraid that this parliament might threaten democracy, or are you really afraid that it would actuate it?[1]

Suddenly I woke up with a start. Wait a minute, I thought: Precisely what emotion are all these arguments appealing to? To our empathy for fellow human beings? To our compassion? Our sense of fair play?

Because we don't feel any of these things—and that's precisely where the problem lies.

What we are all running on is the system of compulsive self-reference we call the ego. Me, me, me. If there's nothing in it for us personally, we couldn't care less. Other people aren't even truly real for us—not special the way we are. Like it or not, but that's the truth.

Western civilization is based on, and cannot escape from, the isolated individual. We are all inveterate narcissists, incapable of responding to anything that does not concern us personally.

In her magnificent *Shikasta,* Doris Lessing traces all our problems back to the same source, the absence of what she calls "the substance of we feeling." If at first the phrase sounds clumsy, on closer examination it proves very precise. We are all emotionally contracted. We are caught in what Krishnamurti, another veteran left-winger, called "our isolating, self-enclosing activity." The issue of self and other isn't some fancy bit of philosophy tagged onto political activism, it's at the very heart of the matter; and for someone as bright as Monbiot to try to work out egalitarian political systems without addressing the problem of the ego is political pie-in-the-sky at its worst.

Historically, the Left has never reexamined its own basic assumptions. Buying into middle-class atheism and materialism, nineteenth-century revolutionaries were forced willy-nilly to accept the concept of the separate self and all that it entailed.

> *I, a stranger and afraid,*
> *In a world I never made.*

But how can you hope to build communism on such a basis? Doomed to be forever alone, what can any of us do but look out for ourselves? Grab all we can during pitiably short lives, and to hell with anyone else. Logically the political philosophy to draw from materialism is fascism—which, of course, is precisely the philosophy everyone has drawn from it, both individually and collectively—whereas the philosophy toward which revolutionary communism gravitates is Dionysian and deeply religious.

During those brief periods when ordinary people seize power, the ego is the first thing out of the window. Not a demonstration, not a riot, not an occupation that does not testify to the end of "isolating, self-enclosing activity." Boundaries dissolve: boundaries between people, boundaries between people and their world. Read any eyewitness account of historic revolutions, and that first vast surge of collective energy is always characterized by the appearance of a radically different ontology. Expressing it verbally may be difficult, but you can sense it immediately in the streets. There's exuberance, magic in the air. Time dilates. People give things away. Friends and lovers meet. You do things for the hell of it . . .

Perhaps '70s split-brain theory did come very close to the mark, and psychologically speaking, political revolutions always entail a revolution of hemispheric dominance. Unmistakably, that was one of the most striking features of the world that materialized briefly in Hyde Park: not only were all the old ground rules overturned, but instinctively, without a moment's hesitation, everyone knew what the new ones were.

36

"Another World Is Possible"

(continued)

THE DEMONSTRATIONS IN HYDE Park were at their peak when I heard of a psychedelic conference scheduled shortly in San Francisco. Many of the writers I had been reading for the past eighteen months were due to be there, and I thought: If there are any answers to all the questions buzzing around in my head, then perhaps that's where I can find them.

The West Coast was in the same state of political ferment as Europe. For the first time in decades grassroots protest was breaking out, not on the epical scale of the demonstrations in Europe but more confrontational, the police reacting with typical American brutality. The drug conference was in Berkeley, slap in the middle of the university campus, and the sense of excitement was like old times.

Most of the celebrities were there: Ralph Metzner, who with Leary and Ram Dass had been one of the original Harvard Three Musketeers who had kept LSD in the headlines in the '60s. Myron Stolaroff, also from the early days, editor of *The Secret Chief.* Artist and South American *ayahuascero* Pablo Ameringo. Alex Grey, Robert Venosa, and a surprising number of other psychedelic painters. Alexander Shulgin, the psychedelic drug research chemist initially responsible for the diffusion of MDMA. And Stan Grof himself, very much the patrician European scholar, listening courteously to the stream of people buttonholing him.

A well-established, even well-heeled cult I had been expecting, but not one thriving like this. The hall was so packed you could barely move. Of all the revolutionary groups of my youth—the hippies, the New Left, the students, the blacks, the feminists—it was, however improbably, the druggies and the druggies alone who had made it through in one piece. And not just survived, but boomed.

Culturally, psychedelics had been vindicated. After the death of his wife, Gordon Wasson, putting archaic cultures behind him, had proceeded to write two elegantly subversive studies of the role plant hallucinogens could have played in the evolution of major world religions. In the first, *Soma: Divine Mushroom of Immortality* (1968), he attempted to identify the enigmatic *soma,* which had played so prominent a part in the genesis of Hinduism. Again he found *Amanita muscaria* the most likely candidate: a hypothesis, which, so far as I know, has been accepted by scholars from a number of widely different disciplines.

Subsequently, joining forces with Albert Hofmann and classics scholar Carl Ruck in *The Road to Eleusis* (1978), he examined the equally mysterious *kykeon,* the sacred potion drunk at the climax of the Eleusinian Mysteries. With initiates including Sophocles, Plato, and Aristotle, the possibility that *kykeon* was psychoactive (Hofmann was to suggest a further ergot-based hallucinogen, ergonovine maleate, which could be produced by water infusion) would mean that an organic psychedelic could have helped catalyze an experience of transcendence informing the whole philosophy of classical antiquity.

Ethnobotany had become a legitimate branch of science. Psychedelics, far from being the handful of high-tech mind-benders they had seemed in the 1960s, had a pedigree stretching back to the dawn of human history. Far from being toxic, with unknown long-term effects, they appeared disconcertingly safe. LSD itself had been tested for more than three generations now—ironically enough, there were few other drugs on the market with so clean a bill of health—and a variety of independent psychologists had suggested that altered states of consciousness were, just as much as dreams, vital to human health and sanity. "Our failure to incorporate hallucinogenic experience into our culture," wrote Paul Devereux in *The Long Trip,* "puts us out of step with the entire record of human experience. It is our culture that is eccentric."

An aberration, which, if the Berkeley conference was anything to go by, was being vigorously put to rights. The fastest-selling publication on the bookstall was the fourth edition of Jon Hanna's *Psychedelic Resource List,* a compendium of websites, organizations, and mail-order businesses dealing in organic and synthetic drugs. The variety of items for sale was mind-boggling. Live plants, cuttings, seeds, spores, and dried herbs were just the start of it. There were grow lights and hydroponic systems, research chemicals, digital scales, and capsule fillers. Books, bookstores, and publishers abounded, as did magazines and newsletters, films, CDs, and DVDs. There were websites (with Erowid, the giant, sprawling over more than 16,000 pages), free online libraries, and chat rooms. And legal, political, and religious bodies to back things up should they prove necessary.

Never had I dreamed there was an underground community of this size and sophistication, nor such a bustling black-market economy stretching from one end of the States to the other. What was disconcerting, though, was that nobody appeared to know what to do next.

Throughout the '80s and '90s the drug lobby's strategy had been to try to dislodge psychedelics from their Schedule A classification and to resume research, on however modest a scale. But since the early 1990s the huge popularity of both cannabis and Ecstasy had largely outflanked the relevance of any such approach: recreational drugs were well on the way to being one of the mainstays of Western leisure. Over the same period every government in the West had seen its credibility disappear almost without a trace, to the point that they were seen as little more than PR firms representing the interests of increasingly despised and hated capitalist corporations. By mid-2003 the possibility that the Bush administration itself was responsible for the destruction of the World Trade Center was looking more and more likely, and the idea of approaching anyone employed by such a regime, cap in hand, would deter all but the most hardened of U.S. academics. In any case, why bother? The *Psychedelic Resource List* proved even the most recondite drugs were easily available; and there were websites bulging with perfectly competent research.

No, the problem wasn't one of making sure that psychedelics were not relegated to a cultural and spiritual *oubliette,* not any longer. Now the problem was how to explore their constructive uses and publicize them—that, and keeping gatherings like the present conference out of the limelight. By the third or fourth day at Berkeley I was looking around the auditorium and thinking: Listen, if you guys don't get something together soon, you are all going to get busted; it's as simple as that. You'll get done as part of this bullshit War on Terror. Your one chance of survival is to join forces with the radical Left, and right smartly.

Such a coalition could prove of enormous benefit to both parties; nor was I, by any manner of means, the first person to have mooted the possibility. Years before Terence MacKenna had declared, "I am a political activist, but I think the first duty of a political activist is to become psychedelic." Fighting words—and the snowballing antiwar movement had, as it had done in the '60s, lent them potential mass resonance—but what could they mean in practice?

individual healing

Enough has been said earlier about the importance of the Left evolving its own in-house approaches to psychotherapy and the prominence this should be given in its propaganda—a prominence no one, with the sole exception of Wilhelm Reich and his Sex-Pol clinics, has even tried to address.

boundary loss and the transpersonal

At the end of the previous chapter I suggested that the nature of the ego and its transcendence are now at the heart of revolutionary politics. LSD psychotherapy is particularly promising in this respect because it leads organically from the personal dimension of healing into the collective one. Boundary loss is at the heart of the psychedelic experience: and boundary loss leads to our rediscovery of what we truly hold in common. Remember Gordon Wasson and his *velada* with Maria Sabina. "I was seeing the archetypes," he exclaimed, "the Platonic ideas, that underlie the imperfect images of everyday life." What he was seeing was the point before self and other divide: Doris Lessing's substance-of-we-feeling. Our common roots: our generic, our species nature.

revolutionary sacrament

And remember that Maria Sabina's *velada* was no isolated, introverted experience. It was a ceremony, a group, and a social event. *Agape* is the word Wasson keeps using to describe that night; and surely it's not too high-flown for something that could bring the vice president of the J. P. Morgan Bank and an illiterate Mazatec peasant face to face in awareness of their common humanity. Heart to heart. What else could have done this? Is it possible that psychedelics could be fashioned into a new sacrament?

At first my own trips seemed so demented, I doubted that any such thing were possible; but now I am no longer so sure. The peyote ceremony, by any standards one of the most aesthetically satisfying rituals ever devised, seems able to field the full range of psychedelic experience; so, for that matter, do the Santo Daime ayahuasca churches. Trying to forge such flexible, dynamic ceremonies would at least get the enormously important concept of *revolutionary art* on the road again: it would pose a true creative challenge light-years from the suffocating entertainment culture into which the West has long since sunk.

transition rites

To be down to Earth about it, you could start with rites of passage: with puberty rites, in particular. Every generation since the '60s has turned instinctively to psychedelics in search of such a demarcation line; and the Left's failure to throw itself wholeheartedly behind rave culture must count among the most dismal of its long catalogue of missed opportunities (and that's saying something).

Or, if you really wanted to come to grips with things, with rites of dying. Such rites are far more threatening, since they entail direct confrontation with the basic repression that has driven the entire civilization insane, repression of awareness of death.

From what I saw of Anna's death, psychedelics could have helped in so many ways: as a crash therapy for integrating the family and childhood issues that worked free during her last weeks alive, and for forgiving the individuals concerned; as a way of saying good-bye to friends and lovers, of bridging the terrible bedside chasm that opens between the living and the dying; as the closest, in fact the only, analog we have of what death may conceivably be like: as a way of learning to surrender, to let go into the utterly, inconceivably unknown . . . and to see that after all this may not be so very terrible . . . not so very terrible at all . . .*

radical vision quest

"The extraordinary development of Western technology . . ." "Our unprecedentedly high standard of living . . ." I cannot believe it, but there are still people churning out this crap. Our technology? Global

---

*In purely medical terms, the relevance of LSD to dying is highlighted by the drug's unexplored anesthetic properties. One- third of a terminal cancer ward treated with LSD experienced complete remission of pain for several days or longer; another third, pronounced palliative effects; the remainder, little or nothing. That any one drug capable of producing so wide a range of positive results should have been banned out of hand, and by people with no medical or psychiatric qualifications whatsoever, would be derisory were it not so shocking.

warming alone would suggest that it is an unmitigated disaster. Our high standard of living? You have to be kidding, right? This squalor? This angst? This stupidity? This toxic diet, and crap culture? In comparison with what, pray, is this "high"? Measured against what definition of happiness?

Our whole concept of evolution is up for grabs. Ultimately this is the reason psychedelics are such political dynamite. They offer the tools with which ordinary people can explore entirely different concepts of what progress might consist of . . . In my generation, the only model of counterculture we had was that of the Romantic rebellion—and clearly the great weakness of the Romantics was that they were bogged down in an "art" that had allowed their vision to be sequestered in the inoffensive sphere of "culture." We had believed that this vision could be liberated from its form and applied directly to the revolutionary recreation of reality itself—though exactly how this was going to be done, we never quite worked out. But the reappearance of "archaic techniques of ecstasy" amid a by now blatantly disintegrating civilization has changed all that. Listen to Maria Sabina:

> There is a world beyond ours, a world that is far away, nearby, and invisible. And there is where God lives, where the dead live, the spirits and the saints. A world where everything has already happened and everything is known. The sacred mushroom takes me to the world where everything is known. That world talks. It has a language of its own. I report what it says.[1]

What's happening is that a different dimension is edging its way into this one—a dimension against which the relevance, let alone the desirability, of industrial technology can be measured. Doors that have been closed for centuries are swinging open . . . and from what I have glimpsed through them, I would say that Western technology could be pruned back, and pruned back hard. Most of it strikes me as having gone off at a tangent; it's not even relevant. Personally, I want an apartment and a job like I want a hole in the head. You can shove your cars and your planes and your creepy nerdy Internet. Come to it, you can shove your precious electricity itself—or three-quarters of it, anyway. For myself I'd stand by the hippie yardstick, that the purpose of technology is to reduce the amount of labor we are forced to do to survive. The working day could be shrunk immediately to four hours a day, the rest of the day being for people to do whatever they see fit.

a modest proposal

How could such a beneficial state of affairs be brought about? As it happened, Asha, just over from the States, and I were discussing precisely this question on the two-million-strong February demonstration. Looking around us on the march, we were struck by the quantity of leaflets and little magazines being handed out . . . and wondered, why not hand out some acid trips too? Put, say, two 100-mike squares of blotter in an envelope, along with a few printed commonsensical suggestions as to set and setting. Target one or two columns of university students, pull up your hoodie, and Bob's your uncle. You'd be gone before anyone knew you had been there. What's more, you could (we were getting quite open-handed by now) add an Ecstasy trip to the envelope and suggest that taking it two hours or so before the acid would provide the best possible introductory set and setting for a first acid trip. Whatever the young students thought, one thing you could be sure about is that they would keep the envelope and take it home to show their cronies. And the tale would spread like wildfire, leaving quite a few young daredevils looking at their two squares of blotter with a dreamy light in their eyes. Just a thought.

37

Toward a Sacramental Vision of Reality

COULD WE BE SEEING some of the first features of Arnold Toynbee's new "higher" religion here?

If so, then I am not sure how true it's going to run to Toynbee's model, essentially because no previous religion has ever been formed in identical circumstances: that is, amid a society conditioned relentlessly for the past five centuries to "scientific" materialism, to atheism, and, push come to shove, to plain nihilism.

Consider, for instance, Evelyn Underhill's account of traditional religious awakening. As the reader may remember, she broke this down into three major stages: (a) Conversion, (b) Purgation, and (c) Illumination, the last two being closely interrelated. But how could any such thing happen today? To what could anyone convert? To a previous world religion? Multicultural society has brought the world's major religions face to face and there they stand, an increasingly wan and woebegone-looking collection, all mutually undermining the claim of the others to the unique credibility on which their dynamism depends.

Paradoxically, it is here that the much-maligned "recreational" quality of psychedelics suddenly takes on surprising spiritual originality. Because psychedelics are basically an adventure—an adventure in a world without any. Because, despite the hair-raising moments, they are fun. They are celebratory. They reveal their own incandescent spirituality, and their anarchism is something that cannot be defended against. They get in under the atheist radar . . .

Referring back to Underhill for a moment, we would find her model stood on its head. Rather than (a) Conversion leading to (b) Purgation/Illumination, we would see that, if anything, (a) Purgation/Illumination might well lead to (b) Conversion. Or, if that were overstating the case, we'd certainly find that Purgation/Illumination was beginning to call geek "science" into some serious question. You'd only need one strong trip to think, yes, well, materialism might well be accurate, that's true; but by the look of things it might equally well not . . . Initially, a contemporary "higher" religion would seem more likely to start as paganism than anything else: *as a conversion away from something rather than toward anything* . . .

OSHO'S MAP

Earlier we saw that Advaita Vedanta was putting down roots in the West and beginning to develop into a new nondualistic philosophy. This is the context in which I'd like—very briefly—to prospect a possible psychedelic/spiritual interface, particularly in terms of the two spiritual teachers perhaps most characteristic of the late twentieth century, Osho and Adi Da.

Much of *The Mystic Experience,* Osho's first and most closely argued book, revolves around demystifying Hindu Tantra. Obviously I can only touch on the subject here, but one of the main themes Osho pursues is the nature of kundalini energy and the meaning of the Tantric chakras.

The chakra system, he suggests, is a blueprint of humanity's possible evolution. The first three chakras (technically *muladhar, swadhishtan,* and *manipur*) symbolize the physical body, the emotions, and the intellect, respectively. Evolution-wise, these three chakras, or "bodies" as

Osho prefers to call them, are already in existence and functioning, albeit erratically. And, like Gurdjieff before him, Osho argues that the first step in spiritual life lies in their integration: in getting body, heart, and mind to function harmoniously.

In the measure that this begins to take place, *anahat,* the fourth chakra or evolutionary level, starts to become active. And it is with Osho's descriptions of this "fourth body" that we are concerned here, for they bear very close resemblance to Grof's descriptions of the transpersonal.

Paranormal powers (*siddhis*) have always been integral to Tantra. Osho cites telepathy, clairvoyance, bilocation, and most of the other phenomena to which Grof also calls attention. The fourth-body person can smell perfumes other people cannot smell, hear music others cannot hear. Such people can travel in forms far subtler than the physical body as we know it, visiting heaven and hell realms, meeting gods and goddesses, and so forth.

Osho and Grof—both of them opposed to almost all traditional religious teachers in this—believe that the raptures, visions, and preternatural powers associated with this realm could prove an enormous boost to human evolution. Osho in particular plays up the attraction magic and esotericism have always had for ordinary people, suggesting that the role they could play in the breakup of a rigid materialistic society might be something of much greater spiritual significance than the role they have played in ages of faith.

For a classic example of Osho's fourth-body person, one need look no further than Carlos Castaneda. The phenomenal popularity of Castaneda's books would indicate he has put his finger on the pulse of something very widespread indeed—something not far from a nascent fourth-body culture—which orthodoxies of any sort have always found deeply threatening. Including, be it noted, psychedelic ones. Carlos Castaneda is the sole creative artist of the first rank psychedelics have produced . . . despite which, he didn't rate a single mention at the Berkeley conference, despite its being billed specifically as a showcase for psychedelic art.

THE ESOTERIC AND THE MYSTICAL

In fact, Grof's and Osho's maps almost entirely corroborate one another. What difference there is comes from the fact that Osho, drawing on both his own meditation and on centuries of Tantric philosophy, takes his model much further. So far as he is concerned, the esoteric or transpersonal are but early days. Spiritually, it is the next level of evolution—*visuddhi,* the fifth body—around which his teaching revolves.

For Tantra *visuddhi* symbolizes "awakening." The fifth body stands for what is loosely referred to as enlightenment, and which, according to Osho, essentially means no more than living totally in the present moment. "Find what you have never lost," Nisargadatta said; and the fifth-body person has done just that. No longer are they spread-eagled between conscious and unconscious, between past and future, between subject and object. They know that the one dimension to their lives, which has never changed, is consciousness itself; and that if they have anything that can be called an identity, this is what it is: self-conscious consciousness.

What Osho is particularly concerned with are the dynamics of the relation between these two great stages of spiritual life—between the esoteric and the mystic.

In point of historic fact, there has barely been a single mystic, Eastern or Western, who hasn't passed through a stage during which one or another preternatural capacity was not activated. Yet the advice of the Christian spiritual advisor or Buddhist meditation master has always been the same: Don't get bogged down in the occult. This is not the goal. Return to your practice.

But Osho isn't going to be fobbed off with this. What we are faced with is the possibility of a new religion appearing in circumstances very different from traditional ones, circumstances in which the esoteric can have a cutting edge nothing else can rival. What Osho is trying to do in *The Mystic Experience* is situate the transpersonal within terms of an overarching spiritual evolution, one in which the transpersonal is the bridge, the missing link between normal and awakened consciousness.

It represents the necessary consummation—inseparably fulfillment, understanding, and transcendence—of esotericism, and the opening to a much deeper understanding of the sacred nature of Being.[1]

THE AWAKENING OF ADI DA

Perhaps the distinction between the esoteric and the mystical would be clearer in terms of a concrete example. The following is an account of the "awakening" of Osho's great contemporary, the American Adi Da.

It is from *The Knee of Listening*—also Adi Da's first book—in which he tells his own story. In the early chapters Adi Da recounts how he devoted his youth to an obsessive search for truth—to, in Ouspensky's phrase, a "search of the miraculous"—and describes the insights and ecstatic experiences that he did experience through a variety of spiritual practices. However, once the initial excitement faded, he had to admit that whatever had happened had failed to leave any lasting change. But, as spiritual adventure after spiritual adventure piled up, he began to notice a strange phenomenon. On each occasion that he was forced to admit his latest "miracle" had proved yet another dead-end, a profound sense of relaxation swept over him. His mind emptied, and for a moment he seemed to glimpse an entirely different order of reality.

The first time this occurred he was still a philosophy student at Columbia. The night he finished reading the last of his philosophy texts, he closed the book, sat back, and had to admit he was as confused as when he started. But the moment he did so, his mind cleared.

> In that great moment of awakening I knew the truth was not a matter of seeking. There were no "reasons" for joy and freedom. It was not a matter of a truth, an object, a concept, a belief, a motivation, or any external fact. Indeed, it was clear that all such objects are grasped in a state that is already seeking and which has already lost the prior sense of an absolutely unqualified reality.

It was late at night, and the young Adi Da wandered through the streets, intoxicated by what he had glimpsed:

I saw that we are, at any moment, always and already free. I knew that I was not lacking anything I needed yet to find, nor had I ever been without such a thing. The problem was the seeking itself, which created and enforced contradiction, conflict, and absence within. Then the idea arose that I am always already free.[2] [my italics]

This is totally at odds with all traditional approaches to religion. Only Zen—Zen with its denial that any practice can ever be of any ultimate help—reflects the same intuition, that there is nothing you can do to find God because God is not an object that was ever separate from you in the first place. God is an understanding, not an experience. God is simply That Which Is. "Truth is always already the case," as Adi Da tried to sum up his understanding in a phrase . . . Yet the paradox running through *The Knee of Listening*—as through Osho's *The Mystic Experience*—is that the unchanging can only be revealed through change itself. "There's nothing you can do about it," as they put it in Zen with customary helpfulness, "but you can't do nothing either." Adi Da's "prior sense of an absolutely unqualified reality" that ends all spiritual seeking can only be discovered by understanding the mechanics of seeking itself. As the old proverb has it, "If you want to find yourself, get lost."

THE ESOTERIC AND
THE MYSTICAL (CONTINUED)

In summary, I would suggest that, yes, psychedelics and the magic they access could possibly prove a key factor in the birth of a new universal religion. They are coming from an angle outflanking all our materialistic conditioning—and doing so with a speed and to a depth nothing else can command.

But this is only half the story. In the mid-1950s Aldous Huxley wrote *Heaven and Hell,* an attempt to produce a sequel to *The Doors of Perception,* in which he observed:

> Visionary perception is not the same as mystical experience. Mystical experience is beyond the realm of opposites. Visionary experience is still within that realm. Heaven entails hell, and "going to heaven" is no more liberation than is the descent into horror.[3]

In light of such a distinction, I'd say that while psychedelics can produce transpersonal, esoteric, or even—using the word loosely—religious experience, they cannot access genuine mysticism. Not directly. They can take you right to the door, give you a glimpse through, but not propel you any further. Their forte is to decondition: after that you are on your own . . . But that's just my personal opinion. Awakening is subtle, dialectical, and unexplored. I'll come back to all this and try to look at it in more detail toward the end of this report.

38

Meltdown in God

BY THE TIME I got back from California it was high summer in London: a summer already remarkable for its soaring temperatures, due to become the hottest summer in England ever recorded. The woodland on the Heath was all the more attractive for it, with a coolness and freshness nowhere else could rival; and a few days later I was back in the clearing, leaning up against the beech, watching the sunlight filter through the branches as I waited for my trip to come on.

For the first time I had increased the dose to 300 micrograms. With all due respect, I didn't want to go back to spending the next three hours shaking like a leaf . . . though all that appeared to have been left far behind, and instead something quite different started to happen. As the minutes went by, I found that I was losing any personal sense of identity. At first I could remember bits and pieces about my life, but it was getting more and more difficult to join them up into any coherent whole . . .

Abruptly I found I had no idea who I was at all. When I looked inside I saw pictures of dozens of different people, men and women of all ages, whose images succeeded one another so fast they began to blur. Could I be several different people at one and the same time? I wondered. A group whose separate individual consciousnesses interpenetrated? That could explain a lot of things, I thought . . . but then found I couldn't remember what the things were that it would explain.

The extra 50 micrograms made much more difference than I had anticipated. My legs were thrashing in the leaf mold. The purple flowers reappeared in the air, but in much larger quantities, almost banks of them now, and lit in a stagy apricot light. They were nodding smugly to themselves, presumably in an otherworldly breeze, and I realized how thoroughly I had come to detest them. Even the cough did a cameo.

The glade was starting to warp, becoming more like a series of thoughts than a solid three-dimensional place. I remember holding my hands in front of my face and inspecting them, as though they might offer a clue as to who or what I was. They appeared to be emerging from pure void. They were puffy, and of an unpleasant purple complexion; the nails were broken and had soil under them. Suddenly I was scared to turn them over because I knew what I would see if I did . . .

Fur!

My heart sank. I couldn't be that, could I? Not some kind of animal that lived in the woods? I reexamined my grubby paws more closely and in a moment of pure insanity thought, Am I a mole?

So over the top was this, I was shocked back into normalcy. The phantasmal flowers vanished, and I found myself thinking coherently again. But blind to it as ever, I had merely been taken over by the illusory sobering-up routine. Step 1 was looking at my watch (I can still remember it was 2:20 in the afternoon). Then Step 2, which was thinking to myself, Phew, well, the peak's over, and things are beginning to settle down a bit. Admittedly the glade didn't look its best, but all that remained of my earlier mania was ongoing identity loss. So muddled had I become I didn't just not know whether I was a human being or not, but I didn't know what human beings were, period. So I thought, Why not go for a walk and see if you can observe some from a safe distance?

Step 3 was repacking the daypack, wading back through the

bracken, and climbing over the fence. I must have felt apprehensive about having to face "people," whatever they were, for when I found some sunglasses I'd bought in the States in my pocket I promptly put them on. I thought they would give me an air of detachment, even sangfroid, but after a couple of paces I found I could barely see anything and nearly tripped. It was like the middle of the night. But when I took them off again I couldn't find the pocket they had come from—indeed, pockets seemed to have disappeared from my clothes entirely—and I had to walk along carrying the sunglasses in one hand, which I felt made me look somehow conspicuous.

Why this should have bothered me I cannot imagine, for by now the woods on both sides of the path had begun to surge backward and forward, choppy as an incoming tide. To my amusement I found I could exert a measure of control over the flux. Walking down the writhing sun-dappled path, something prompted me to say out loud, "Eighteenth century," and to my delight the bushes and saplings transformed into an elaborately gardened eighteenth-century walk—classic *Louis Quinze* with clipped box and wrought-iron bowers. Wow, I thought . . . pie-eyed hippie to the last.

Turning a corner in the path, Step 4 struck with blinding clarity. I knew exactly what I was.

I was everything.

There was the same huge influx of energy as the previous summer. The same astonishment that all my life I could have overlooked the utterly obvious. The same roaring vortex.

Whatever I beheld, I was.

Perhaps I was more observant than before. I remember stopping and listening to the roar in my head, as attentively as though I had a stethoscope and was trying to establish whether the sound could be the circulation of my own blood. What made observation tricky was that, so self-evident was the way things now were, I could not remember how they had ever seemed any different.

Everything was equal.

The *I* was out there: it was an integral part of the world, and on the same footing as everything else.

There was no inside.

By now I had left the deep woods and was back on the central track bisecting the Heath; I turned right, following the path toward the Vale of Health pond.

I was shifting back and forth between two clearly differentiated modes of perception. The first, the main one, was a state of effortless meditation, of Krishnamurti's "choiceless awareness." I was detached and without personal characteristics. "A disembodied eye," as Gordon Wasson had said, "invisible, incorporeal, seeing but not seen." But then, without warning, another vast surge of molten lava–like energy would sweep me up, and everything would fuse. Intuitively I knew that this second state was so intense that if it went on for more than ten seconds or so there would be no coming back.

Whenever I had approached such intensity before there'd been a whirring, then cracking sound in my head; this time, however, it wasn't sound but sight that started to disintegrate. Vision went pointillist. It began to break down into pixels. The world started to go grainy, wobbling somewhat, like a handheld camera.

As though I was seeing sight itself.

The insight was so shocking I thought I was going to throw up. Was such a thing possible? Could I be seeing the brain from the outside? Was I withdrawing from the body and beginning to see its most intimate processes as mechanisms out there in the world? Literally waking up from my identification with it? Was I disincarnating?

Excarnating—was that a word?

As I left the shade of the last trees, the heat hit me like a blow. Shit, I thought, as I strode unsteadily through the glare towards the Vale of Health pond, this is as hot as India.

I ducked into the shadow of the willows overhanging the waterside. I've indicated already the possibility that there's some kind of occult connection between water and acid: as though the acid is so corrosive, so yang, it needs the yin of water to soothe and balance itself out. At any rate, the pixilated world I had been seeing, with its sudden blurring and jamming of areas of the visual field into jerky rectangular masses, became fluid once more. And the pond before me that was conjured up was beautiful to die for . . . Where the willow roots plunged under the surface they became the subtlest shades of pink and orange and crimson; and there were the same amber rays of underwater sunlight I remembered so vividly from the ponds at Gran's. There was the identical pond-side waft of rotting leaves—and with a rush it all flooded back. At long last I had come home. Deep in my heart I knew that I would do anything, go through it all once more, through all the humiliation of a human life, just to be a child again.

Just to go back to those ponds one last time.

Then, with a gasp of amazement, I realized that was exactly what was happening.

The moorhens were gliding toward me across the burning black water. Somehow they were both moving and staying still at one and the same time. There was a flash of pure heaven. I felt absurdly weak; my knees were starting to give way. In his *Duino Elegies,* the poet Rainer Maria Rilke had written:

> *for Beauty's nothing*
> *but beginning of Terror we're still just able to bear,*
> *and why we adore it so is because it serenely*
> *disdains to destroy us*

Perhaps that's what happened to me. Like Rilke, I just wasn't able to bear it any longer, because after that moment of watching the moorhens both still and moving simultaneously, there's just a blank.

I must have made it back to the apartment, but I can't remember a thing about the journey there. I guess I soaked in the bath and chilled out; at which point jumbled memories start to join up again. But not until early evening, when the day was beginning to cool down, did I venture out once more, this time for a leisurely—and, as I fondly believed, post-trip—ramble through the back streets up to the top of Hampstead Village. I still had no idea how much more powerful the 300-microgram dose was to prove.

Whitestone Pond is at the top of Hampstead Hill. If you're not familiar with the city, it's the highest point in London. There's a broad, cemented-in pond there, where in olden times the horses that had dragged carts and carriages up from the West End would stop to cool down and have a drink before continuing on the road to the north.

I decided to stay there and watch the sunset.

On the far side of the pond there's a small green with a few scattered benches and a flagstaff. Lying down on the grass and joining my hands behind my head, I stared up into the evening sky. It looked unbelievably huge. For the first time I realized that the sunsets had been growing more and more panoramic all summer. It must be the temperature, I reflected: the hot air is carrying the clouds up much higher than normal.

The vast dome was empty apart from two crisscrossing vapor trails, which the rising air had flattened out and bent into cryptic hieroglyphs. By now I thought I was almost completely sober again and was merely amused when a tiny pink-and-blue airplane, way up there, entered my visual field. The plane was catching the last rays of the sun, dragging a perky little trail of psychedelic afterimages in its wake, and I was smiling to myself in a fatuous, self-congratulatory way when the acid kicked back in.

Two things happened with gut-wrenching speed and violence. First, sky, giant hieroglyphs, and plane became one and the same thing as the brain registering them—a single indivisible unity—and I was standing apart as pure witness. Then witnessing consciousness too was gone. Simply, there was nobody.

The physical body jerked upright on the grass in horror. A shudder more profound than any earthquake ran through creation. An eternal instant passed; then the world lurched heavily back into place.

39

Out of the Body?

RIGHT FROM ALBERT HOFMANN'S famous bicycle ride, there have been reports of out-of-the-body experience. Describing the climax of that first trip, Hofmann wrote:

Occasionally I felt as being outside my body. I thought I had died. My "ego" was suspended somewhere in space and I saw my body lying dead on the sofa. I observed and registered clearly that my "alter ego" was moving round the room, moaning.

And right from the first, the reports have been ambivalent. "Occasionally I felt as being outside my body." What exactly is that supposed to mean? Is Hofmann using a metaphor, or is he saying that he felt he was literally outside his physical body? Or isn't he certain which it was himself? The contortion of the sentence would suggest the latter. The same ambiguity runs through *The Doors of Perception*.

My body seemed to have dissociated itself almost completely from my mind. . . . It was odd, of course, to feel that "I" was not the same as these arms and legs "out there," as this wholly objective trunk and neck and even head. . . . In my present state, awareness was not referred to an ego; it was, so to speak, on its own.

There's more in the same vein; but Huxley, like Hofmann before him, avoids coming to grips with what he is half-suggesting—unlike the hippies who, bless their hearts, didn't suffer from any such inhibitions. They were flattened on the surgery ceiling along with the best of them.

> I lay in the bed, totally immobile. Then I suddenly started feeling very cold, and that's when the switch took place. Suddenly everything was okay. Another part of myself kicked in and told me, "It's all right." At that moment, I noticed I was looking down on myself. I was up on the ceiling, floating above the room. I could see everyone else sitting in a circle on the floor, listening to the music. I saw myself lying on the bed, looking up at myself looking down at myself. It was uncanny. I realized I was dead. There was no other explanation. I was very, very cold.

That's from Charles Hayes' *Tripping,* which features several other similar or related reports, such as the following:

> It was as though I were a discorporate being looking down at this "other" body . . .
>
> It was as though I were a third person watching myself along with the concert . . .
>
> I believe I left my body, because it went completely out of control. It was in violent motion and could not be restrained. It seemed as if I were watching myself in a movie, as my body, separated from my consciousness, went its directionless way . . .

What is out-of-body experience? Are our terror of death and desire to survive it capable of manufacturing an illusion of ongoing postmortem existence? Are such stories simply wish fulfillment, on a par with wish fulfillment in dreams? That would be the materialistic explanation of such phenomena, and no one could deny that it may very well be the case.

Yet at the same time, subtlety and ambivalence could be of the essence. There's something almost willfully obscure about the experience. "As though . . ." "As though . . ." "It seemed as if . . ." Such phrases run like leitmotifs through people's stories. Once again we are confronted by the basic ambivalence of the transpersonal, by the virtual impossibility of distinguishing what we are observing from what we are creating, and perhaps by something more than that. The young Freud's vehemence that the unconscious mind does not acknowledge the distinction between true and false comes to mind. as does Osho's "fourth body" and his thesis that the imagination is a more highly evolved faculty than reason, one to which literal-minded forms of either/or fail to apply. "You imagine the truth," as he said. Perhaps the way you "leave your body" is deeply interrelated with the imagination?

Nor, pharmacologically speaking, should it be forgotten that lysergic acid is not classified as a true hallucinogen: not in the sense that DMT or psilocybin are. Your sense of your own subjectivity remains intact, it's just that you suddenly find yourself on Alpha Centauri or cavorting with the wee folk. Lester Grinspoon and James Bakalar, two of the most level-headed commentators in the field, try to summarize the available data:

> People may sense internal organs and physiological processes usually kept out of consciousness. Some drug takers can project images of themselves onto walls; a few see their bodies as if from above or to the side, or even perceive themselves as having left the body behind to travel in the almost immaterial "astral body" of occult literature. One of the most powerful effects of this kind is the total dissolution of the body or some part of it into the environment. Like the emotions associated with distortions of the body image, the sense of transcending the self that often accompanies bodily dissolution can lead on to more profound experiences.[1]

"People may sense internal organs and physiological processes usually kept out of consciousness." That was exactly what had just happened to me when I felt I was seeing the internal structure of the eye.

Then I began to wonder whether the same mechanism couldn't have been behind my experience earlier in the trip (and behind the identical and equally electrifying insight the previous summer) that "I had become everything." At the time I had interpreted this, in a distinctly woolly minded way, as meaning that I had become one with everything in some "mystical" nondual sense. Now I began to wonder whether the experience couldn't be interpreted differently.

Bear with me a moment. So far as I understand it, it is a commonplace of scientific thought that "the world" is in fact generated in our brains from data the objective nature of which we are, strictly speaking, almost entirely unaware; and that is then projected by us collectively as a solid three-dimensional world "out there." Could what happened to me last summer have been that I suddenly glimpsed this processing at work?

When I said "I am everything I behold," the remark had been perfectly accurate, because my brain and the world are inseparably interrelated. "Processes usually kept out of consciousness" were abruptly laid bare. I was creating the trees, the bracken, the path—the holly bush under which I sheltered—just as surely as they were creating me. I was the world, and the world was me. This was objective "scientific" fact, there was nothing mystical about it.

But what was it that had seen this?

Bowled over by the intensity of the experience, I had entirely overlooked the nature of the experiencer. Had I always been a "witness" or "pure consciousness"—or a soul, or Love itself, if that sits better with you—entirely independent of the physical body, as though all my life I'd had my eye so tightly pressed to the sensory keyhole through which I was peering that I had long forgotten there was a keyhole there at all? Could I step back from the keyhole, back from the lock, from the door . . . and finally realize that I was something else entirely?

Were we a qualitatively different entity that did not so much separate from the physical body at death as realize that it had never been one with it in the first place?

40

Session 45

At Judges Walk

AS I SCRAMBLED BACK to my feet that night at Whitestone Pond, I was shaking so badly I had to lean against the flagpole. Furtively I snatched a glance upward . . . only to see the plane, still sporting its dinky little trail of afterimages, continuing imperturbably on its way through the evening sky. I leaned against the flagpole until my pulse had stopped hammering quite so madly, then stood there watching the plane as it dwindled and finally disappeared from sight.

Repeatedly over the following days I tried to relive those few apocalyptic seconds. For a timeless moment I had stood apart from everything. From absolutely everything. Then there had been nothing. But it had been so fast, so brutal, so like the proverbial bolt of lightning . . . yet that was exactly what it had been like. A flash, a blinding flash. Now I could see why Tibetan Buddhists called the ultimate vision "the Clear Light of the Void" and why they insisted that seeing it naked inevitably meant recoiling in mortal terror.

But it *had* been blinding! Had I caught a glimpse of what I really was, something beyond time and space? Or was all that truly childish wish fulfillment? Was what I had seen precisely what I thought I saw, the last agonized instant of consciousness as the universe plunged darkly into oblivion? And now I was doing my damnedest to talk myself out of it.

That evening I hadn't walked more than a hundred yards away from the flagstaff and the pond before I knew I was going to have to repeat the whole session again . . . You know, even after all this time, high-dose tripping still scares the living daylights out of me. But, or so I told myself as I walked down the hill, it's not going to be too long before the doctor looks up with that "I'm afraid I've got some rather worrying news for you" expression on his face . . . and that is going to scare me still worse, isn't it?

So what the hell?

I stuck with the 300-microgram dose, though it was more than I could even make a pretense of handling. The earlier stages of the trip, while I was still in the woods, were so drunken, so Dionysian; I cannot remember much of what happened. Again it was a day of phenomenally high temperatures, so hot that by midafternoon I was driven back across the Heath to the apartment for shelter. Not until a couple of hours later did the heat begin to subside, and I thought it was cool enough to wander up to the top of the hill.

What was genuinely spooky was that the trip proper didn't start until I'd reached exactly the same place, Whitestone Pond, at exactly the same time of day, late afternoon, and with the same intention of finding a secluded spot to sit and watch the sunset . . . If you are walking up the hill from Hampstead Village when you reach the pond and look to your left, you can see an overgrown, virtually neglected part of the Heath. Clipping a Josquin mass into the Walkman, I ducked across the road and took the narrow path through the nettles and long grass that leads deeper into this wasteland. After a moment you turn past a tall, back-garden fence and see the feature giving the place its name: a row of ancient chestnut and lime trees called Judges Walk.

Reputedly, these are all that remain of a once-fashionable eighteenth-century mall marking the northern boundary of the village. Beneath the trees, to your right, the ground drops steeply to a small oval meadow. The secret about Judges Walk is that it's probably the best spot in London to watch the sunset. Coleridge used to walk over from Highgate, and Constable lived just around the corner. Today, however, hardly anyone ever ventures there. Just a few lovers, the occasional tramp sleeping rough, or, when it snows, local kids who use the steep slope to toboggan.

No sooner did I take the path through the nettles than to my surprise (for it was the sixth hour or more since I had taken the drug) I felt the acid kick back in. Not violently, like last time—far from it. On the contrary, this was pure magic. I felt as though I had stepped through a real but invisible portal. The path, the long grass, and the trees started to shimmer, as though a breeze had crossed them, and there was a weird sense of slipping back in time, as though I was leaving the contemporary city and was returning to the country as it had been several centuries before. Bleached blond by the long summer's sun, the tall grass was on the verge of turning into a field of corn. The light was peculiarly golden. The is-ness of everything was becoming more pressing by the moment. I knelt to examine a clump of grass and found myself transfixed by one single arching blade. It was pure Plato: the first and last blade of grass; the original stroke of genius.

At my feet, the ground fell away to the little meadow. The slope was a mass of wildflowers, in prodigal quantities, and of a beauty that took my breath away. The end of the bowl where I stood was dense with rosebay, just coming into flower in shades of pink and mauve, while the main slope was an Impressionist blaze of whites with purple splashes of thistles. Perfectly on cue, the Josquin mass burst into the *Gloria*.

I had never known a trip to be so stable. There was no flickering, no sense of being on a drug. Faerie was substantial flesh and blood. Physically I felt superbly well, and as I wandered down the side of the bowl I could feel that my body was functioning in a different, somehow more integrated manner. Each step was fully conscious; and the multiplicity of sensations as my foot pressed down on the earth was something I had long forgotten.

Bees alighted on the flowers or rose into the air in perfect time to the Josquin. All awareness of Walkman and earphones was gone, and the Mass appeared broadcast by the landscape itself. The organic quality of Josquin's polyphony, the way it branched and quivered like a living thing, was what I had always loved about it; and that evening it was like an X-ray of nature in terms of sound. Finally, all I was doing was playing and replaying the *Agnus Dei,* which didn't just sound as though someone had composed it yesterday, more that someone was about to compose it tomorrow . . . and deeper and deeper emotional levels started to open up.

The first thing was that in such a perfect world I finally felt free to die.

Why, or so it was impressed upon me that evening, we hang on to life so desperately is because we are enjoying it so little; but once we are living life to the full, then the meaning of death changes entirely. Somehow it becomes the consummation of life. Before, whenever I compared joy to sorrow—to sorrow that seems so endlessly sensitive— joy had always appeared relatively flat and one-dimensional. Now I saw that this was because I had always missed the vital connection between beauty and death. But Keats had put his finger on it in *Ode to a Nightingale:*

> *Now more than ever seems it rich to die,*
> *To cease upon the midnight with no pain,*
> *While thou art pouring forth thy soul abroad*
> *In such an ecstasy!*

Once again early childhood flooded back. Dying nobly, the sheer life affirmation of it, had been one of the secret games I had played when I was alone. How could I have forgotten? The way honor and self-sacrifice were so deeply interrelated? For if there isn't something more valuable to you than living, then what value can life itself have?

Another paradoxical thing about the space I was in: There was no data about the existence or nonexistence of the soul. During what was one of the most sustained occasions in my adult life of ability to regard death without flinching, there was no concern with whether the "I" transcended death—not even any interest in the subject. Back to normal, I cannot understand this at all, *but the question simply did not arise.*

Focus, if focus there could be said to be, was on the aesthetics of dying itself. And, while I can no longer understand this either, the emotion suffusing this was one of almost infinite tenderness. Never before had I felt so gentle. Yet Keats (to stay with a local lad, he lived just down the road) captured this too in his *Ode:*

> *Darkling I listen; and for many a time*
> *I have been half in love with easeful Death,*
> *Called him soft names in many a mused rhyme,*
> *To take into the air my quiet breath.*

Paradoxically again, along with the idealism came a graphic, perhaps overly graphic, degree of realism.

As the shadows lengthened I found myself looking around the little meadow with . . . well, a speculative eye. How would you do it, then? Sitting under that tree over there? Under that rambling rose that had climbed up into the hawthorn? Normally I am hopelessly squeamish, but that evening I found myself drawn quite naturally to the idea of opening my veins. To return what had been given—with gratitude, and with courage. Often I have been struck by the strange luminosity color assumes in fading light. Red, red blood in green, green grass. The last birdsong being sung at more and more spacious intervals . . . and each time, as it were, more and more carefully. . . .

41

BPM 4

TO MY EMBARRASSMENT, I have to admit that a long time was to pass before I fully understood what had happened at Judges Walk.

Not until work on this report was nearly complete and I was double-checking details about Grof's perinatal matrices did I chance on the following passage. Describing BPM 4, the climactic moment of the baby's delivery, Grof lists some of the salient features of reliving this matrix.

[The subject] is struck by visions of blinding white or golden light and has feelings of enormous decompression and expansion of space. . . . The general atmosphere is that of liberation, redemption, salvation, love, and forgiveness. The individual feels cleansed and purged. . . . The individual tuned in to this experiential realm usually discovers in himself genuinely positive values, such as a sense of justice, appreciation of beauty, feelings of love, self-respect, and respect for others. These values, as well as motivations to pursue them and act in accordance with them, seem to be, on this level, an intrinsic part of the human personality.

Basic Perinatal Matrix 4 is the matrix of spiritual rebirth. Its typical themes run through all religious conversions, from

Road-to-Damascus-type theophanies to the quietism of many ordinary people's nature mysticism. As an erstwhile hippie, I had been especially dumb, for that evening should have thrown a flood of light on my own generation's experience with LSD. The passage continued:

> Symbolism characteristic of BPM 4 selectively displays situations . . . such as spring landscapes with melting snow or ice . . . luscious meadows and idyllic pastures in springtime . . . trees covered with fresh buds and blossoms.[1]

What Grof was describing was Flower Power!

My first response to this was equally discreditable. I was pissed off that it had taken me some fifty trips to arrive at the point many of my contemporaries had reached on their first excursion. Swanning around in their party gear to the Grateful Dead, and regarding "bad trips" incredulously . . . as from the worldview of BPM 4 you would be bound to do.

Mulling it over afterward, however, I saw that it did allow me to reframe the question of why some people had "good" and others "bad" trips. All along Grof had maintained that the typical order in which the matrices tend to manifest is BPM 2, BPM 3, BPM 4 . . . and only then BPM 1. Surely one could argue that this sequence was based too strictly on his personal clinical experience with severely traumatized individuals, already in many, if not most, cases substantially regressed, and that such would not necessarily be the case with the fresh-faced teenagers we once were? Perhaps in many instances of recreational LSD use, the first trips tended to be BPM 4, and only in later sessions did the drug begin to eat through to the darker realms of BPM 3 and BPM 2? Obviously that's no more than a suggestion; but understanding why some people have positive experiences straightaway while others have nightmarish ones will remain a key issue if we are going to try to reintroduce psychedelics as a major countercultural force.

More importantly—though this didn't occur to me until even

later—I would say that trip at Judges Walk also reflected motifs of BPM I, that is to say of intrauterine or possibly preincarnational states of being. Definitely Keats's *Ode to a Nightingale,* to return to that benchmark of Romantic vision, would testify to close connections between the two matrices. "Fade far away, dissolve, and quite forget." If that's not unabashed Nirvana, I would be glad to know what is.

Only during the time I have been finishing this report has the profound importance of death, and of consciously embracing it, struck me as being at the very heart of the Romantic Rebellion. "Our birth is but a sleep and a forgetting," wrote Wordsworth; while the priority of Nirvana, of existence outside form, is still more pronounced in Shelley: "That Beauty in which all things work and move / That Benediction which the eclipsing Curse / Of birth can quench not, that sustaining Love / Which through the web of being . . . " and so forth.

With late Shelley the theme becomes explicitly suicidal:

> *Why linger, why turn back, why shrink, my*
> *Heart . . . ?*
> *No more let Life divide what Death can join*
> *together.*

The dimension to Romantic politics this could open up (down to self-immolation as being the convergence point of "internal" and "external" proletariats) would take us too far afield to consider here.

However, BPM 1 themes were unmistakably to become more pronounced during my next session at Judges Walk. This trip, though I didn't so much as suspect it at the time, was to be my last acid trip (though looked at from another angle, it was to prove the start of one long trip lasting not weeks so much as months). But before I come to that, there's a bit of early childhood background without which it won't make sense—about, of all things, a long and very high stone wall . . .

On those afternoons when Gran and I had exhausted Crosby's most recent double-bills of U.S. war movies and films noirs, we would set out for long walks together in the countryside. Just after the war, Windle Hey was literally on the very outskirts of Liverpool, and slipping out of the back gate, we were in the open fields.

We always went the same way, a round trip to the hamlet of Little Crosby. Down a narrow path hedged with hawthorn, through the fields, then for a long way under the shadow of a forbiddingly high wall enclosing what seemed to the little child I was to be a vast forest. Then over a stile, and on through more fields to Little Crosby. It was a lovely walk, blithe in summer, lost in enchanted sea fogs and flooded fields in the winter.

Our arrival at the giant stone wall marked the point where we stopped for a rest. Gran would smoke a Craven A in silence, then, as she finally twisted the stub out of the cigarette holder, turn and stare balefully up at the wall.

"There are man-traps in those woods!" she would say, with what I reconstruct as authentic republican disgust. Then she would fish bleakly in a bag of sugared almonds that she produced from somewhere on her person, making a big show of offering me one, since she knew I detested them. (Unlike the box of fancy Belgian chocolates she bought on the sly and would hide in ever-changing places in Windle Hey, refusing to share them. This stinginess with the violet creams was the one cloud on our otherwise unconditional love.)

Then we would continue on our way over the stile and across the fields to Little Crosby.

My last trip started off identically to the one preceding it. The afternoon in the woods remains an almost complete blank, and the drug didn't kick in until after the time it would normally have ceased. Once again I had walked up to Whitestone Pond, crossed the road, and taken the narrow path to Judges Walk and the sunken meadow.

All the high summer, the sunsets had been of a magnificence I had never seen before, not even in the East. Presumably they were a freak combination of the soaring temperatures and rocketing pollution of the city: but whatever the chemistry, each evening London was crowned with a sky that looked like heaven. Subsequently, that day turned out to have been the hottest day in England since meteorological records were first kept, and the clouds had risen to such a height that the sheer scale of the sunset dwarfed anything I had ever seen before.

Again the grasses, flowers, and trees were breathtakingly pretty . . . but this time there was something subtly interdimensional and, for all the loveliness, more brooding about the place. The bowl beneath the trees had the quality of an ancient, long-forgotten temple site tucked away at the very summit of London. Most of the trip I spent sitting in the long grass, leaning up against one of the chestnuts, at the top of the slope. This time I had a Lassus mass on the Walkman, and finally I was just staring up into the sunset with my thumb on replay, listening time after time to the *Agnus Dei.*

With early polyphony, the convention is that there are three versions of the *Agnus,* each one capping the preceding in its beauty: and emotionally this is where they sock it to you. A cappella had always been associated with sensations of soaring for me—with inner ascent, with Eliade's magical flight—and as I played and replayed the *Agnus Dei,* I became more and more exalted. Almost bodily I seemed to be rising higher and higher, and everything around me was growing darker and falling away . . . and in my heart I was glad to see it go. Again I remembered another long-forgotten game I used to play as a child: sitting and staring into sunsets at Windle Hey. I would try not to blink until I was half-hypnotized. I had thought that when I grew up I would be able to fly, and I would journey deep, deep into the heart of setting suns—through those unmapped continents of massed clouds, through their mountains and chasms, their steep shafts of epic or holy light, entering another world that was my true home.*

Despite the Valhalla in the sky, the daylight was still clear when I hit replay for the Lassus one last time and got back up to my feet.

I was leaving Judges Walk by a different route from the way I had

---

*See Grof on BPM 4: "Very typical of this perinatal matrix are visions of gigantic halls with richly decorated columns, huge statues of white marble, and crystal chandeliers."

come, down a tiny cul-de-sac. If you go that way the first thing you pass is a tall old red-brick wall, over the top of which you can glimpse some trees. At its foot were clumps of nettles, limp and dusty with the heat, and as I walked along beside them, I glanced down. As I did so I froze—then felt as though I had been picked up and hurled bodily back through time.

This was just the way it had been by the huge wall on those walks with Gran to Little Crosby!

The two walls rushed together. Everything staggered; my mind opened on vast empty space. I gazed around, in silence and slow motion. There was no more time. All these years I thought I had betrayed and lost everything—but now I saw that nothing could have been further from the truth.

Nothing had changed. Nothing had been lost. Nothing had been lost at all. More than that. Nothing ever could be lost—because nothing ever happened. All my life nothing had ever really happened to me.

Nothing ever did.

I felt like a drowning man who finds that all along his feet have been a fraction of an inch from the Rock of Ages. Finally, finally I had become what I always had been. Again there was that shock of recognition, as though something at the very root of memory had been jarred.

Indeed, as thought began to return, that was the first thing I asked myself. *How could I possibly have forgotten?* And, as though I had consulted an oracle and if you ask a real question you get a real answer, I had the most graphic hallucination. For the first time in months I felt the slimy cobwebby stuff trailing out of the corner of my mouth . . . perhaps more vividly than I had ever felt it before!

I cracked up, and was laughing out loud to myself (was the answer as straightforward as that, then?) as I set off down Hampstead Hill, in the direction of a sunset-lit Mount Vernon.

42

The Long Flashback

ANOTHER STUNNINGLY HOT DAY dawned the next morning, and not until early evening did I decide it was cool enough to go out and get some fresh air.

I had a hit of grass, clicked an a cappella CD in the Walkman, and headed up the hill to Whitestone Pond. I took the same path through the nettles and rosebay until once again I was standing at the foot of the row of ancient trees, and once again London was crowned with otherworldly fire. And as I looked around me I saw, to my surprise, that there was the same psychedelic edge to everything as there had been the previous evening. I'm on a trip again, I thought incredulously. But it was true—I was! By no means with the searing quality of the previous day . . . but trip it unmistakably was, with the same freshly minted quality to nature, with the same almost absurdly high ideals.

"Flashbacks" get a mixed response in the literature. By and large, they are held to be an abrupt recurrence of the drug state during the days or weeks following a trip: and typically unpleasant rather than not. But what started to happen to me that evening wasn't anything like that. Far from being negative, my flashbacks (or more accurately flashback, for all were almost entirely homogeneous) were overwhelmingly positive. A further passage I found in the *Realms* was much more apropos.

> If the subject is under the strong influence of one of the perinatal matrices at the time when the pharmacological action of the drug is wearing off, he can experience the influence of this matrix in a mitigated form for days, weeks, or months after the actual session has ended.

I returned to Judges Walk the second evening after the trip . . . and the third . . . and the fourth . . . and each time there was the same dazzling afterglow. "The glory of the Lord," as old Handel sang, "shone round about." What was strange was that it had to be the same place, Judges Walk, at the same time of day, sunset; and it had to be preceded by a toke of grass, and a track or two of a cappella. If I didn't repeat this precise formula, then nothing happened.

I don't think the trigger was the grass so much as the music.

Since then I've met others who have told me they too can reaccess psychedelic space through music alone. "According to shamans of the entire world," writes Jeremy Narby in *The Cosmic Serpent,* "one establishes communication with spirits via music." Only now, at the end of my third summer with the acid, did I see that this had already been happening for a long time. Early polyphony wasn't just an arcane aesthetic taste psychedelics had left me with. Like the peyote songs in the Native American Church, or the *icaros* of South American shamanism, it was an integral part of my tripping. For me, a cappella was a psychic tool.

While I was high, it worked as a way of navigating: as a means of entering psychic space, of centering amid it, and finally of offering a bridge back to the everyday world. I had three or four tracks which, played at the end of a trip, always made me cry: like a woman, I found tears to be the most effective of exit strategies. Post-trip, a cappella frequently allowed me to recapture some of the subtlest and most elusive emotional perceptions of a session. In general, it always drew my attention back to a subtle ascending or rhapsodic current of energy, which now never seemed very far away.

Exactly the same thing happened every evening for the following five or six weeks. I would go up to Judges Walk and wander through the autumn sunsets playing and replaying my Top Ten motets.

Overall there was a profound sense of completion. I understood that the acid had worked as rites of passage for me, rites of passage from late middle age to old age. My "Saturn return," or whatever it had been, had left me freaked and embittered by what seemed a wasted life in a doomed civilization and scared stiff of dying: what the acid had given me was the space to confront and live through this. I had analyzed and come to terms with the individual and collective factors that had made me the way I was and which, like it or not, was the only way I could have been. Now it felt as though a great burden had fallen away.

My life was something "out there," far more a part of the world than it was of me. I had to admit that I couldn't remember that much of it anyway. Not really. Matter was thinning out, and the energy draining out of it was backing up inside me, the way a receding wave is hauled up into an incoming one. Sometimes I had an odd sensation of being just behind and above myself in space, and the moment before myself in time. Simultaneously with this sense of depersonalization, there was a very marked sense of empathy with others. I had always imagined that compassion was a "virtue" that rare individuals managed to cultivate: this no longer seemed to be the case. Compassion appeared much more of a reflex instinct, one almost automatically associated with ego loss. *Poor people,* I murmured to myself as I wandered through the drunken evening. *Poor, poor people!*[*1]

---

[*]Over-the-top idealism is perhaps the archetypal effect of acid. There's a trip reported in Masters and Houston's *Varieties of Psychedelic Experience,* a classic case of a young student who overdosed and "turned into everything," too long to quote here, but the conclusion

If music had played the role of spiritual compass, then the trip journals had provided an equally vital space in which the sessions could be logged, their details recorded, and the process of working-through initiated.

Here we are face to face with perhaps the single most important factor setting psychedelics apart from any previous spiritual path.

Traditionally, spiritual breakthrough would have been preceded by years of devotion and steady practice. It would have been rooted, contextualized, in daily life from the first, whereas with psychedelics everything works the other way around. First there's the breakthrough, then the devotion and the practice. I guess that's the only way it can happen in a society of such doctrinaire materialism—but it puts unprecedented emphasis on keeping memory of the breakthrough alive and working through its implications.

During that autumn I read a slim volume, basically no more than a monograph on art, that I had bought at the Berkeley Conference but hadn't settled down to read until now.

Drawing It Out: Befriending the Unconscious was written by American artist Sherana Frances and told the story of the single high-dose LSD trip she had taken, which had revolutionized the course of her life.

The reason she had turned to psychedelics was that she felt driven half-mad by an inner war between her desire to be a full-time artist and her responsibilities as a wife and a mother. Her session was supervised professionally, and clearly something of major importance happened to her . . . but during the days, then weeks, after her session, she found that she could not even begin to put into words what had occurred.

(*continued from page 235*) to which reads eloquently: "There was the sense that one must speak to beauty and commune with beauty in all of its forms. . . . This imperative was part of a larger imperative that seemed to stand out absolutely from all other thought as the one overriding imperative statement: That one must seek God. The beautiful is part of the imperative that one must approach the Godhead. This was the ultimate procedural prescription. All the rest of thought was dispensable and this prescription alone could guide one."

Pressure built up and up . . . until one night she sat down and for more than a month worked on producing a series of eighteen drawings. The first is of her lying back and seeing mandala-like patterns as the trip comes on . . . then of her being seized by an energy with the force of a whirlpool that sucks her down into the underworld. Terrified, naked, dismembered, the drawings record her shamanic journey through the halls and caverns of death, through frightful visions of mythological and religious themes, before she finally reemerges, reborn and triumphant.

As art, the drawings are a sort of cross between Blake and the Surrealists, but executed in black and white with a raw visceral power neither commanded. What fascinated me was not the artistry but the method, the way Sherana Frances had found to express and keep the material from her session alive. A psychotherapist friend of hers writes in the introduction to the book:

> The concept of the container, as used here, springs from the practice of depth psychotherapy. . . . The container holds the rich chaos of conscious and unconscious experience, allows a multitude of fragmentary images to be sorted out and deeply felt, to interrelate and be held in consciousness. The container provides a framework for the bridging of split worlds, for the recognition of revolutionary insights which the socially conditioned ego might otherwise avoid.[2]

Sherana Frances herself added that even years later, the drawings continue to provide ongoing inspiration. She refers to them as "unfailing guides, healers, prophets, and teachers." I wished she had developed her ideas on this subject, because this was exactly what I had been trying to do with the trip journals . . . and, as I turned from one of her drawings to the next, I was beginning to feel that for me this could be done only by writing a book.

In a general sense I suspect that the exploration of psychedelic space is going to entail the development of something much more supple and dynamic than just Terence McKenna's "diaries of explorers," though at the same time not necessarily by anything as traditionally "artistic" as Sherana Frances's drawings. Perhaps by some kind of ceremony. Perhaps by prayer: the prayer to which acid had repeatedly drawn my attention, and to which I had equally repeatedly refused to respond.

At any rate, we could witness an extraordinary burst of imagination and artistry in this context, one transcending anything previously considered "art."

43

Interim Report

THE LEAVES WERE FALLING, the days growing darker, and I felt increasingly cooped up in the London apartment. Weeks of being high on natural beauty had left the city looking cheaper and more tawdry than ever, and finally I decided to scrape together whatever money I had and move to Cornwall, to a village in West Penwith, close to Land's End.

Once there I settled down to edit the trip journals and montage the entries into coherent narrative. At first this proved straightforward enough . . . though as I did so, something completely unexpected happened. I found I had lost all desire to trip. It had just vanished; nor, as the weeks, then months, went by did it show any sign of returning. I didn't know what to make of this. Was hands-on experiment behind me? Was I faced now with making some kind of psychological and philosophical sense out of everything that had happened? I couldn't tell. All I knew was that if I wanted answers to these questions, I would have to work through them in this report.

Otherwise, my obsession with psychedelics continued unabated. If anything it got more intense. Only now, trying to grasp the past three years as a whole, did I begin to question what psychedelics might mean . . . mean in terms of the individual, in terms of society, in terms of the planet.

Historically, the background to this report has been the decline and fall of the middle classes. The civilization that ruled Europe for five hundred years is dead and buried and has been replaced by a corporate capitalism indistinguishable from fascism.

Politically, the joke was very much on my generation. In our innocence we believed ourselves to be a new revolutionary avant-garde, while in fact we were the last-ditch stand of the old middle classes. In the absence of any mass support, we, like every other revolt since the Luddites or the first Romantics, never stood a chance. Everything we tried to do was co-opted, commercialized, and put through a 180-degree turn to function, even flourish, as an integral part of the society it had been intended to destroy. Our despair when we saw what had happened was terrible. Three close friends, including my oldest and best, were to kill themselves in the course of a single year.

Utter political hash we may have made of our "youth revolt," but about one thing we had not been wrong. As a society, the West found its goalposts had been moved. The problem was no longer exclusively, or even primarily, one of physical survival: the problem was the meaning of life. Obviously the economy had to be revolutionized, obviously the little shits responsible should be strung up on the nearest lamppost—but the basic problem was, what were we living for? The dynamics of culture had become involved with those of revolution to an unprecedented degree.

Gurdjieff and Lenin walked the same streets . . . streets of a civilization all of whose values were in ruins. We weren't just angry that anything once called art or philosophy had been commercialized into a 24/7 barrage of entertainment and useless information set on brain stun. No, the rot went deeper than that, a lot deeper. What my generation zeroed in on was the very form of the culture, the unquestioned premise underpinning it all: the spectator/show model. And evil isn't too strong a word for what we saw there.

For media work in one direction only. By definition they cannot "communicate" anything, because communication is based on a dialog moving freely between two individuals, in terms of that most basic of all Western inventions, democracy. Media that work in one direction express one thing and one thing alone—fascism. Communication has been reduced to consumption of page or screen or stage or canvas or DVD or concert, it's all the same . . . the point is that you cannot respond. Such culture is inherently passive; and because it is passive it's isolated, and because it is isolated it's impotent. Essentially, the media work as *a system of isolation:* as a creative curfew, the implications of which are directly political.

If you want to figure the philosophical small print, then read '60s and '70s insurgents, read Guy Debord, read Herbert Marcuse. If you want to see it with your own eyes, go down in the subway and take a look at the posters. "Stunning . . ." "Riveting . . ." "Electrifying . . ." "Un-put-downable . . ." "Nerve-shredding . . ." "Obsessive . . ." This is the language of hard-drug addiction. In fact, the culture is a hard drug, period. Or, to use the correct pharmacological term, it is a *dissociative anesthetic.* That is, it potentiates, speeds up mental activity to the point that you cannot feel anything at all. The medium is the message, as someone once observed; and the message is, Fuck you.

Right from the first pages of the trip journal, there is a fascination with the nature of true communication. How do I communicate with myself? How do I communicate with others? How do we all communicate with one another and with our common heritage? At first it is mostly in reference to Jung's concept of the collective unconscious . . . and consists of delight at the bravura of what I began to call *psychedelic language.* Then a growing awareness of the didactic edge to this communication begins to appear; and finally acknowledgment that I appeared to be being taught something, something specific, albeit in a densely symbolic manner. Several times the same observation is made: that psychedelics are like a book, only one that you live rather than read.

Not that those early sessions did much more than dust off the cobwebs from Jung's concept. The first trip that truly shocked me, shocked me to the core, was the one where I turned into the passerby on the street. That flouted everything. Perhaps because it demonstrated that reality appeared to be indefinitely plastic. Perhaps by the implication that its nature wasn't so much material as linguistic (for what other remotely sane interpretation could be coaxed out of the afternoon: *that what I was experiencing was a living metaphor from a more highly evolved language?*). Perhaps because of the corroboration that someone or something was indeed trying to communicate with me: me personally, with driving urgency.

From this point, my tripping didn't look back.

I picked up on South American and Mesoamerican shamanism. In the initiatory vision of Maria Sabina, I found the first symbol for psychedelics that had genuine resonance for me.

> On the Principal Ones' table a book appeared, an open book that went on growing until it was the size of a person. In its pages there were letters. It was a white book, so white it was resplendent. One of the Principal Ones spoke to me and said: "Maria Sabina, this is the Book of Wisdom. It is the Book of Language. Everything that is written in it is for you. The Book is yours, take it so that you can work." I exclaimed with emotion: "That is for me. I receive it."[1]

Psychedelics tuned us into a waveband of information otherwise scrambled. That was their evolutionary significance. To some surprise, I found that this wasn't just some daffy theory of my own. In his study of ayahuasca, the Western professor of religious philosophy Benny Shanon makes the same assertion, if anything more forcefully.

> First and foremost, it dawned on me that what I was actually entering was a school. There were no teachers, no textbooks, no instructions; yet there was definitely structure and order to it. The teacher was the brew; the instruction was conducted during the

period of intoxication without the assistance of any other person. And what was quite remarkable—there were grades. Each series of sessions centered on a topic or a problem. At times, I realized what the topic was only in retrospect. But there was always an order. I have heard the same impressions from other people.[2]

If this is beginning to sound alarmingly esoteric, there are other writers in the field who have done their best to keep their bearings in relation to contemporary Western scientific thought—Jeremy Narby in *The Cosmic Serpent,* for instance.

Earlier I quoted a passage in which Narby stressed the sophistication of the chemistry called upon to produce curare, the Amazonian arrow poison, and questioned how indigenous tribes could conceivably have stumbled on such a complex process through trial and error. Narby ends his elegant and subversive piece of detective work with the hypothesis that *ayahuasceros* have somehow found a way to crack what we in the West would call the DNA code. Readers are referred to Narby's book for his arguments, which, though wild, aren't that over the top; and it does look as though we are confronted with something along the lines he is suggesting—a timeless, spaceless dimension of pure information.*[3]

However mad it may be, personally I have found the closest reflection of my own experience in Terence McKenna's *The Archaic Revival.*

Somewhere in that extraordinary collection of essays, McKenna invents the term "the generation of three-dimensional languages" apropos of South American shamanism; and while he is using the phrase specifically in the context of DMT and psilocybin, I can only add that something very similar has been my experience with acid. To use—most

---

*Recently, support for Narby's thesis came from an unexpected quarter when it was revealed that Francis Crick, the Nobel Prize–winning father of modern genetics, was a closet acid-head and indeed *in flagrante delicto* when he first envisioned the double-helix structure of DNA. Mmm.

probably abuse—Jacques Lacan's celebrated phrase: "The unconscious is structured like a language." If you wanted to push your luck, you could go so far as to suggest that the unconscious, or at least its human interface, is structured like a narrative: that the unconscious is telling a story.

Needless to say, McKenna jumps in the deep end. We are faced, he announces magisterially, with . . . *the return of the Logos*. With "The Word" of St. John's Gospel, the Word made flesh and struggling to return to its prior nature as Spirit. Wacko it may sound, but I can only affirm that in psychedelic outer space the ancient religio-philosophic language rings true. I touched on the Platonic tone to those last trips at Judges Walk; and during the final stages of this report, I felt I was being drawn to the study of philosophy between Socrates and Plotinus as a framework within which psychedelic experience could possibly be approached. Unfortunately, pursuing this was something else that had to be shelved until the present manuscript was done with.

Looking back on my whole adventure, the feeling I am left with is overwhelmingly one of having been healed. "This stuff gives you what you want," Aldous Huxley says somewhere; and in my observation the remark, far from being flippant, gets close to the way the psychedelic works.

First the acid took me back to a total sense of failure, to the terrible intellectual wound of having staked everything on a rebellion that failed: a rebellion that had truth and beauty and justice on its side . . . and that didn't make a blind bit of difference. Acid didn't just soothe this pain, didn't just take it away. *It didn't just console, it redeemed.* Again the old religious terminology conveys the experience best. It didn't just restore my ideals to the state before they were trashed, it renewed and transfigured them; it gave them a richness, a sinew, a twice-born quality they had never known when I was young.

On top of which, I felt I had unearthed the most vital piece of unfinished countercultural business left by my generation—and got to play with it all on my own. I hope that at least I've managed to convey that: Boy, did I have a good time!

Could this conceivably have been something just for me? I find it hard to believe. McKenna was once asked whether he thought psyche-delics were for everybody. "No," he replied after a moment. "Not for everybody . . . but for nearly everybody."

The purpose of this report has been to inspire the research to explore McKenna's thesis. Should it still not be clear, I can only stress that nothing here is meant to be a model to be followed. All I have wanted to do is to give one concrete example of—er—constructively approaching the subject, essentially just to show that it can be done. Since the '60s rebellion, true creativity has struck me as being the cre-ation of creativity itself; and at the end of the day, this is a profoundly political book.

Never mind political—it's straight agitprop.

44

Interim Report

(continued)

EARLIER I LOOKED AT the idea that awakening today might break down into two stages. The first is a kind of deconditioning, a reenchantment of daily life; the second something subtler and more elusive, a growing awareness of the unchanging, the quality of is-ness running though everything.

Well, what seems to have happened to me is that I have gotten stuck between the two worlds, with a foot in each, as it were. As I've just been saying, the sense of magic has come back, and brilliantly, but the second stage—the steady self-awareness, the moments of merging—has been fugitive at best. Measured up against Nisargadatta, I am still asleep on my feet. So the last question I'd like to look at is: Can psychedelics help complete this process?

Should I go back to working with acid the way I have been doing—or can psychedelics by definition be no more than a preparation for something you have to go through on your own? And if so, how do you know when that preparation is complete?

Earlier we looked briefly at the career of the American teacher Ram Dass. Here was someone who had been deeply involved with psychedelics who, while continuing to acknowledge the importance of the role they had played in his life, returned to more traditional forms of religion . . . and insisted there was a clear cutoff point, beyond which psychedelics were no longer beneficial.

After some three hundred trips, Ram Dass said the drug stopped doing anything much: "I found that if I kept taking LSD every month, I'd plateau, I'd get the same experience over and over again, and I'd get bored with it all." His conclusion was that psychedelics could decondition, heal, and initiate, but that was the extent of their power. "They are a catalyst, a door opener," he said. "I will still do it, all things being equal, but I don't feel like I'm learning something that new anymore."[1]

Accordingly, Ram Dass adopted a more traditional approach to spiritual life: first devotion to a guru, to Neem Karoli Baba; then, after Neem Karoli's death, to various awareness-training practices in the Buddhist vipassana and *dzogchen* traditions. To the best of my knowledge, he never defined more precisely what he meant by "catalyst" or "door opener," nor mentioned whether he had explored the possibility of using psychedelics and awareness practice in tandem. More significantly, he overlooked another teacher who, in mid-twentieth-century India, at any rate, was unmistakably towering head and shoulders above the rest—Ramana Maharshi.

I can't but feel that photos of Ramana overdo the saint. Surely he must have had the most beautiful, certainly the most eloquent, smile of anyone who ever lived, but all those photos of him in his diapers blissing out with the ashram cow end up making me feel . . . well, that I am having my leg pulled somewhat, more especially in view of a teaching that is little short of spiritual bolshevism. For what Ramana was trying to do was to revolutionize the Hindu tradition. To undercut every aspect of Vedic culture . . . study of the scriptures . . . morality . . . ritual . . . single-pointedness of mind . . . samadhi . . . in favor of one thing alone: direct confrontation with who, or what, we are.

Who are you? Ramana asked.

Just that. Who are you? Find the quick of your sense of identity, of your most intimate sense of you-ness, and see what you consist of for yourself. "You are awareness," he said.

> Awareness is another name for you. Since you are awareness there is no need to attain or cultivate it. All that you have to do is to give up being aware of other things: that is of the not-Self. If one gives up being aware of them then pure awareness alone remains, and that is the Self.

That was it. That was Ramana's entire practice—if practice it could be called. To be wary, not just of the glamour of the esoteric, but of the glamour of religion, period. For what we are looking for is right under our noses.

> The Self is ever-present. Each one wants to know the Self. What kind of help does one require to know oneself? People want to see the Self as something new. But it is eternal and remains the same all along. They desire to see it as a blazing light and so forth. How can it be so? It is not light, nor darkness. It is only as it is. It cannot be defined. The best definition is "I am that I am."[2]

When I was first trying to sit vipassana, I would run into these kind of Zen bon mots and get really wound up. I thought they were trying to make a joke. The trouble was that for the first moment I read them, they seemed blindingly self-evident truth: then, equally abruptly, whatever meaning they had disappeared entirely. Yet over the years I continued to bump into these same mocking, almost nihilistic outbursts and had to admit that they could be traced back to the very roots of the mystical impulse: most clearly in the Chinese Ch'an and Japanese Zen traditions, where they formed an acknowledged way to freedom, referred to as the "sudden or abrupt path," in terms of which understanding doesn't build up incrementally but strikes in spontaneous lightning bolts.

Toward the end of *The Way of Zen* Alan Watts even quotes the Buddha himself as observing:

I obtained not the least thing from unexcelled, complete awakening, and for this very reason it is called "unexcelled, complete awakening."[3]

Surely Buddha had the most impeccable credentials of any world teacher—so what was he trying to say? Years were to pass before I began to understand. Largely by chance I discovered the work of the contemporary Western teacher, the American Adi Da, who was trying to express the same understanding, and I found I had a skeleton key to ultra-left mysticism in my hand.

Earlier I quoted Da's satori while he was still a student at Columbia. But what he had glimpsed that night didn't become life-transforming until a further decade of near-hysterical seeking had passed. At which point Da, now in his early thirties, was meditating furiously in the Hollywood Vedanta Temple, attaining levels of ecstatic trance he had barely touched upon before. "These experiences," he wrote—indeed a trace archly—"exceeded any kind of pleasure that a man could acquire."

Then without warning, something snapped. After a particularly intense session he returned to the Vedanta temple.

The next day I sat in the temple again. I awaited the Shakti to reveal herself as my blessed companion. But as time passed there was no sensation, no movement at all. There was not even any kind of deepening. There was no meditation. There was no need for meditation. There was not a single element to be added to my consciousness. I sat with my eyes open. I was not having an experience of any kind.

In an instant, I became profoundly and directly aware of what I am. It was a tacit realization, a direct knowledge in consciousness itself. It was consciousness itself without the addition of a communication from any other source. I simply sat there and knew what I am. I was being what I am.

Over the course of writing *The Knee of Listening,* Adi Da articulated the implications of what he had experienced with a clarity which, for me at any rate, has remained unrivaled.

At the Vedanta Society Temple tacit knowledge arose that I am simply the consciousness that is reality. The traditions call it the "Self," "Brahman," identified with no body, realm, or experience, but perfect, unqualified, absolute Reality. I saw there was nothing to which this nature could be compared, differentiated, or epitomized. It does not stand out. It is not the equivalent of any specialized, exclusive, perfected spiritual state. It cannot be accomplished, discovered, or remembered.

All paths pursue some special state or goal as spiritual truth. But in fact reality is not identical to such things. They only amount to an identification with some body, realm, or experience, high or low, subtle or gross. But the knowledge that is reality, which is consciousness itself, which is not separate from anything, is always already the case, and no experience, realm or body is the necessary or special condition for its realization.[4] [my italics]

Compared with an understanding as radical as this, what Ram Dass is talking about is barely religious at all. Or, to be fair, it's esoteric but not mystical. So as far as Ramana or Da are concerned, discovering a new master, or going deeper into trance, or any of it is just more of the same. It's continuing to avoid the full horror of the situation, expressed so ruthlessly by the Upanishadic "Where there are two, there is fear."

Yet the shift or leap of faith or whatever it is between the esoteric and the mystical is complex—so idiosyncratic, so explosively dialectical—how can one come to grips with it?

None of it is straightforward. When I first read *The Knee of Listening* I was still sitting vipassana—from under which Adi Da elegantly pulled the chair. No way could I say I was trying to sit down quietly and observe things with "bare attention." I was trying to control and manipulate my own fine nervous states and live in realms of subtle rapture. I was in search of the miraculous; I was trying to get high, and after a few years in India I was beginning to get the hang of it. But I was so bowled over by Adi Da that I overreacted wildly and threw any form of awareness practice out the window—which, in retrospect, I can see was a disastrous mistake. I never lived through those desires properly, and longing for rapture continued to haunt me. (Truly there are "experiences exceeding any kind of pleasure that a man could acquire." Promise.)

In much the same vein, during the Advaita boom of the late twentieth century, there were a number of long-term meditators who came close to the same breakthroughs as Ramana and Adi Da and promptly declared themselves enlightened . . . only to return to normal a few weeks or months later, looking distinctly silly, which wasn't really fair, since all that had happened was that the process had gone off half-cocked.

Much of the nuts and bolts of the Zen tradition was designed to check whether satori was stable or temporary self-inflation; and, on a closing note, perhaps one could suggest that in the absence of a steady supply of qualified Zen mad people, a dose of Dr. Hofmann's potion might ferret out any last traces of spiritual ego. A veritable Acid Test, passing which could be assessed in terms of Daisetz Suzuki's famous definition of satori:

"Just the same as before—only six inches off the ground!"

45

Mutual Immanence

I DON'T SEEM TO be able to drop this. I guess what I am asking is, *How close can acid bring you to that point of letting go?* . . . and there simply isn't enough data to go on.

But perhaps there are further aspects to the information we have already if we dug away at it. We could look, for instance, more attentively at those last trips of Ram Dass's, the ones on which he based his assertion that psychedelics couldn't form a spiritual path in their own right. There seem to me to be several features to those sessions that Ram Dass himself didn't notice.

When all's said and done, what did his objection to LSD amount to? That after some three hundred trips the drug failed to reveal anything new. "I'd get the same experience over and over again, and I'd get bored with it all." It's a pity he doesn't expand on this because—at least in terms of a number of religious models—quite different, in fact much more positive, interpretations of his own experience could be put forward.

Several times already I've referred to Evelyn Underhill's analysis of individual religious evolution, but largely only in relation to the stages of Conversion, Purgation, and Illumination. But these constitute only the introductory steps to a full spiritual life (which Underhill calls "the first religious life") and are followed in fully mature cases by two further dimensions of a much more profound and dramatic nature: The Dark Night of the Soul and Unity with God.

"The Dark Night of the Soul" was the term coined by St. John of the Cross to describe the spiritual devastation recorded by many of the world's mystics immediately before their final awakening. Without warning a great, apparently integrated contemplative is split in two by the insight that all their spiritual "attainments" are without the slightest value. They are vanity, pure vanity. If anything, they are spiritually pernicious. From feeling they were on the verge of finally dissolving into God, such a person becomes tortured by feelings of the most intense worthlessness.

For Underhill, the Dark Night is the door between the first and second religious lives. In a sense the Dark Night is the return of Purgation—only this time without any attendant Illumination. Religion is all self-delusion; neither God nor meaning to the universe exist.

Could this have been what Ram Dass was suddenly catching sight of during those last seemingly dud sessions? In fact, far from revealing nothing new, was the acid starting to mirror something that was horribly so? That everything he had been priding himself on was no more than self-inflation? Was he being ushered into the shadow of the Dark Night?

Never mind Ram Dass. Didn't something comparable happen to many of us at the time? Didn't LSD begin to prove too much? Wasn't this what lay behind the large-scale defection of the first acid-heads during the early '70s? Wasn't what was really happening that we were being shown that acid plays for keeps: that we were going to have to let go of everything, absolutely everything . . . and just wait, wait without fear, wait without hope, wait in true humility of heart for That Which Is to have its way with us? The bitterness and sense of betrayal (the recourse to smack or fundamentalist Buddhism) are totally in accord with Underhill's descriptions of the Dark Night.

For only true self-obliteration—the old medieval *self-naughting*—can leave us totally, unconditionally open for the final stage of religious life, total surrender to the will of God.

Is there any other way we can learn that, in the end, there is only Grace?

Such phenomena return us to a distinction that has bedeviled this report, that between the *via positiva* and the *via negativa:* concepts like the Dark Night clearly belonging to the latter category. Perhaps this kind of possible culmination to sustained use of LSD could be offset by something very different created by a sustained *via positiva* approach?

All along there's been a trip I have wanted to quote but never found the right place to work it in. Perhaps this is it, for the story illustrates the feasibility of psychedelic experience melting into ordinary being through pure joy. For a long time I had been surprised that the most famous trip of them all, Aldous Huxley's in *The Doors of Perception,* had never produced the sequel for which it manifestly cries aloud. Late in the day I discovered such a sequel did exist, though it is little more than an extended sketch, and barely known.

Shortly after that momentous May morning in the Los Angeles hills, Aldous Huxley's wife, Maria, had died of cancer. Huxley nursed her devotedly through her last days, but during the months following her death he found himself increasingly attracted to a younger woman, Laura Archera. During this period Huxley had a second mescaline trip in the company of two friends, though this appears to have fallen far short of the intensity of the first one; and for his third experiment he asked Laura to sit for him.

Nominally this was because Laura was a psychotherapist, and Huxley, who could remember next to nothing of his early childhood, wanted her to help him probe for these lost years. Predictably enough, no such thing took place. A few days after the session, Huxley wrote to Humphry Osmond, the doctor who had supervised his first mescaline trip and subsequently become a close friend, as to the distance separating that first session from what had just happened.

Instead there was something of incomparably greater importance; for what came through the closed door was the realization—not the knowledge, for this wasn't verbal or abstract—but the direct, total awareness, from the inside, so to say, of Love as the primary and fundamental cosmic fact. The words, of course, have a kind of indecency and must necessarily ring false, seem like twaddle. But the fact remains. I was this fact; or perhaps it would be more accurate to say that this fact occupied the place where I had been.

The letter launches into an analysis of taking a psychedelic in the set and setting of falling, moment by moment, more and more deeply in love with the person you are with.

Love deobjectifies the perceived thing or person. At the same time it de-subjectifies the perceiver, who no longer views the outside world with desire or aversion, no longer judges automatically and irrevocably, is no longer an emotionally charged ego, but finds himself an element in the given reality, which is not an affair of objects and subjects, but a cosmic unity of love. . . . Love deobjectifies and desubjectifies, substitutes the primordial fact of unity and the awareness of mutual immanence for a frenzy heightening to despair by the impossibility of that total possession . . . at which the subject mistakenly aims.

Intuition bordering on telepathy, attested to equally by Laura Archera in her own write-up of the session, was an integral part of the lovers' experience that afternoon. More's the pity Huxley never approached the subject with the drive and literary passion of *The Doors of Perception,* for such a conflation of lysergic acid, love, and Advaita could have drawn the themes of his earlier work into a breathtaking finale. "Mutual immanence"—was there ever a phrase that wedded our spiritual and political longings so gloriously?

Among the by-products of this state of being the given fact of love was a kind of intuitive understanding of other people, a "discernment of spirits," in the language of Christian spirituality. I found myself saying things about [Laura] which I didn't know but which, when I said them, turned out to be true. Which, I suppose, is what one would expect if one happens to be manifesting the primordial fact of unity through love and the knowledge of mutual immanence.[1]

46

Sanctus

POLITICALLY, WHAT'S GOING TO happen next is anyone's guess—but the odds are clearly in favor of disaster.

Corporate capital is the doomed attempt to impose control on a situation that has unmistakably, on every level from the personal to the planetary, spiraled totally out of control. To read the papers or watch the TV is enough to make you want to puke.

The world seems run by creatures from the Pit—and yet there still isn't any trace of opposition. Is it too late for anything even remotely resembling traditional political organizations to form? To call a spade a spade, the population of the West is apathetic and apparently almost unbelievably stupid. Long ago Nietzsche predicted that capitalism would succumb to an age of mass nihilism, and his prophecy appears to have been borne out by events.

Yet at the same time there have been rays of light as dazzling as the international peace movement of 2001–03. This was a flowering of *agape* on a scale unprecedented in history, and to dismiss it as a "failure" is to miss the point entirely. Massively positive outcomes have been triggered by equally desperate straits. Primitive Christianity is clearly a case in point, as is Mahayana . . . and such spiritual insurrection can appear apparently out of the blue and spread with extraordinary speed.

How harebrained is the suggestion that such a movement could be catalyzed by psychedelics remains to be seen . . . but we are, let's face it, down to the long shots.

On the one hand we have a civilization in mortal crisis; on the other a fountainhead of visions of a New Heaven and Earth. Suggesting that sooner or later the two are likely to come into contact does not seem that far-fetched . . . though the way in which this could happen remains in my opinion entirely unpredictable.

Truth to tell, I slightly exaggerated my sabbatical from drugs during the time I was working on this book. I did do a few low-dose trips, but just to touch base. Only once did my patience snap, and I downed a higher dose than ever before.

Late one summer's night I took 350 mikes, alone in the little studio outbuilding where I was living at Cape Cornwall; and it was the events of that night and the following dawn that made me see that, whatever my aspirations for a "way beyond form," my own trip with acid was still far from over.

Not that the trip got off to a good start.

At first I thought I had just been greedy, for all that happened was that I felt fainter and more nauseated than ever before. What seemed an eternity was spent dry-retching over a plastic bucket, while I became more and more confused about who or where I was.

Finally, I crawled over to the bed, and collapsed there, utterly exhausted.

But as I lay there, the room slowly began to fill with the most exquisite music. Never had I heard anything so pure . . . so pristine. Hopelessly corny as the phrase is, it sounded just like angels singing.

I shut my eyes, and, fading in and out of the voices, a series of visions came into focus. An ornamental garden was revealed. The garden was laid out formally with level walks, many-bowled fountains, and parterres brimming with flowers. Mostly these were old damask roses, though there were others, perhaps a species of poppy that I could not recognize. Despite the sumptuous color, the garden itself was severe, almost geometric in conception. Medieval Arabic, I remember thinking. Sufi.

At times the roses and fountains were normally three-dimensional, at others they began almost imperceptibly to stiffen and become stylized like illustrations from an old illuminated manuscript . . . a manuscript through which light was pouring. "The Book of Wisdom," I thought. "The Book of Language." The fountains pulsed and the hue of the flowers flushed in time to the choir. (Weird how detached parts of your mind continue to function per usual on trips: instinctively I knew that such coincidence of color and sound was called *synesthesia* and that, while I hadn't the slightest idea who "I" was, this was something I had never experienced before.)

Wherever the singing was coming from, it was qualitatively different from anything I had ever previously considered to be music. This was more like a sacred language, one proper to another sphere. Through my mind flashed the memory of the first time I had ever truly *heard* music. One afternoon Gran and I had been at the Odeon watching the Disney cartoon at the start of the program when, without missing a beat, *the sound track suddenly turned into something else altogether.*

"What's that, Gran?" I whispered, electrified.

"'Greensleeves,'" she whispered back.

"Yes . . . *but what is it?*" I asked again.

"It's called 'Greensleeves,'" she repeated, getting rattled and starting to shout in the dark.

"Yes . . . *but what is it?*" I tried one last time, already knowing she wasn't going to understand . . .

That night in my little room at the Cape was the same, as though a royal road to the heart of creation, one whose very existence I had never even so much as suspected, lay shining before me.

I rose from the bed and, walking unsteadily across the room, opened the door leading to the yard.

The softest of rains was falling, and the first light of dawn was in the sky.

Abruptly I realized what the music was.

It was the birds! It was the dawn chorus!

I stood there transfixed. The drizzle was falling on the wooden fence surrounding the yard, on the washing line bare apart from a few plastic clothespins, and on the roof of the garage next door. This was Terrible Beauty, again—but this time far more terrible than ever before.

The world was transfigured, and I was looking into the Godhead.

All strength had drained from my body, and I just stood there in the rain. I thought I was going to cry, or black out. For this was all I had ever wanted: to know that this world and the holy are one and the same: to know that we are not abandoned, nor have we ever been. Nor, so far as I could see standing there that dawn in the rain, was it possible that we ever could be.

Magnified enormously, this was the same vision as those last sessions at Judges Walk, that to die would be very heaven. Though in reality there wasn't any question of living or dying, or change of any sort. All of that was part of the old world. All that was important was That Which Is. The reality of That alone mattered.

Not That. Thou. Only Thou.

Only Thou.

APPENDIX

Ergot and the West

AFTER GORDON WASSON PUBLISHED *Soma,* his study of the dawn of Indian religion, he turned to the possibility that plant hallucinogens could have played a comparable role in the evolution of Western mysticism.

Wasson was particularly fascinated by the "Mysteries" celebrated at the Temple of Demeter at Eleusis in ancient Greece. With a history spanning more than two thousand years, from 1500 BCE to the early fourteenth century CE, when it was sacked by the Christian Church, Eleusis was probably the most influential temple in the history of the world. Initiates included Homer (reputedly), Plato, Aristotle, Sophocles, Aeschylus, and Pindar; and the temple retained its preeminence during the Roman Empire, with Cicero, Hadrian, Marcus Aurelius, and other emperors all figuring as initiates.

Everyone attending the Mysteries was sworn to secrecy; and effectively, since next to nothing is known of the crucial ceremony save that it climaxed with drinking a sacred potion, the *kykeon.* Initiates claimed the transfiguration brought about by *kykeon* was the key psychic event of their lives. Again, Wasson's hypothesis was that the active ingredient in the *kykeon* was a plant hallucinogen—only in this case not *Amanita muscaria,* but ergot.

And the obvious collaborator for Wasson vis-à-vis the botanical and chemical aspects of any such detective work was Albert

Hofmann. Not only had ergot been the source of the lysergic acid used by Hofmann in his original synthesis of LSD, but the two men had already worked together on the extraction of psilocybin from Mexican magic mushrooms.

What exactly is ergot? Ergot is the fruiting body or *sclerotium*—commonly described as a "dark horn or spur"—of the *Claviceps purpurea* fungus. *Claviceps purpurea* grows as a parasite, particularly aggressively on rye, but also on barley or wheat and on certain wild grasses. It owes its unique notoriety to the fact that it combines some of the most healing and some of the most lethal of all the features ascribed to fungi. While small doses were employed throughout the Middle Ages in folk medicine, if higher doses were accidentally consumed—as for instance when ergot-infested rye was inadvertently milled and baked into bread—epidemics of ergot poisoning or *ergotism*, known widely as St. Anthony's Fire, could result. Characterized by vomiting, gangrene of the fingers and toes, and what is described medically as "convulsive ecstasy," thousands died horrific deaths during such outbreaks.

Albert Hofmann responded enthusiastically to the challenge, and within a year was to write back to Wasson:

> What suitable kinds of ergot were accessible to the ancient Greeks?
> No rye grew there, but wheat and barley did and *Claviceps purpurea* flourishes on both. We analyzed ergot of wheat and ergot of barley in our laboratory and they were found to contain basically the same alkaloids as ergot of rye, viz alkaloids of the ergotamine and ergotoxine group, ergonovine, and sometimes also traces of lysergic acid amide.[1]

Nor had Hofmann's research been purely theoretical. Some of these alkaloids could be produced by chemistry as simple as water infusion, and Hofmann prepared one such, ergonovine maleate, and subjected himself to a series of tests. Should he have hoped to repeat his breakthrough with LSD, he was to be disappointed. While he established that ergonovine maleate had definite mood-changing and hallucinatory effects, estimating its potency at about one twentieth that of LSD, his lab report was definitely an anticlimax.

A profound feeling of frustration resulted, and, as Peter Stafford records in *Psychedelics Encyclopedia,* the following year Jonathan Ott and two friends made an attempt to explore stronger doses. As against Hofmann's 2 mg dose, they took 3 mg; then a fortnight later, 5 mg. Both sessions were hallucinatory, but only mildly; and even, a week later, stepping the dose up to 10 mg didn't attain anything like the experience intimated by the ancients. "Thrice happy are those of mortals who having seen these rites depart for Hades," observed Sophocles. "For to them alone is granted to have a true life there. For the rest, all there is evil." Stirring words; but since then no one has stepped forward to continue experiment in situ . . . which, given the history of ergotism, is perhaps understandable.[2]

Wasson's hypothesis, Hofmann's research, and a commentary by classics scholar Carl Ruck were written up as *The Road to Eleusis* and published in 1978, but the book proved something of a dead end. In 1973, five years earlier, Michael Harner's *Hallucinogens and Shamanism* had zeroed in on the Solanaceae, the potato family, particularly datura but also mandrake, henbane, and deadly nightshade, as being the plants most likely responsible for the visionary dimension of witchcraft. All contain hallucination-rich alkaloids, and Harner's research popularized the hypothesis that combinations of these were applied as an unguent, or "flying ointment," going so far as to suggest that the stock-in-trade broomstick was in fact a vaginal applicator.[3] Subsequently, fascination with ayahuasca and South American shamanism edged the prehistory of LSD still deeper into the shadows.

Yet, while researching this book, I was struck by repeated references to the use of ergot in popular medicine during the Middle Ages. The context was always midwifery. Ergot in high doses could produce abortions, in lower ones accelerate contractions, and in yet lower ones stanch postpartum bleeding. This must have been enormously important in the medieval context, and ergot would have been one of the mainstays of the shamanic/wise-woman's pharmacopoeia. Over the centuries the drug must have been explored extensively, with especial sensitivity to doses, and it seems inconceivable that psychotropic effects produced by simple water infusion could have escaped attention.

But speculation about possible ongoing use of acid in the Middle Ages isn't what concerns me here. What does is the clear evidence that ergot has been used in midwifery for a very long time indeed, and the probability that such use was already established in ancient Greece. The hypothesis I am looking at is that the breakthrough at Eleusis was the same one the twentieth century was also to make:

The discovery that ergot can work in two directions.

Ergot derivatives cannot only ease our way into the world, but they can also ease our way out of it. They loosen up birth. They can allow us to retrace our steps: to recall early conditioning, the shock of birth, or even the womb life preceding it. To glimpse the mechanics of our incarnation . . . even the incomparably vaster identity coming before and after it. The Idealist poet Shelley wrote:

> *Life, like a dome of many-colored glass,*
> *Stains the white radiance of Eternity.*

Did Eleusis birth the basic concepts of Western and Near Eastern metaphysics—the "Forms," the "Ideas," the "Archetypes"? The concept of another world, prior to, more pristine than this, from which we journey forth and to which we return in a richer, more highly evolved form?

That was as high as I was to get anyway. During one of those last trips at Judges Walk, I remember gazing spellbound at a single blade of grass. "The first and last blade of grass," I wrote, "the original stroke of genius." That stalk of grass held a different cosmic status to anything I had ever known. Literally, it was The Idea of a blade of grass: I could no longer distinguish the thought of it from its full-blown material reality. It participated equally in two dimensions of reality, like a revolving door.

Furthermore, discovering the archetypal world was inseparable from discovering what holds us apart from it.

In Plato's cosmogony, this role is played by what he named *anamnesis:* his theory was that we have always been aware of, have always been at home in this prior world . . . *but have merely forgotten.* Here again there would seem to be an explicit tie-up with the conscious reliving of birth at the heart of the psychedelic experience. Surely, by and large, birth is the worst pain we as individuals undergo—and as such could present a plausible etiology for *our universal state of post-traumatic amnesia.*

Such are the basic parameters of Western religion and philosophy. On the one hand, our most basic awareness—our "substratum consciousness," as the Advaita teacher Poonja described it—is that everything is perfectly all right the way it is, in fact it is ecstatic, because on our deepest level we are still symbiotic with the cosmos. And on the other hand, that there is always something wrong with everything: some niggling little thing to which we overreact mechanically, rather than seeing as a playful wake-up call bringing us back to our true business, the desire and pursuit of the whole.

Notes

PREFACE

1. Terence McKenna, *The Archaic Revival* (San Francisco: Harper, 1991).

CHAPTER 1. BATCH 25

1. Albert Hofmann, quoted in Peter Stafford, *Psychedelics Encyclopedia,* 3rd ed. (Berkeley: Ronin Publishing, Inc., 1992), chapter 1, "The LSD Family: The First LSD Experiences."

CHAPTER 3. *THE DOORS OF PERCEPTION*

1. Aldous Huxley, *The Doors of Perception* (New York: Harper, 1954).

CHAPTER 4. PSYCHOPOLITICS AND THE SIXTIES

1. Martin Lee and Bruce Shlain, *Acid Dreams: The CIA, LSD, and the Sixties Rebellion* (New York: Grove, 1985), chapter 5, "The All-American Trip: Acid and the New Left."

CHAPTER 10. THE FIRST GROUP OF TRIPS

1. Stanislav Grof, *Realms of the Human Unconscious* (New York: Viking, 1975), "General Introduction."

2. For what remains, probably the best introduction is Robert Ornstein, *The Psychology of Consciousness* (New York: Penguin, 1975).

CHAPTER 12. BPM 2

1. Marlene Dobkin de Rios and Oscar Janiger, *LSD, Spirituality, and the Creative Process* (Rochester, Vt.: Park Street Press, 2003), chapter 3, "(Un) Characteristics of the LSD Experience," sections titled "Anxiety and Fear," "Cramps, Paralysis, and Agony," "Paranoid Feelings," "Depression, Guilt, and Irritation," "Somatic Discomfort," and "Strange Body Feelings."

CHAPTER 15. UNDERGROUND PSYCHOTHERAPHY

1. Myron Stolaroff, *The Secret Chief* (Sarasota, Fla.: MAPS, 1997), chapter 3, "The Individual Trip."

CHAPTER 16. SET, SETTING, AND HISTORY

1. Frances Cheek, Stephens Newell, and Mary Sarett, *The Illicit LSD Group: Some Preliminary Observations,* reprinted in *Psychedelics: The Uses and Implications of Hallucinogenic Drugs* (Garden City, N.Y.: Anchor Books, 1971), ed. by Bernard Aaronson and Humphry Osmond.

CHAPTER 18. "I SAW A MAN CLOATHED WITH RAGGS . . ."

1. Nisargadatta Maharaj, *I Am That* (Bombay: Acorn Press, 1973), trans. by Maurice Frydman.

CHAPTER 19. RESISTANCE

1. Stanislav Grof, *LSD Psychotherapy* (Alameda, Calif.: Hunter House, 1980), chapter 5, "Critical Situations in LSD Sessions."

CHAPTER 20. PSYCHEDELICS SINCE THE SIXTIES

1. R. Gordon Wasson, "Seeking the Magic Mushroom," *Life,* May 13, 1957, quoted in Jeremy Narby and Francis Huxley, *Shamans Through Time* (London: Thames and Hudson, 2001).

2. Valentina Wasson and Gordon Wasson, *Mushrooms, Russia and History* (New York: Pantheon, 1957), chapter 5, "The Mushroom Agape."

3. Mircea Eliade, *Shamanism: Archaic Techniques of Ecstasy* (Princeton: Princeton University Press, 1951), chapter 2, "Initiatory Sicknesses and Dreams."

4. Ibid., chapter 8, "Shamanism and Cosmology."

5. Jeremy Narby, *The Cosmic Serpent* (New York: Tarcher/Putnam, 1998), chapter 4, "Enigma in Rio."

CHAPTER 25. THE TRANSPERSONAL

1. Grof, *Realms of the Human Unconscious*, "Transpersonal Experiences in LSD Sessions."

2. Paul Devereux, *The Long Trip: A Prehistory of Psychedelia* (New York: Penguin, 1997), Introduction, "A Head of the Times."

3. Christopher Mayhew, "An Excursion Out of Time," *Observer* (London), October 28, 1956, reprinted in *The Drug Experience* (New York: Grove Press, 1961), ed. by David Ebin, "All the events in my drawing room between one-thirty and four existed together at the same time . . ."

4. Charles Hayes, *Tripping* (New York: Penguin/Compass, 2000), "The Narratives: Jason, The Shining Ones."

CHAPTER 29. "ECSTATIC JOURNEY . . ."
(CONTINUED)

1. Carlo Ginzburg, *Ecstasies: Deciphering the Witches' Sabbath* (New York: Doubleday, 1991), part 2, chapter 2, "Following the Goddess."

CHAPTER 31. "NOT THE TRUE SAMADHI . . ."

1. Suzanne Segal, *Collision with the Infinite* (San Diego: Blue Dove Press, 1996), chapter 8, "The Secret of Emptiness."

2. Ram Dass, *The Only Dance There Is* (Garden City, New York: Anchor Books, 1974), chapter 3.

CHAPTER 35. "ANOTHER WORLD IS POSSIBLE"

1. George Monbiot, *The Age of Consent* (London: Flamingo, 2003), chapter 4, "We the Peoples."

CHAPTER 36. "ANOTHER WORLD IS POSSIBLE . . ." (CONTINUED)

1. Maria Sabina, quoted in John W. Allen, "Chasing the Ghost of Maria Sabina: Saint Mother of the Sacred Mushroom," in *Psychedelic Illuminations,* vol. 1, no. 6 (1994).

CHAPTER 37. TOWARD A SACRAMENTAL VISION OF REALITY

1. See Osho, *The Mystic Experience.* Reprinted as *In Search of the Miraculous,* vol. 2, chapter 3, "The Path of Kundalini."
2. Adi Da (writing as Franklin Jones), *The Knee of Listening* (Middletown, Calif.: Dawn Horse Press, 1972), part 1, "The Life of Understanding."
3. Aldous Huxley, *Heaven and Hell* (New York: Harper, 1956).

CHAPTER 39. OUT OF THE BODY?

1. Lester Grinspoon and James Bakalar, *Psychedelic Drugs Reconsidered* (New York: Basic Books, 1979), chapter 4, "The Nature of Psychedelic Experience."

CHAPTER 41. BPM 4

1. Grof, *Realms of the Human Unconscious,* chapter 4 "Perinatal Experiences in LSD Sessions."

CHAPTER 42. THE LONG FLASHBACK

1. Sherana Frances, *Drawing It Out: Befriending the Unconscious* (Sarasota, Fla.: MAPS, 2001), Prologue.
2. Ibid., Introduction.

CHAPTER 43. INTERIM REPORT

1. Maria Sabina, *Maria Sabina: Selections,* ed. by Jerome Rothenburg (Berkeley: University of California Press, 2003), chapter 6, "The Life of Maria Sabina."

2. Benny Shanon, *The Antipodes of the Mind: Charting the Phenomenology of the Ayahuasca Experience* (New York: Oxford University Press, 2002), Prologue.

3. Alun Rees, "Nobel Prize Genius Crick Was High on LSD When He Discovered the Secret of Life," *Mail on Sunday* (London), August 8, 2004.

CHAPTER 44. INTERIM REPORT (CONTINUED)

1. See "Ram Dass: the Gnosis Interview," *Gnosis,* Winter 1993.

2. Ramana Maharshi, *Be As You Are: The Teachings of Sri Ramana Maharshi* (London: Penquin, 1985), ed. by David Godman, chapter 1, "The Nature of the Self."

3. *Vajracchedika,* quoted in Alan Watts, *The Way of Zen* (New York: Pantheon, 1957), part 2, chapter 1, "Empty and Marvellous."

4. Adi Da (writing as Franklin Jones), *The Knee of Listening,* part 1, "The Life of Understanding."

CHAPTER 45. MUTUAL IMMANENCE

1. Aldous Huxley, *Moksha* (New York: Stonehill, 1977), ed. by Michael Horowitz and Cynthia Palmer, chapter 16, "Letter to Dr. Humphry Osmond," October 24, 1955.

APPENDIX. ERGOT AND THE WEST

1. Albert Hofmann in Gordon Wasson, Albert Hofmann, and Carl Ruck, *The Road to Eleusis* (New York: Harcourt, Brace & Jovanovitch, 1978), chapter 2, "A Challenging Question."

2. See Peter Stafford, *Psychedelics Encyclopedia* (Los Angeles: Tarcher, 1983), chapter 1, "The LSD Family: Botanical Sources of Lysergic Acid Amides and Their Histories and Effect: Rye and other Grasses."

3. See Michael Harner (ed.), *Hallucinogens and Shamanism* (New York: Oxford University Press, 1973), chapter 8, "The Role of Hallucinogenic Plants in European Witchcraft."

Bibliography

A Chronology of
Psychedelic Literature

PRINCIPAL WORKS DEALING WITH
PSYCHEDELICS, IN ORDER OF PUBLICATION

1954   Aldous Huxley. *The Doors of Perception.* New York: Harper.

1957   Valentina Wasson and Gordon Wasson. *Mushrooms, Russia and History.* New York: Pantheon.

1961   Constance Newland. *My Self and I.* New York: New American Library/Signet.

1966   Robert Masters and Jean Houston. *The Varieties of Psychedelic Experience.* Rochester, Vt.: Park Street Press, 2000.

1966   David Solomon (ed.). *LSD: The Consciousness Expanding Drug.* New York: Putnam.

1968   Carlos Castaneda. *The Teachings of Don Juan.* Berkeley: University of California Press.

1968   Gordon Wasson. *Soma: Divine Mushroom of Immortality.* New York: Harcourt, Brace & Jovanovich.

1970   Bernard Aaronson and Humphry Osmond (eds.). *Psychedelics:*

The Uses and Implications of Hallucinogenic Drugs. New York: Doubleday/Anchor.

1973   Michael Harner (ed.). *Hallucinogens and Shamanism.* New York: Oxford University Press.

1975   Stanislav Grof. *Realms of the Human Unconscious.* New York: Viking.

1977   Stanislav Grof and Joan Halifax. *The Human Encounter with Death.* New York: Dutton.

1977   Aldous Huxley. *Moksha: Classic Writings on Psychedelics and the Visionary Experience.* Ed. by Michael Horowitz and Cynthia Palmer. New York: Stonehill.

1978   Albert Hofmann, Gordon Wasson, and Carl Ruck. *The Road to Eleusis.* New York: Harcourt, Brace & Jovanovitch.

1979   Richard Evans Schultes and Albert Hofmann. *Plants of the Gods.* Rochester, Vt.: Healing Arts Press, 2001.

1979   Lester Grinspoon and James Bakalar. *Psychedelic Drugs Reconsidered.* New York: Basic Books.

1980   Stanislav Grof. *LSD Psychotherapy.* Alameda, Calif.: Hunter House.

1983   Albert Hofmann. *LSD, My Problem Child.* Trans. by J. Ott. New York: McGraw Hill.

1983   Peter Stafford. *Psychedelics Encyclopaedia.* Los Angeles: Tarcher.

1985   Martin Lee and Bruce Schlain. *Acid Dreams: The CIA, LSD, and the Sixties Rebellion.* New York: Grove.

1991   Terence McKenna. *The Archaic Revival.* San Francisco: Harper.

1996   Wade Davis. *One River.* New York: Simon and Schuster.

1997   Myron Stolaroff. *The Secret Chief.* Sarasota, Fla.: MAPS.

1997   Antonio Melechi (ed.). *Psychedelia Britannica.* London: Turnaround.

1997   Paul Devereux. *The Long Trip.* New York: Penguin.

1998   Jeremy Narby. *The Cosmic Serpent.* New York: Tarcher/Putnam.

2000   Christopher Bache. *Dark Night, Early Dawn.* New York: SUNY Press.

2000   Nicholas Saunders, Anja Saunders, and Michelle Pauli. *In Search of the Ultimate High: Spiritual Experience Through Psychoactives.* New York: Random House.

2000   Charles Hayes (ed.). *Tripping: An Anthology of True-Life Psychedelic Adventures.* New York: Penguin/Compass.

2001   Sherana Frances. *Drawing It Out.* Sarasota, Fla.: MAPS.

2002   Benny Shanon. *The Antipodes of the Mind: Charting the Phenomenology of the Ayahuasca Experience.* New York: Oxford University Press.

2003   Maria Sabina. *Maria Sabina: Selections.* Ed. by Jerome Rothenberg. Berkeley: University of California Press.

2003   Marlene Dobkin de Rios and Oscar Janiger. *LSD, Spirituality, and the Creative Process.* Rochester, Vt.: Park Street Press.

BOOKS OF RELATED INTEREST

DMT: The Spirit Molecule
A Doctor's Revolutionary Research into the Biology of Near-Death and
Mystical Experiences
by Rick Strassman, M.D.

Tryptamine Palace
5-MeO-DMT and the Sonoran Desert Toad
by James Oroc

LSD: Doorway to the Numinous
The Groundbreaking Psychedelic Research into Realms of the Human
Unconscious
by Stanislav Grof, M.D.

Plants of the Gods
Their Sacred, Healing, and Hallucinogenic Powers
by Richard Evans Schultes, Albert Hofmann, and Christian Rätsch

The Psychotropic Mind
The World according to Ayahuasca, Iboga, and Shamanism
by Jeremy Narby, Jan Kounen, and Vincent Ravalec

Salvia Divinorum
Doorway to Thought-Free Awareness
by J. D. Arthur

The Encyclopedia of Psychoactive Plants
Ethnopharmacology and Its Applications
by Christian Rätsch

The Psychedelic Journey of Marlene Dobkin de Rios
45 Years with Shamans, Ayahuasqueros, and Ethnobotanists
by Marlene Dobkin de Rios

INNER TRADITIONS • BEAR & COMPANY
P.O. Box 388
Rochester, VT 05767
1-800-246-8648
www.InnerTraditions.com

Or contact your local bookseller